Pickett's Charge

Pickett's Charge

A Microhistory of the Final Attack
at Gettysburg, July 3, 1863

By George R. Stewart

HOUGHTON MIFFLIN COMPANY
Boston

To C. S. F.

In Memory of Twenty Years
of Friendship

Copyright © 1959 by George R. Stewart
Copyright renewed © 1987 by Theodosia B. Stewart

ALL RIGHTS RESERVED

For information about permission to reproduce selections
from this book, write to Permissions, Houghton Mifflin
Company, 2 Park Street, Boston, Massachusetts 02108.

Library of Congress Cataloging-in-Publication Data

Stewart, George Rippey, date.
Pickett's charge : a microhistory of the final attack at
Gettysburg, July 3, 1863 / by George R. Stewart.
p.   cm.
Includes bibliographical references and index.
ISBN 0-395-59772-2
1. Gettysburg (Pa.), Battle of, 1863.   2. Pickett, George E.
(George Edward), 1825–1875.   I. Title.
E475.53.S86   1991   91-24117
973.7′349—dc20   CIP

Printed in the United States of America

AGM 10 9 8 7 6 5

Contents

Illustrations

following page 146

vii

MAPS AND DIAGRAMS

Foreword

IF WE GRANT — as many would be ready to do — that the Civil War furnishes the great dramatic episode of the history of the United States, and that Gettysburg provides the climax of the war, then the climax of the climax, the central moment of our history, must be Pickett's Charge.

Thus to hold, indeed, is not to maintain that a different result, there by the clump of trees and the angle in the stone wall, would of itself have reversed the course of the war and decisively altered history. The moment is, rather, a symbolic one, not even recognized at the time, but gaining significance in retrospect. This significance, moreover, is a part of world-history, since the existence of two rival republics would probably have prevented the United States from turning the balance of two World Wars and becoming a global power.

There are those who would not call it by the usual term, maintaining that it is neither Pickett's nor a charge. Such double-dissenters usually prefer Longstreet's Assault, thus attaching it to the one man of all men who most thoroughly disowned it. But in the ordinary language of the time, by the men participating, it was known as a charge, no matter what restrictions the dictionaries and manuals may put upon that word. As for Pickett, he was the senior officer who advanced (at least, part way) with troops, and it seems certain that he was entrusted with the command of all the brigades engaged.

The sources of information about the charge are amazingly rich and varied, permitting not only the reconstruction of a military movement, but also of the adventures of individuals, and even of their thoughts and feelings. On one point the author would insist — he has read both sides. While this may not render him unique, it at least makes him a rare bird. Almost universally, even in the mid-twentieth century, writers have approached this war, not as over-all historians, but as Northerners or Southerners.

Careful consideration of the documents of both sides leaves the writer with no choice but to reject, here and there, the shining legend. Patriotic sentimentalists to the contrary notwithstanding, not all men were heroes in the Army of the Potomac, or in the Army of Northern Virginia. Yet, why should this pain us too much — to learn that we are not puny descendants of demigods, but that our ancestors, too, sometimes went to the rear? But let it be known that for Southern derelictions there is no need to accept Northern testimony; and similarly, for Northern derelictions.

There is, also, in the generally accepted story of the charge something of the massive simplicity that arises with time, as blurred actuality sharpens into folk-tale and legend. In studying the documents, however, one is continually struck by the complexities and complications of the action. It was seldom simple. Moreover, its key-note was confusion — of smoke, fear, excitement, and broken ranks. Through all these the historian must try to pierce, toward truth, though at the same time he must remember that the confusion is itself a part of the truth.

The action here presented lies wholly within the day of July 3, 1863, covering about fifteen hours. Even so, the mass of material is such that severe concentration is demanded. You will, then, find here no general history of the war — no discussions, for instance, of the populations of North and South, and their production of pig iron. Important as such matters were, they made not a hair's difference, once the armies had met. So, also, we may forget the long march northward and even the heroic fighting of the first and second days. Now the battle has been joined and the dead lie quietly on Oak Ridge and in the Peach Orchard.

Nevertheless, let us remember one or two matters, not so small. This, we should not forget, may be considered the "classical" battle of the war. Like well-trained athletes, never before and never again, we may believe, were the two armies in such unsurpassed condition. Far behind were the blundering battles between armed mobs; still ahead lay the dreary months of war to be waged by combat-weary veterans and half-hearted conscripts. With few exceptions the men at Gettysburg were there by their own decision.

Partly for this reason there is little need to write of the horrors of war. Horrors there were in plenty — men struck in the eyes, through the intestines, in the genitals. Men were carried away maimed for life, and at least one wounded man drew his revolver and shot himself. But to write of Gettysburg in terms of the Somme or of Monte Cassino would be a painful falsification of history. Nothing is more striking in the sources generally than the absence of gloom. The armies suffered casualties such as few modern armies have endured, but the men did not seem to feel sorry for themselves. Did some primitive spirit of combat sustain them? Or a romantic sense of glory? Or an intense patriotism? Or was it a more imminent hint of immortality, as when a private of Brown's battery died in a religious ecstasy. Perhaps as the best symbol of this spirit we can take the letter of Captain Charles Phillips of the Fifth Massachusetts Battery, written to his "little nephew" in which he went into great detail about the glorious battle, described the shelling as being "pretty lively" and mentioned that a battery was "throwing case shot at us very carelessly." One doubts whether such a letter could be matched after the year 1914.

Let us approach the charge, then, as a microcosm. Thus we may be able to see the war as clearly by looking minutely and carefully at a period of a few hours as by looking extensively and dimly throughout four years. And may it not supply more than a mere vignette of military history? Much of human nature, good and bad, displays itself on a battlefield. In a sense, even, the charge may stand for all of human life. Some time in the years, if not daily, must not each of us hear the command to rise and go forward, and cross the field, and go up against the guns?

Pickett's Charge

PART I

Early Morning — Mostly Confederate

The enemy is there, and I am going to strike him.
— GENERAL R. E. LEE

ON THE BATTLEFIELD, in their tens of thousands, the men slept, or lay resting. The night was mild, forecasting a warm day to come. The moon, a little past full, illumined the shot-torn fields and pastures with a dim and silvery splendor. So quiet it was that an officer of the 19th Massachusetts, wakeful, near a clump of small oaks and a good mile from town, clearly heard the courthouse clock strike three. Years later he remembered, and added a trite comment on the contrast between the stillness of the night and the pandemonium of the day that followed.

But battles, or the preparations for them, are likely to begin at an early hour. Well in front of that clump of oaks the Union pickets kept their watch, and even before the moon began to grow pale, they must have heard sounds that had a homelike familiarity about them. A farm boy in the 8th Ohio would have thought of wagons creaking across a far-off hay field; a Philadelphian in the 106th Pennsylvania, of drays clunking upon cobblestones. But this was too far front for wagon trains. Those sounds could only mean that in the moonlight the Rebs were putting artillery into position.

2

The guns were moving under the orders of young Colonel E. Porter Alexander, commanding a reserve battalion of the artillery

1

of Longstreet's corps, but at the moment acting in a position of higher authority. For, we would judge, Colonel J. B. Walton, Chief of Artillery for the corps, was not held in the highest estimation by Lieutenant General James Longstreet, who had quietly assigned him to a rear echelon, so that a more skillful officer could take over the important duty of emplacing the artillery. "I was directed," Alexander wrote in his report, "to prepare for a general attack upon the enemy to our front and left."

On this morning of the third day of battle the Confederates were still on the offensive. As Lee stated it, "The general plan was unchanged." On the Union right, Ewell had gained and still held an excellent position. On the Union left-center, Longstreet had almost broken through, but had finally been repulsed; still, his position was favorable for a renewed offensive.

The plan, as part of which Alexander was placing his guns, was apparently this. . . . Longstreet was to drive ahead for the Taneytown road, not more than a thousand feet behind the main Union line. Simultaneously Ewell was to strike for the Baltimore Pike, having rather less than that distance to go. With the cutting of these two roads, the whole Union front could be expected to collapse in disaster. Meade's army was shaken by two days of heavy losses. Another pole-ax blow, an hour's fighting, and the war might be won!

Like most plans this one had its weaknesses. One of these was, obviously, the Union army. It might not be as badly stricken as was hoped. Moreover, the plan called for co-ordination in time, but communications were poor. The two points of attack were distant only about a mile by air-line, but by the route that a courier must follow they were at least five miles apart.

Placing his guns in the favoring moonlight, Alexander may have wondered about the infantry that was to make this attack. Out in front, somewhere, was a skirmish line of Mississippians, and off on the right were Wofford's Georgians and other brigades. But these troops had already assaulted the position in front, and had been repulsed with heavy losses. Thus weakened, they could hardly do in the morning what they had failed to do the evening before.

Years later — in the time of bitter controversy as to why the Lost Cause was lost at Gettysburg — the Confederates debated the question of this proposed attack with much heat. Fortunately, to tell the story of Pickett's Charge, there is no need to become involved in this controversy. The charge must be conceived as a substitute for this early attack, not a part of it. As far as Longstreet was concerned, any practical possibility that he could launch a dawn attack had already vanished before midnight. Since no orders had been issued by that time, he would lack at dawn the essential element for a successful assault — a large and compact body of fresh infantry. He would lack, in fact, the third division of his corps, Pickett's three brigades.

3

Their absence at this juncture, although it is in some ways so strange as to be called mysterious, can be easily enough explained at a superficial level. On the preceding day, to complete the concentration of the army, the division had made a forced march beneath a blazing sun, and about six o'clock had arrived at a point some three miles from the battlefield. The men were close to exhaustion. Ahead they could hear the crash of battle, as their comrades of Longstreet's corps fought their way through the Wheat Field and attacked Little Round Top. Pickett sent an aide forward to report to Lee that the men, though tired, could still be pushed on, to take their part in the fighting. But Lee — strangely, it seems — replied that Pickett was not now needed, that his division could go into bivouac and be ready for action on the following day. Thankfully, the weary men collapsed into a grove of oaks at the side of the road.

In miles, they were at no great distance from the point of intended attack. By time — according to the rate at which large bodies of men can march across country, make the necessary preparations, and finally go into battle — they were four hours away. To co-operate with Ewell in a dawn attack, the men should have been routed out, after an inadequate night, not later than midnight.

Whatever plan existed for a co-ordinated battle thus miscarried sometime before midnight. Either Lee gave no orders for Pickett to break camp, or Longstreet failed to transmit them. But in the time of controversy, after Lee's death, Longstreet maintained vigorously that he never received orders for an early attack, and no one proved that he had. Possibly Lee, who was a very tired man on the evening of July 2, neglected to give the necessary orders. More likely, he decided at the last moment against the plan, thinking that Pickett's men would be better off with more chance to recuperate. He had already instructed Ewell to attack at dawn, but this was no reason for worry because he could send orders for postponement.

Actually, reveille for Pickett's division was about three, somewhat before daybreak.

4

They awoke, a little stiff and footsore from the preceding day's hard march. In the moonlight they heard the insistent bugles and the sergeants shouting, but no sound of guns.

Of those who were there, more than one left a record; if no one told much, they told different things. So one noted that the stars were still twinkling, though some clouds hung around the horizon, and he recalled that as the men fell in for roll call, the flags hung limp in the still morning air. And, another remembered, the men had their usual jokes, and "no gloomy forebodings hovered over our ranks." But, a third noted, by the luck of the march, the artillery having gone on ahead, Kemper's brigade took the lead, and then came Garnett's and then Armistead's. (But he did not know what that would mean, later on.)

Before daylight, the march began — a little way eastward on the main road, and then turning off to the right. At that turnoff a tall gray-bearded man in general's uniform sat on horseback, silent and motionless, to look at them passing. So Robert E. Lee watched Pickett's men march to the field of Gettysburg.

Thus they left the main road. More than a mile long, the column wound along the lanes and across the fields, in the still doubtful light, seemingly as aimless and uncertain as a huge blind snake, except that at its head rode someone as a guide, sent back, doubtless, by Lieutenant Colonel Moxley Sorrel, Longstreet's Chief of Staff, one who did not forget details. By now the marching men might have been able to see the first showing of dawn.

5

By now, too, as fast as he could over uncertain roads and in the half-darkness, a courier was galloping with Lee's message to Ewell, that Longstreet could not attack until ten o'clock.

And by now, also, near Culp's Hill on the extreme Union right, Brigadier General John W. Geary, a former mayor of San Francisco, was standing, about to give the signal for the Union batteries to open fire.

At Geary's order, twenty guns spoke. Artillery preparation, attack and counterattack — the fat was in the fire!

Meade, by thus opening the fight, had forced the issue. No longer was Lee in serene control of the battlefield. Ewell was already forced to engage, but Pickett was still at least three hours away.

When Lee's courier pulled his sweating horse up to deliver the message to Ewell, his information had become only an ironic comment on history.

6

No one kept a log-book of Lee's movements. On the authority of Captain John Dooley of the 1st Virginia, we have reported him as watching the march of Pickett's division. Not only was Dooley an officer, but also he later studied for the priesthood, so that we may consider him truthful — but it is, indeed, a little strange that no one else mentioned Lee's presence there.

In any case, he next rode to meet with Longstreet. Somewhere on the way, the blast of artillery fire from the Union right must have brought him up short. During a battle an occasional outburst was likely at any time of night, when some nervous battery-commander opened against imagined assailants. But now many cannon thundered together — the *spang* of smooth-bores mingling with the *slap* of rifled guns.

At once Lee would have been certain that Meade had seized the initiative. The realization must have come to him with some chagrin. Like most generals, but with more justification, he considered himself to have an ability at judging what the other general was like and what he would do. When informed of the change of command in the Union army, he had remarked that Meade would "commit no blunder." Though these words are sometimes quoted as being a compliment, they were certainly not better than a compliment second-class, for they implied that Meade would not do much in a positive way. This, it would seem, was exactly Lee's opinion, and he took long chances at Gettysburg, apparently trusting that he would not be caught off-balance by a counterattack. Now the thunder of the guns proclaimed that this was just what had occurred, and that even Meade could not be altogether trusted to remain on the defensive.

As soon as he could reach some point of vantage (and that should not have taken him many minutes), Lee knew that the cannonade was directed against Ewell's left, and he must have realized that his plan of co-ordinated battle had been ruined. Ewell could not be told to hold his attack off. He was already engaged, but Longstreet could not be ready until ten. Still, as an experienced and practical soldier, Lee was not one to be too much concerned with not being able to do what he had intended to do. If a plan miscarried, then you worked out a new one. Possibly, even, Meade would weaken himself by trying to take the offensive.

So Lee, with his staff, rode toward his meeting with Longstreet, the most skilled and experienced of his corps-commanders. Since he was headed southward, we may assume that he rode slightly in front of his own battle line on Seminary Ridge, where he could look out eastward, in the gray dawn, across the fields, and see the Union lines and the rising smoke of the guns firing near Culp's Hill. He certainly studied the Union lines to see whether any changes had occurred during the night. Moreover, by the time he was to meet with Longstreet, he would apparently have worked out a new plan of battle, and he could scarcely have done so without careful consideration. So we may suppose that at times Lee halted, and gazed through his field-glasses.

About half way along the ridge, on its gentle eastward slope, is a spot which is sometimes mentioned in the Confederate accounts as "the point of woods." From near this spot Lee viewed many of the events of the third day's battle. It is high enough to afford an excellent view, and yet not so high that a man standing there shows against the skyline. Trees offer a neutral background, and staff-officers and horses can be conveniently hidden among them, so as to offer no temptation to the enemy's artillery.

If Lee halted somewhere, let us assume that it was here. But rather than looking with him let us first look at the general himself. On this day no one else was destined to bear so great a responsibility for such momentous events.

7

So we see him stand there, field-glasses in hand, fifty-six years old, gray-bearded, "tall, broad-shouldered, very well made, well set up." On the Gettysburg campaign he favored a well-worn long gray jacket, and blue trousers tucked into horseman's boots; he usually wore a high black felt hat. He bore no arms, not even a sword. Only the stars on his collar proclaimed his rank. He needed no bedeckment of uniform, for he easily dominated men, as many have testified, by his mere presence.

Thus we may easily catalogue the exterior. But to tell what he really was — that can tax all men's ingenuity. Some bits of morning mist, they tell us, still hung about the battlefield, and if a little of that mist swirled about him, half-concealing, we may take that as a symbol; for even yet the man, whatever he was, is blurred by the shifting mists of his legend. Gentleman without flaw, "Marse Robert," father-figure to an army, replacing even Washington as the ideal Southerner!

For our purposes here, however, we need not consider the whole man. We have but one question to ask, "Why did Lee order Pickett's Charge?"

8

As he stood there, Lee could reflect upon two days of fighting throughout which, as reckoned in the dark ledgers of war where all the entries are in red, he had operated at a profit. The Army of the Potomac had seven corps of infantry. Of these Lee knew that he had smashed the First, Third, and Eleventh. He had also damaged — rather badly, he could believe — the

Second and Fifth. At this very time, Ewell was fighting the Twelfth, and he could be counted on to wear it down. Only the Sixth remained. Actually, Lee had no certain knowledge that the Sixth Corps had reached Gettysburg, but as a wise commander he could only assume that it had. Still, that corps was not invincible.

In his own army, Lee had Pickett's division intact, and several brigades that had not been heavily engaged. But the rest of the army had suffered severely — more, indeed, than Lee himself realized. This may seem an incredibility, but more than once during this day, Lee's ignorance of the state of his own troops is apparent. This can perhaps be put down merely to poor staff-work. More deeply considered, it may be connected with the romanticism of the Southern character, a refusal to face realities, an unwillingness to admit that the despised Yankees were really dangerous. At the same time, from a military point of view, this state of mind had much to recommend it. The Southern soldier was thus endowed with a feeling of invincibility.

This high and serene sense of confidence should not, even for a moment, be forgotten in any appraisal of Gettysburg. A few of the many possible citations can demonstrate it. Colonel Fremantle, the Englishman who was traveling with the army, mentioned it three times in his diary within a few days — "all full of confidence and in high spirits . . . everyone, of course, speaks with confidence . . . the universal feeling in the army was one of profound contempt." A private in Pickett's division remembered: "How joyous, how buoyant, how frolicsome we all were!" A Union prisoner reported, "The enemy are arrogant." Eppa Hunton, senior colonel of Garnett's brigade, recalled that he was not so confident at first; after talking with Lee, "I threw away my doubts and became as enthusiastic as he was." Hunton reported of Lee, "he believed his army could whip anything on the planet." One of Mahone's men remembered "each soldier feeling himself superior to three of the enemy."

The confidence of the army in its general was almost a religious faith, as a curious ancedote illustrates. While Pickett's division was passing through a Pennsylvania town, an old lady called out, "You are marching mighty proudly now, but you will come back faster than you went."

"Why so, old lady?" an officer called back.

"Because you put your trust in General Lee and not in the Lord Almighty."

All will agree that mutual confidence and a sense of invincibility are good for an army and its general. But there is a subtle line between confidence and over-confidence. Before Gettysburg this feeling of contempt for the enemy (one Confederate writer later compared it to a cancer) had spread high and low, among all ranks.

Two days of hard fighting had undoubtedly made some difference. If you had interviewed the men of Brockenbrough's brigade on the morning of July 3, you would probably have found few who maintained that one of them could lick three Yankees, or even that one of them could lick one Yankee, if he held a good defensive position. But most of the army was still confident, and Lee retained his confidence in it.

Closely allied to this assurance, or over-assurance, was a tendency toward wishful thinking, often expressed in over-valuation of successes. Thus General A. P. Hill reported the "almost total annihilation of the First Corps of the enemy" on July 1; this would have been news for the nearly two thousand men of that corps who were now waiting on Cemetery Ridge, and for the four thousand others who were still under arms in other parts of the field. Another highly exaggerated report was that of General A. R. Wright, whose Georgians had attacked Cemetery Ridge on the afternoon of July 2. Similar reports are also to be found in the Union records, as well as in those of the British, French, and Russian armies — and doubtless in the Martian records too. But with the Confederate army at Gettysburg attaining, as another officer reported, "the zenith of assurance," such reports were the more likely to be taken at face value.

On this morning, then, Lee faced the inevitable three possibilities for a general — to attack, to retreat, to stand still. The last had nothing to recommend it; Meade, with his lines of communication open, could win at a waiting game. Similarly, to retreat after two days of what could be counted success was unthinkable. Such action would present the North with victory on a silver platter. Besides, the prospect of a long and harassed retreat was not pleasant. Therefore, for a fighting general in command of a fighting army, there was only one choice — attack!

Another factor cannot be altogether neglected. Lee himself was naturally aggressive, quick to take the offensive. Longstreet thought that the real reason for the attack thus lay in Lee's character, in the excitement of combat that took possession of him, "when the hunt was up." Most people have agreed that Longstreet went too far, and the same admirers of Lee have become very violent about it. In Longstreet's support, however, another opinion may be cited, that of Major General Harry Heth, who was close to Lee on July 3 and who had no particular reason to side with Longstreet. Heth wrote — of Lee at Gettysburg:

> This determination to strike his enemy was not from the position he found himself [in], consequent upon the invasion, but from a leading characteristic of the man. General Lee, not excepting Jackson, was the most aggressive man in his army.

Nevertheless, as far as the morning of July 3 is concerned, there seems to be no need to draw heavily upon Lee's special personality for an explanation. Faced with the situation, having the inescapable three choices, any good soldier would — in some way or other — have attacked.

The probabilities are that Lee himself never considered anything else. As he looked out eastward toward the dawn, the real question was — "Where?" His plan for co-ordinated attack was ruined. What could be substituted?

He scanned the now familiar profile of the Union line — for disposition of troops and batteries, signs of fortification, evidences of change since the evening before. The shape of that line has been conventionally and aptly compared to a fishhook. At the Point of Woods, Lee was a little less than a mile away, and could look, southward, along the shank of the hook to his right, and to his left, northward, could see the first part of the curve. At that northern end rose a hill where there was a cemetery, so that it naturally bore the name Cemetery Hill. It was a strong position. At the southern end of the line rose the hills for which the Confederates had no certain names, but of which the two highest are now known as Round Top and Little Round Top. These were also strong positions, not attractive for assault. Between the northern and the southern hills, the distance of about a mile, the land was low, offering no serious physical barrier. The main attack of yesterday had been launched against the southern end cf this portion of the line, the Union left-center. Now Lee must have looked at the northern end, the Union right-center.

First of all, at that time of the morning, he may have noticed the many smokes from the little fires where "those people" — as he generally called them — were boiling their coffee. So also he may have noted puffs of white smoke where the two lines of skirmishers, in that ceaseless and often senseless activity which is war, were shooting at each other. But Lee studied, rather, the essentials, with the practiced eye of an engineer officer, trained in reconnaissance from the days of the Mexican campaign. The crest of the ridge was a good artillery position, and several batteries were in full view. But the slope was not steep enough to hinder the advance of infantry. Some trees and

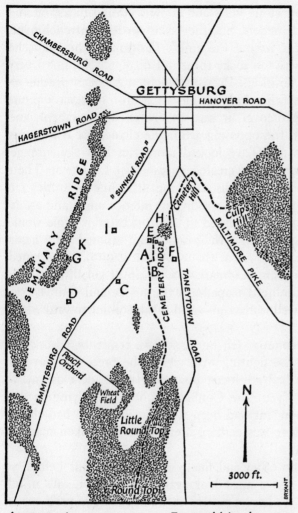

GENERAL
MAP

*Battlefield
of
Gettysburg*

CHAMBERSBURG ROAD

GETTYSBURG

HANOVER ROAD

HAGERSTOWN ROAD

SEMINARY RIDGE

"SUNKEN ROAD"

Cemetery Hill

Culp's Hill

BALTIMORE PIKE

I

H
E
F
A
B

CEMETERY RIDGE

TANEYTOWN ROAD

K
G

C

D

EMMITSBURG ROAD

Peach Orchard

Wheat Field

Little Round Top

N

3000 ft.

Round Top

BRYANT

A   The Angle
B   Clump of trees
C   Codori house and barn
D   Spangler house and barn
E   Bryan house and barn

F   Meade's headquarters
G   Point of Woods
H   Ziegler's grove
I   Bliss barn
K   Lee's position

🌲 Woods

----- Union line

bushes, some low stone walls and a few scattered rocks, offered
shelter to the defenders, but there was no real entrenchment,
not even lunettes around the guns. The top of the ridge, he
would assume, was too rocky to permit digging. No, not a very
strong infantry position! Even its height was not altogether in
its favor; troops firing from an elevation are notoriously prone
to overshoot. Moreover, it was in a small way a salient, and
therefore offered the opposing artillery a chance for converging
fire. Also — he may have looked more closely — the arrangement of the stone walls created an essential weakness. There
was a jog, and for some distance, the little line of stones ran
almost directly toward him, making an interior angle and an exterior angle. Any troops placed to hold the exterior angle would
essentially be fighting with their right flank exposed. If a heavy
attack could be launched at that spot — ? Also of importance,
the place had a plain landmark — a clump of smallish trees of
peculiar form, umbrella-shaped. In the smoke and confusion of
an assault, it is well to have an unmistakable point toward which
to advance.

As a careful commander, he must have remembered another
detail. During the fighting with which the preceding day had
ended, Wright had advanced his Georgia brigade close up to
the stone wall. Even now, Confederate dead were lying on that
slope. The Georgians had been repulsed, but they had shown
that the way there was certain, unimpeded by sunken roads or
by marshy land.

There was one other and finally great point. But before we
can appreciate it, we must look again into the general's mind.
Here, for once, we have a matter about which he himself spoke.
As he stood there at Gettysburg, he was weary of victories. He
might well, he realized, victory the Confederacy to death. As
he later told a friend, after Fredericksburg and again after
Chancellorsville he had been "much depressed." The South
had been wildly enthusiastic, but Lee himself, with deeper

penetration, had known the barrenness. Northern casualties, pretty well balanced (considering the disproportionate population) by Southern casualties! "Those people" forced to relinquish a few square miles of exhausted Virginia countryside!

Pyrrhus, Hannibal, even Napoleon — they had won their famous victories. In a few years, where were they? Schooled by defeats, an army may quickly become more skillful. This came close home. With all its reverses, the Union army had shown by two days of heavy battle that it was perhaps a more dangerous opponent than it had ever been before. So, on this third day, Lee was undoubtedly not so much trying to win another victory as to create — while there was still the chance — a disaster!

The situation was favorable. The opposing army had been driven back, and hard hit, and — especially with so many defeats to reckon with — its morale should be badly shaken. Historians would later expatiate upon the advantages which the fishhook position offered to Meade. But if Meade had met with disaster, historians would in their wisdom point out that the fishhook invited catastrophe. If the line could be broken — say, at the clump of trees!

Here, indeed, we have the best explanation of why Lee had so confidently and so strangely told Pickett that he would not be needed on the afternoon of July 2. Lee could have planned all the fighting on that day merely to weaken and to fix the Union army — as the matador wears the bull down, before he goes in for the kill.

Now he could plan for the final day. First, the devastating and demoralizing bombardment; then the grand assault! The Union line crushed at that critical point; a third of Meade's army surrounded and captured; the rest of it streaming down the road to Baltimore in irretrievable rout, harried by Stuart's cavalry! A great and war-ending stroke, in the Napoleonic tradition of Austerlitz, Jena, and Wagram!

To us, knowing the answer, such thoughts may seem fantastic. At that time, no man knew.

Again, also, we must remember the supreme sense of confidence pervading the Confederate army. Only a few failed to have their judgments impaired by this headiness. Only here and there a few still demanded facts, and looked steadily at time, space, and number. Of these the chief was James Longstreet, whom Lee was riding to meet.

9

By now the brightness of the sun must have been showing beyond the Round Tops. On Culp's Hill the sound of fighting rose and fell. Across the fields the men of Pickett's division came marching on.

10

Longstreet had sent scouts during the night to feel out the way around the Union left flank. This was characteristic of the man; he wanted facts.

He was in his prime at Gettysburg, forty-two years old — "a soldier every inch, and very handsome, tall and well proportioned, strong and active." This sounds like a younger Lee, but the two were very different — the Virginian and the man from the farther South. There was about Longstreet nothing of the god-like aura. Even more than Lee, he was a soldier's soldier. He liked his liquor, and an occasional riotous party — as on the occasion when he stood on a table with another high-ranking general and the two sang the duet from *I Puritani*. He was a devoted and dangerous poker player. As Lee did not wholly, Longstreet accepted such failings in others. On one occasion, as they rode through a camp, Lee noted sorrowfully that some of the men were actually playing chuck-a-luck, a primitive form of crap-shooting. Longstreet said he would do what he could to end such devilish practices. But no one noticed that he did anything. He was no man to try to stop a rat-hole by poking moon-beams into it, and only such a man will try to keep American soldiers from gambling.

He had been West Point '42, and shown off well in the Mexican War. Later the routine of army life wore him down; as he declared, he lost aspirations for military glory; he became a pay-master, ranking as major in 1861. Under the Confederacy he had military glory thrust upon him by an appointment as briga-dier. So here he was at Gettysburg, a lieutenant general and second in command of the army.

In battle some said that he was slow to start, but that is easy to say, and hard to prove. Once engaged, all agreed, he was a magnificent fighter — handling his men well, getting from them everything they had, never happier than when he himself could lead an attack, but "like a rock in steadiness, when sometimes in battle the world seemed to be flying to pieces."

His relationships with Lee were intimate and friendly. Each was large-minded enough to appreciate the capacities of the other, different though they might be.

Such a man was this James Longstreet — a healthy animal, powerful, virile, seemingly tireless, possessing that natural and tenacious courage of the bulldog to which his admirers com-pared him; a man who attracted nicknames — Dutch, to his West Point friends; Pete or Old Peter, to his men; "my old war horse," as Lee once called him; not a quarrelsome man, but a man who created a considerable retinue of enemies, largely be-cause he weighed evidence and therefore frequently committed the unforgivable sin of being right; most of all, perhaps, a real-ist, trying to base his judgments upon determined fact, and then stubborn to maintain them.

11

The place of their meeting has been described, vaguely enough, as "on the field in front of and within cannon-range of Round

Top." Another has stated that the time was "soon after sunrise." Several persons who were present have written of this "conference." They did not write until years later, when their memories were dull, and when controversy may have perverted their recollections. To reconcile them all is impossible, and the best we can do is to give some account that will square with events as they later occurred. On the whole, more seems to have been made of the incident than is warranted. It was not a council of war, but merely a brief meeting, between the commanding general and his senior corps-commander — an interchange of views, followed by the giving of some orders.

Being within cannon shot, they doubtless sent the horses back with the orderlies, and then gathered at a point where they would have a view of the Union lines and yet themselves be inconspicuous. Lee and Longstreet were there. Also present were Lieutenant General A. P. Hill, commanding the corps holding the Confederate center, Major General Harry Heth, and several members of Lee's staff. Colonel Alexander was there, unless what he reports came to him at second hand.

Longstreet took the lead, perhaps realizing that in a moment of uncertainty the first proposer of a definite line of action is likely to be successful. During the night, he said, his scouts had discovered a possible route around the Union left flank. He could sidle his corps in that direction, and thus force the Union army to abandon its strong position. In fact, he had already given orders to start this movement.

That a corps-commander should thus commit the army to a particular action seems high-handed, but Longstreet thus wrote in his official report, seeming to consider it nothing extraordinary. Perhaps what he had done was to give orders to prepare for such a march, rather than to begin it.

Lee's reply was decisive. Though the exact words of a conversation as reported a dozen years later are not to be trusted, still they probably represent, in simplified form, what was expressed.

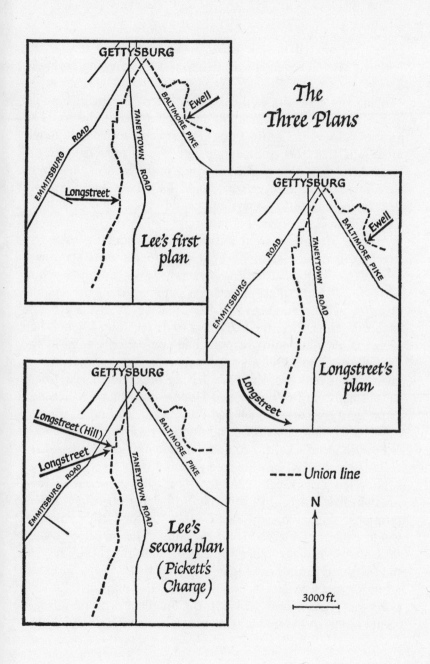

The Three Plans

GETTYSBURG

Ewell

Longstreet

Lee's first plan

GETTYSBURG

Ewell

Longstreet's plan

Longstreet

GETTYSBURG

Longstreet (Hill)

Longstreet

Lee's second plan (Pickett's Charge)

EMMITSBURG ROAD

TANEYTOWN ROAD

BALTIMORE PIKE

- - - - Union line

N

3000 ft.

Longstreet quoted Lee as saying, while he pointed toward the Union lines, "The enemy is there, and I am going to strike him."

Being the commander, Lee had no need to explain himself. Yet, as an eminently reasonable man, he probably did so. The most obvious objection to Longstreet's proposed flanking movement was that the Confederate line was already dangerously long. Moreover, though Lee may not have said this, merely to have forced Meade to retreat would have been nothing more than to win a victory. Gettysburg would have been only another Chancellorsville, as barren of results.

An aide, doubtless, went hurrying off to countermand Longstreet's orders, and then Lee put forward his own plan, as a proposal and not as an order. As nearly as we can make it out, what he set forth must have been approximately the original plan, for which Alexander had been placing his artillery before daybreak. In essence, the battle was to be taken up where it had been left off the evening before. The ever-present sound of the fighting on Culp's Hill must have lent support to what he was saying, for Ewell was obviously having his troubles. As troops to be employed, Lee mentioned Hood's and McLaw's divisions, of Longstreet's corps, which had done heavy fighting on the preceding afternoon. By thus using troops already in position without waiting for Pickett to come up, Lee could have launched the attack very quickly, in time to co-operate with Ewell.

Now was Longstreet's time to object. He came out flatly — his two divisions could not safely be taken from their present positions. They already faced strong forces; their removal would easily be observed from the hills. The maneuver would thus invite Meade to strike the Confederate right. Besides, the sounds heard during the night indicated that Meade, in expectation of renewed attack, was fortifying the position. In addition, the ground over which the Confederates must advance would be swept by the fire of the batteries on the smaller hill.

Longstreet may not have felt it politic to present another reason. But his men had suffered heavy casualties, and were scarcely fit to resume the offensive. As he wrote some years later, "To have rushed forward my two divisions, then carrying bloody noses from their terrible conflict the day before, would have been madness." There was, indeed, little of the glory-hunter in Longstreet. His implied but unspoken question must certainly have been, "Why don't you let Hill's corps win some renown today?"

The obvious evidence for the strength of Longstreet's arguments is that Lee was convinced, and dropped the idea of using those two divisions. He also seems to have accepted the arguments against the place of the attack, and he now, we must assume, began to develop the idea of what would be known as Pickett's Charge.

This involved a considerable change of plan. First, the point of assault was shifted to the Union right-center. Second, all idea of direct co-ordination with Ewell's attack was abandoned. Third, the troops to be employed were different. Pickett's division was now definitely earmarked, and to this Longstreet could raise no objection. The other troops were to be drawn from Hill's corps. Lee mentioned a total of three divisions, about 15,000 men.

At that moment, in the brightness of the newly risen sun, the old was clashing with the new. On the one side stood Lee — tall, slender, patrician. Behind him loomed in spirit the romantic warriors of the past — charging knights with waving plumes, gentlemen of the English Guard, "Light Horse" Harry. Essentially, one may think, Lee believed that victory rested in superiority of morale, in the brave hearts of his soldiers.

On the other side was Longstreet, heavier-set, younger. Behind him mustered the warriors of the future — men with repeating rifles, machine guns, and electronic computers. Longstreet was no man to decry courage, but he was deeply convinced that assaults must be calculated in terms of numbers, distance, and fire-power.

He had met the infantry of the Army of the Potomac often enough to have a considerable respect for it, and he did not believe that a frontal attack on a well-placed Union line could be successful. In this he differed from his commanding general, though he was not in a position to say much more, having already made as many objections as a second-in-command could well make. Nevertheless — perhaps, merely for the record — he expressed himself, and we can quote the words as he remembered them:

> General, I have been a soldier all my life. I have been with soldiers engaged in fights by couples, by squads, companies, regiments, divisions, and armies, and should know, as well as anyone, what soldiers can do. It is my opinion that no fifteen thousand men ever arrayed for battle can take that position.

At these words a coldness must have fallen upon those assembled. The corps-commander had gone a little too far. He had declared a basic lack of faith in his chief's plan of battle. As a modern soldier has stated, Longstreet's reply was "dignified, yet verging on insubordination."

Lee probably felt no personal offense. He was not one to stand much on rank, and he had great respect and friendship for the man who was opposing him. The suggestion has been made that Lee should at that moment have relieved Longstreet of command. But this would have been making a mountain out of a molehill, especially since Lee had no one available who was capable of handling a corps half so well as Longstreet could. What Lee might well have done, however, was to have put Hill in command of the assaulting troops. This would have been reasonable, since two-thirds of them were to be from Hill's corps. But Lee retained Longstreet in command, thus obviously indicating that he considered the remark to be nothing more than an expression of professional difference of opinion, and that he preferred Longstreet, recalcitrant, to Hill, co-operative.

Lee then gave orders that preparations should begin. Several hours must necessarily elapse before the infantry could advance, and in that interval many things might happen. For instance, Ewell might gain a striking success. Or, Meade himself might decide to attack. Or, new information might cause Lee to change his mind. Longstreet could still hope that he would not have to throw his infantry against Cemetery Ridge.

12

Pickett's men were getting closer. Fifteen regiments, Virginians all! There were companies recruited from every part of the state — some from the northern fringe which had been an occupied zone for most of two years; others from counties which had now seceded from secession to become West Virginia.

One memorialist of the division emphasized its "sprinkling of restless, roving adventurers." But certainly this could not have been more than a thin sprinkling. The vast majority of the soldiers were from the small farms and little towns. There were units from Richmond and Norfolk, but even those places were not very large. Most of the "men" were scarcely old enough to justify the word. A sergeant of the 7th Virginia, himself eighteen, later ventured the opinion that the average age, men and officers, of his regiment at Gettysburg did not exceed nineteen years. In appearance the division cannot have been highly military. By 1863 the Army of Northern Virginia had decided that comfort was preferable to display. Uniforms were far from uniform, and the headgear in particular was various, consisting of what each man preferred or could get hold of. Except among the officers there was very little wearing of the gray. The prevailing tone was half way between brown and yellow, a color

known as "butternut," from which the "blue-bellies" of the
Union army called their opponents "butternuts."

Though composed of veteran troops, the division, as a division, was neither old nor distinguished. It had been organized
in September, 1862, by grouping one South Carolina and two
Virginia brigades under Pickett. Two more Virginia brigades
were soon added. At Fredericksburg the division was in reserve,
and suffered only forty casualties. It was then sent off on the
"Suffolk campaign," into southeastern Virginia, where it did a
little skirmishing. Chancellorsville was won before the division
rejoined the army for the swift march into Pennsylvania. A
Virginia brigade and the one from South Carolina had been left
behind, so that it now had only the brigades of Kemper, Garnett,
and Armistead.

13

At the head of the column rode Major General George Edward
Pickett. At least, he probably rode at the head, for he was a man
with a certain love of flair, and he would have been likely to be
at the front when approaching a battlefield. Yet we cannot be
sure. Military practice of the time prescribed no definite post for
the general commanding a division, but allowed him to be at
whatever point he deemed most advantageous. This is a detail
amplified in importance by the events of the afternoon.

As he rode forward that day, Pickett was thirty-eight years old
by the calendar, but in his heart he was not a day past twenty-
one, and he was gloriously, head-over-heels, in love with a pretty
Virginia girl in her teens. He came of an old Virginia family,
and was related to practically everybody of importance east of
Richmond. His appointment to West Point, however, had been
from Illinois, where he had been studying law with his uncle.
There he had come to know a lawyer named Abraham Lincoln,
who had liked the youngster well enough to give him some bits

of good advice on his departure. But, then, nearly everybody liked young George Pickett.

The class of '46 was a distinguished one. George McClellan was graduated as #2; Thomas J. Jackson, as #17. In all there were fifty-nine graduates, and Pickett ranked as #59. Academic distinction is perhaps not necessary for a soldier, but still it is disturbing to find Pickett very low even in military subjects — in infantry tactics, #52.

He had a distinguished career as a lieutenant in the Mexican War. He did a tour of duty on the Pacific Coast, and was involved in the so-called Pig War. This border dispute never got to the shooting stage, but Pickett did well, as a captain of infantry, by refusing to yield an inch to the roarings of the British lion.

Naturally he went with his state in 1861. On the Peninsula he was a brigadier — commanding, with considerable dash, the regiments which now marched in the column as Garnett's brigade. He was knocked out with a wound in June, but by fall was back, to assume divisional command, and to be commissioned major general. From that time until Gettysburg his military career was that of his division.

So much for the events of his life — but what was he like? Nearly everybody had liked young George Pickett, and this seems to hold pretty well for the older George Pickett of Gettysburg, at least among those who had known him when he was young. One of these was Longstreet, who was tremendously fond of him. But if the older Pickett had suddenly come into your life, you might have had reservations. One of the best descriptions is from keen-minded Moxley Sorrel, who saw Pickett as he first reported to Longstreet's headquarters as a brigadier — "a singular figure indeed!" He described the newcomer as a medium-sized, well-built man, erect and in well-fitting uniform, an elegant riding whip in hand, of distinguished and striking appearance. This last adjective applied most aptly to his hair —

"long ringlets flowed loosely over his shoulders, trimmed and highly perfumed; his beard likewise was curling and giving out the scent of Araby."

This hair-do amazed, and generally amused, everyone. During wet weather the hair hung lank down to his shoulders, giving him doubtless some resemblance to that redoubtable warrior Sir Andrew Aguecheek. These curls provided the subject of a joke, perhaps the only one, made by Lee during the Gettysburg campaign. When an admiring Maryland lady asked him for a clipping of hair as a keepsake, he replied that he really had none to spare, but that she might ask Pickett. The latter, who was present, did not enjoy the pleasantry. (Also at Gettysburg was Pickett's long-haired Union counterpart, that other George, surnamed Custer.)

What Pickett was actually like at Gettysburg is difficult to determine, because most of the comments about him were written after the war when his later actions, as well as his Gettysburg reputation, were influencing people's judgments. But we may quote Sorrel again, since he seems to write of times before the great battle. He was personally friendly with Pickett, and characterized him as "a good fellow, a good brigadier." Whether the last statement implies that he should never have been made a major general must be left to inference, but Sorrel used words carefully. He added, "taking Longstreet's orders in emergencies, I could always see how he looked after Pickett, and made us give him things very fully; indeed, sometimes stay with him to make sure he did not get astray." Sorrel also mentioned the love-affair and the "fiery, if mature, affections." On one occasion Pickett left his division without leave, to visit the girl. Sorrel concluded, "I don't think his division benefited by such carpet-knight doings in the field!"

An even more severe judge of Pickett was Colonel Eppa Hunton of Garnett's brigade. He was possibly prejudiced, for he wanted to be made a brigadier, and besides he was suffering from a fistula, a type of affliction that does not make anyone likely to be charitable of his fellow-men. Hunton had seen Pickett, during the Suffolk campaign, lie down on his horse's neck and scurry out of the line of fire of a battery. In Hunton's opinion this was below the standard of courage current for a Confederate officer. Nevertheless, Pickett commanded a division, and he was meeting the requirements of Lee and Longstreet.

14

Kemper's brigade led the march — the 1st, 3rd, 7th, 11th, and 24th Virginia. It traced its origin to the spring of 1861. Its first commander had been Longstreet himself, and so it fought at First Manassas. Under a series of brigadiers, including both Ewell and A. P. Hill, it had served gallantly on the Peninsula, and at Second Manassas and Antietam. Though its men had done little at Fredericksburg and had missed Chancellorsville, they could hold their heads high.

Kemper himself was thirty-nine, and not a professional soldier, having held a commission during the Mexican War, but without seeing active service. A lawyer, he had gone into politics, serving ten years in the Virginia legislature. All this had made it easy for him to be commissioned a colonel at the opening of the war, and his regiment had been the 7th, still serving in his brigade. Proving himself a good soldier on the Peninsula, he was soon a brigadier. Something of the political orator lingered about him, and he was given to high-flown language. "Judging by manner and conversation alone," an observer wrote, "he would have been classed as a Bombastes Furioso."

Garnett's brigade marched second — the 8th, 18th, 19th, 28th, and 56th Virginia. In background it was much the same as Kemper's — a fine brigade. Four of its regiments had fought at First Manassas. Pickett himself commanded it on the Peninsula, until he was wounded, and then Hunton took over. Pickett resumed command in the fall of 1862, until he was given the division. Then Garnett was brought in as brigadier, to the disgust of Hunton; he thought he had earned the promotion, but he remained as colonel of his regiment. Still, there was not much chance to impugn the soldierly qualities of the present brigadier.

Richard Brooke Garnett was forty-four, West Point of '41. He had enjoyed an uneventful career in what was called "the old army," and ended as a captain in 1861. He was a strong Union man, and made a public speech against secession. But he followed his state. At the battle of Kernstown something went wrong, and he incurred the displeasure of Stonewall Jackson. He was clapped under arrest and relieved of duty. The matter was cleared up, but Garnett had not recovered from the blow to his pride. He felt that his military honor and his reputation for courage had been smirched.

He was, on July 3, in constant pain from his leg, having recently suffered the indignity of being kicked by a horse. According to Alexander, who knew Garnett and saw him that day, the general was "buttoned up in an old blue overcoat." According to a captain in his own brigade, who also saw him, the general was wearing a "fine new gray uniform." Though an overcoat seems unlikely on that July day, Alexander's description was widely read, so that in dozens of later accounts the blue overcoat appears.

Dick Garnett should probably have been in the hospital, but with the memory of Kernstown in his mind, he could not stay at the rear. So he rode to the battle, carrying with him a touch of the tragic-heroic, a Union man fighting against the Union, a proud and courageous man wounded at heart, a man so much in pain that he scarcely could have had zest for the fighting.

Armistead's was the last of the brigades in the column — the 9th, 14th, 38th, 53rd, and 57th Virginia. It had been Armistead's from its organization in the spring of 1862. Both general and brigade had performed distinguished service at Malvern Hill.

It had shared in the battles of the Army of Northern Virginia, down until the time when Pickett's division had been sent on the Suffolk campaign. Like the other two, it was a brigade that anyone would be happy to have covering his flank.

Lewis Addison Armistead, at forty-six, was the oldest of the three brigadiers. In his hair as well as in his uniform he wore the gray. He came of a military family, and was West Point and Old Army. He served well in Mexico, but in 1861 he was only a captain of infantry. In the Confederacy he was made a colonel, and placed in command of the 57th Virginia. (What was left of it was marching in his brigade now.) Before he saw any fighting, he was promoted to brigadier, and thereafter his career was that of his brigade.

Of him they tell a famous story — one of the archetypal tales of the war, of the spring when the comrade-officers of the Old Army parted, not knowing where or if they would meet again. . . . In a far-off dirty little adobe village called Los Angeles, some Southern officers were leaving to join the Confederacy, and they spent the last evening at the house of a Pennsylvania captain. As the party was breaking up, the wife of a Southern officer sat down at the piano, and sang "Kathleen Mavourneen," that song of parting in the gray dawn:

> It may be for years, and it may be forever.

Then Captain Armistead walked across to his host, and put his hands on his friend's shoulders as the tears streamed down, and said, "Hancock, good-by; you can never know what this has cost me." Now, more than two years later, it was bright morning and not gray dawn, and "Lew" Armistead was riding toward where his friend waited.

15

So Pickett's men drew nearer, and there was, it appears, no sense of urgency. "A shady, quiet march," one of them recalled.

And he went on, "we halted for a short time in the woods, but moved forward pretty soon into a field, near a branch." The Southern word rings strangely in Pennsylvania; almost certainly it was the little stream known as Pitzer's Run, and they were near where it joins the slightly larger Willoughby's Run. The location was a little over half a mile behind the main Confederate line, protected from artillery fire, moderately level, with plentiful water. It was a good spot to establish their base.

The column was halted, and the men were allowed to fall out. In company lots, one-hundred-fifty heaps, they piled their blankets and other extra gear. Then, doubtless, they scattered to attend to their needs. The surgeons and the ambulance-men began to set up the field hospital. Soon the men came straggling back, and went to fill their canteens at the stream. From over the wooded ridge to the east came the far-off sound of cannonading, but that was nothing to disturb veterans. They took it easy. Obviously, no couriers were spurring back with orders to push the march.

16

In the low ground east of the Peach Orchard, there was a Confederate skirmish line, within rifle range of the opposing skirmish line. It was a place where a sensible man kept his head down. That was sufficient reason for Private Gart Johnson of the 18th Mississippi to be surprised at seeing two men in officers' uniforms walking along, bolt upright and stopping now and then to look around. He was considerably more surprised when he recognized them as Generals Lee and Longstreet. The only sign that the two had not completely lost their senses was that they were keeping fifteen or twenty steps apart, so as not to offer a double opportunity to any sharpshooter.

They came close and stopped again to look. Bullets whistled by, showing that "those people" had spotted an attractive target.

The skirmishers were hugging the ground, and one of them spoke: "General Lee, you are running a very great risk."

Lee did not move, but went on "calm and serene as if viewing a landscape." Then he called across to Longstreet in words that Johnson remembered as being, "Mass your artillery behind that hill, and at the signal bring your guns to the top of the ridge and turn them loose." Then the two went on.

Since Lee had spoken at a considerable distance, the Mississippians had heard, and they immediately realized that before long they would be right in the middle of an artillery fight. The result was an outburst of activity, the men digging with bayonets and pieces of board, and anything they could lay their hands on. In this low ground the soil was deep, and soon they had the satisfaction of being well down, two or three men to a hole. . . .

The two generals, some time that morning, also came to General W. T. Wofford, commanding a brigade stationed near the Peach Orchard. Lee asked Wofford whether he could again advance to the ridge marking the Union line, as he had on the preceding afternoon.

"No, general, I think not."

"Why not?"

"Because, general, the enemy have had all night to entrench and reinforce."

These two incidents are of importance as showing that Lee was still open-minded as to the point of attack, that he took pains to reconnoiter, and that he and Longstreet were co-operating closely.

17

We have just seen Lee pointing out a ridge for the location of artillery. Of such features, the best known on the battlefield are Seminary Ridge, held by the Confederates, and Cemetery Ridge, the low southward appendage of Cemetery Hill, held by the

Union army. The two run nearly north and south about a mile apart, and neither is much of an elevation. Generally parallel to them and about half way between, there is a very slight rise of ground, which has also been called a ridge, though it is too insignificant to warrant that designation and has not been given a name. From the Peach Orchard it extends north about a mile, angling across the Emmitsburg road, so that it is west of the road at the south and east of it at the north. The ordinary person can pass along the road without realizing that there is any ridge there. This, however, was the elevation to which Lee had pointed.

The work of moving the guns to this new location devolved upon Alexander, and he doubtless shrugged his shoulders. He had already placed his guns once. Well, it is for generals to order and for colonels to execute!

18

Alexander was a Georgian — West Point, '57. His commission was in the engineers, and he was immediately assigned to duty as instructor at the Academy. All of this means that he was unusually brainy. He was also highly practical, and soon developed the "wig-wag" system of signaling. President Davis appointed him an engineer and Chief of the Signal Service on Beauregard's staff. He did ordnance and signal work for a while, and then Longstreet put his finger on him. By the end of 1862 Alexander, at twenty-seven, was a colonel of artillery. He rendered distinguished service both at Fredericksburg and at Chancellorsville.

His portraits suggest an intelligent but colorless man. Actually, he was something of a "character." In an army passionately addicted to good horseflesh, he was notorious for the sorry nags he rode. In a manner suggestive of the Chocolate Soldier, he eschewed a revolver and carried a big-bored horse-pistol. He kept this loaded with bird shot, and found it very handy for knocking off quail, thus often gaining a toothsome dinner.

Alexander's orders must have been two-fold. (1) Place your guns so as to be able to bombard the position near the clump of trees. (2) Be prepared, later, to advance guns in support of the attacking infantry. We can appreciate better how he went about solving his problem if we know what he had to work with.

19

The artillery of Longstreet's corps totaled, that morning, just about eighty guns. They were grouped into twenty-two batteries, and these into five battalions. This organization was efficient — superior in some respects to that of the Union artillery. The morale of officers and men was high.

In what might be called professional skill, the Confederate artillerists were perhaps lacking. This was partly because there was a chronic shortage of ammunition, and a corresponding lack of target practice. Also, the Southerner, even when an artillery-man, was likely to have a certain disdain for mechanical details. Let the base-minded Yankee concern himself with trajectories and velocities! The Confederate ideal was to rush the guns as far forward as possible, and then go *bang-bang*. In northern Virginia, a country of woods and small fields, the system had worked. It was not so well suited to the openness of Gettysburg.

The Confederate artillery was characterized by the number of different kinds of guns in use. Although creating a problem of supplies, this was not altogether a disadvantage. Under some particular conditions, almost any kind of gun might prove to be just the one needed. The chief reason for the variety, however, was that artillery during this war was in a madly transitional period. On the one hand were little stubby, 12-pound smooth-bore howitzers which might have done their bit at Saratoga; on the other hand, there were two superlatively up-to-date English-made Whitworth breech-loading rifles.

About 10 per cent of the Confederate artillery consisted of the nearly obsolete little howitzers. There were also four 24-pound howitzers, big brothers to the 12-pounders and just about as out-of-date.

The great majority of the guns — and this goes for both armies — were either bronze smooth-bore Napoleons, or iron rifled cannon. Both types remained in use throughout the war, and each had its advantages.

The Napoleon took its name from the current emperor, not from his more illustrious uncle. Being a smooth-bore, shooting a spherical projectile, it might be termed obsolescent, but it was still a highly effective weapon. Its great virtue was the hitting-power that came from its four-and-a-half-inch bore. At canister range, under a quarter of a mile, it was a gigantic and murderous shotgun. Its extreme useful range was less than a mile.

The standard rifled guns were the 10-pound Parrotts and the "3-inch" both shooting elongated, conoidal-nosed projectiles. Since the bore of the Parrotts was 2.9 inches, the difference between them and the "3-inch," for actual combat, was inappreciable. These rifled guns were newly invented, but would soon become universal in the armies of the world. They were accurate up to a mile and a half, or even farther. But they lacked something of the Napoleon's short-range deadliness.

The Parrotts also came in a 20-pounder that was heavy for the horses, but still rated as a field-gun. Both sides had a few of them. The Confederates also had the two Whitworths.

20

Alexander, having got his orders, must have looked the ground over to see what he could do at concentrating fire upon the area around the clump of trees. Northward, three Union batteries were in position, and three others were to the south. The length of line occupied by these batteries and the spaces between them was something over half a mile. The southern part of this he could consider the sector on which to concentrate. Anything to the north, Hill's artillery could take care of. Yet Alexander could not pin-point all his fire. Long and intense concentration would reveal the plan of attack, and warn the Yankees to mass reserves. Besides, farther to the south were many Union batteries; they must be kept under control and prevented from smashing the infantry when it advanced.

Alexander, therefore, left his own battalion, except for two guns, where it already was. It was in a slightly elevated position, east of the Peach Orchard, facing south of east. The guns could not cover the area around the clump of trees; their duty would be to neutralize the batteries opposite them.

He extended this line to the south by bringing up two of Henry's batteries. This was the battalion attached to Hood's division, which held the extreme right. Its two other batteries had to remain on that flank.

North of his own battalion, Alexander bent the line back so that it faced northeast, at the clump of trees. Here, with the left flank touching the Emmitsburg road, he placed Eshleman's battalion (the Washington Artillery) and part of Cabell's. Still to be put into position was Dearing's battalion, which was the artillery attached to Pickett's division and by this time was arriving on the battlefield.

"We shifted about," he wrote, "as inoffensively as possible, and carefully avoided getting into bunches." Such devices worked, and the Union artillery fired only an occasional nuisance shot. This leisurely pace in posting the artillery is another indication that Lee and Longstreet no longer felt themselves pressed for time.

21

On Culp's Hill the sound of the fighting, a mingling of cannonade and musketry, varied from time to time. An experienced listener could tell that the Confederates had seized the initiative and were attempting to capture the hill, and that the intensifications of fire indicated crises of attack.

22

Now, for Pickett's men, the pleasant little twenty-minute halt was ended. Facing east toward the cannonading, they stood in double-ranked battle-formation, captains at company right in the front rank, lieutenants and sergeants as file-closers. The extra gear still lay where the men of each company had piled it; heavy in each man's pockets or in his cartridge-box rested his sixty rounds of ammunition. No one needed to be told that these extra rounds had been issued because of imminent battle, and perhaps the weight was heavy on more than a man's pockets or cartridge-box. Then the command came, "Forward!"

In battle-formation they marched toward the risen sun and the sound of the distant guns. High ground protected them from the enemy's sight. Crossing the fields, their lines must have become disordered, but that was no matter now. They came to where there had been fighting the day before; a few bodies lay scattered. Then they saw other troops and batteries and behind-the-line activities. They were halted finally with a ridge in front still sheltering them from observation. They were ordered to lie down, and to do nothing that would attract the enemy's attention.

Shortly after they were in position, Lee, Longstreet, and Pickett began to ride slowly along the lines of prostrate infantry-men, inspecting. Mindful of their orders, the men refrained from cheering, but by a spontaneous impulse they rose, uncovered, and silently held their hats up while the generals rode by.

23

Pickett's men were not to be the whole; Lee had promised two of Hill's divisions. He rode about the field, making his choices.

Brigadier General James H. Lane, known as "Little Jim," was in temporary command of Pender's division that morning. Lee appeared, and reconnoitered the enemy's lines; when he was about to leave, he remarked that he needed more troops on the right, but did not know where they were to come from.

On that third day of battle, fresh infantry was getting hard to find. Yet Lee was not nearly so badly off as he might have been. Altogether, he had thirty-seven brigades of infantry. At mid-morning of July 3, eight of these were pinned down on the right, and ten on the left. But this means that Lee had been able to concentrate nineteen brigades, more than half his army, in his center, where they could be used to launch or to support the climactic attack.

To consider further, at this time thirty of the brigades were more or less worn down by hard fighting, and seven were fresh or comparatively so. All of these seven were among the nineteen brigades massed in the center. Obviously, Lee had been able to effect this concentration only because he was playing Meade for what he was, that is, a not very aggressive fighter, doubly hesitant at Gettysburg because he had been in command of his army for only a few days. Thus, for the launching of the great attack, Lee had effected a magnificent concentration, especially of fresh troops.

His problem, of which he spoke to Lane, was thus perhaps not so much in finding infantry as in finding a large unit, a whole division, which he could employ. Of Hill's three divisions, Heth's was his first choice. There were two obvious reasons for the selection — the division was already posted in just about the proper position from which to launch the attack, and it had not been engaged on the preceding day.

According to many opinions, this choice was a great error.

Whether any other division would have done better may be argued, but certainly the choice seems to have been somewhat the result of mere ignorance. Though Lee had been himself a staff-officer, he seems to have had a blind spot as to the necessity of an efficient staff. Instead, he surrounded himself with a group of congenial gentlemen, passionately devoted to the Confederate cause and to their chief, but not notably able. After the war, a member of that group made a remarkable statement, "They were terribly mistaken about Heth's division in this planning." Who can "they" mean except Lee and his staff? And why would Lee have been "mistaken" unless his staff had failed to supply him with the needed information?

The division had been formed recently, during the reorganization of the army after Chancellorsville and Jackson's death. Two of its brigades were veteran units of the army, worn down in numbers after many battles. One of these was Archer's — 1st, 7th, and 14th Tennessee, 13th Alabama and 5th Alabama Battalion. The other was Brockenbrough's all-Virginia brigade — 40th, 47th, 55th, and 22nd Battalion. Then there were two big but less experienced brigades. The one was Pettigrew's, of North Carolina — the 11th, 26th, 47th, and 52nd. The other was Davis's — the 2nd, 11th, and 42nd Mississippi, and 55th North Carolina.

Brockenbrough's brigade of Virginians was basically indistinguishable from any of Pickett's. As Field's brigade, it had been a long-time unit of the army, and had fought in most of its battles. Field had been badly wounded, late in 1862. Brockenbrough, as senior colonel, had assumed command, and the brigade, still known as Field's, had remained under this "temporary" command for a period of months. Apparently Brockenbrough was not considered worthy of promotion. At last, Heth was given the brigade, and it assumed his name. Shortly, however, he was transferred to the divisional command, and the brigade reverted to what seems to have been the uninspired leadership of Brockenbrough. It then took his name, even though he remained a colonel. At this juncture, the brigade went into Chancellorsville, fought well, and suffered badly. Again, on the first day at Gettysburg, it attacked with Heth's division, and was repulsed with loss.

The other three brigades were from states where life was somewhat more primitive than in Virginia. Their men were from the hill-country and the mountains, from the bayous and the piney woods. Some have claimed that this touch of the primitive made them even better fighting men than the Virginians were. Many of their men had more than a touch of the backwoods about them, even of the frontier. This again was to their advantage; they had handled firearms since boyhood, and prided themselves on their marksmanship.

Archer's brigade was thoroughly veteran, having fought in most of the battles of the army. It had launched the opening attack at Gettysburg, and had been taken in flank. It had retired in confusion, losing some prisoners, including Archer himself.

Pettigrew's and Davis's brigades had served together, and had much in common. They were new to Lee's army, having been brought up as reinforcements just before the march northward. Of their regiments the 26th North Carolina and the 2nd and 11th Mississippi had previously been with the army, and had good records of battles fought. The other five regiments were not new in service, and had seen some rough-and-tumble fighting along the North Carolina coast. Up until July 1, they had lacked big-battle experience. On that day they got it suddenly and thoroughly, having what can scarcely be called the pleasure of being initiated by experts — the regiments of the Union First Corps, including the Iron Brigade.

The division as a whole had suffered losses of at least forty per cent. In most armies, such a battered unit would have been sent to the rear for reorganization, but here it was being selected for a climactic attack!

Apparently Lee did not find another division that he wished
to employ as a unit, and so he took Lane's and Scales's brigades
from Pender's division and Wilcox's and Perry's from Anderson's.
In the end, however, these last two brigades were not used in
what we may call the charge, and so need not be considered here.

Pender's two brigades were both North Carolinian and both
veteran units of the famous Light Division. Scales's — the 13th,
16th, 22nd, 34th, and 38th — had been in the first day's fighting,
and had suffered hideously, losing all but two of its field officers.
The colonel who took command of it at the end of that day
described it as "depressed, dilapidated, and almost unorganized."
Lane's brigade comprised the 7th, 18th, 28th, 33rd, and 37th
regiments. It had not as yet been seriously engaged at Gettysburg.

Such had been the shattering impact of two days of battle
that both these divisions and four of the six brigades were under
temporary commanders. Heth and Pender being wounded,
Pettigrew and Lane now led the divisions. Colonel J. K. Marshall
of the 52nd had succeeded Pettigrew in command of the brigade.
Archer, taken prisoner, was replaced by Colonel B. D. Fry of
the 13th Alabama. Davis and Brockenbrough remained, though
it is often stated that Brockenbrough had been replaced. Lane's
brigade had been taken over by Colonel C. M. Avery of the
33rd, but Lane was soon to resume command. Since Scales had
been wounded, Colonel W. L. J. Lowrance of the 34th had
replaced him.

24

The three generals deserve a few words. . . . James Johnston
Pettigrew, thirty-five-year-old North Carolinian, practiced military leadership only as one of a host of talents. Sprung of a
prominent family, he was Fortune's child. He had a fine legal
mind, was a scholar in Greek and Hebrew, had published a book

of travels, though a rather dull one. He was an outstanding representative of that not too common type, the intellectual Southerner. Within his reach, people said, lay any goal — Chief Justice, President. The whirlwind of war caught him up. Soon he was a brigadier; now he commanded a division. (Yes, and already the unrustling wings of the Dark Angel hovered above him, though not as closely as they did that morning for many.)

As for Joseph R. Davis, thirty-eight and from Mississippi, one might cynically say that he had one qualification for being a brigadier general — he was a nephew of President Jefferson Davis. At the least, one can say that he would not have been in his present rank without that family background, for he had done nothing remarkable, and had been in only a little fighting, as a lieutenant colonel. His service as colonel had been wholly on his uncle's staff. So there is not much to be said about his military experience, though this is not to say that he was lacking in courage and other qualifications. An observer has described him, personally, as "very pleasant and unpretending."

The third brigadier was James H. Lane — still under thirty, familiarly called "Little Jim," and considered to be the youngest for his rank in the Confederate service. Lane shared two qualities with Pettigrew — both had entered the army from North Carolina and both were intellectuals. Lane, indeed, was of that lowly breed called "professor." Like many short men, "Little Jim" seems to have had a hankering for military life. He entered the army as major, and a year and a half later was a brigadier. Yet, whether for lack of stature or of years or for some other reason, he did not altogether have the confidence of General Lee — for a brigade, yes; not for a division.

Suggestions have been put forward that troubles resulted from the necessity of putting four brigades under colonels. Actually, three of these brigades were small, not individually equaling what one regiment was supposed to be; even Pettigrew's brigade was not much larger than a full regiment. Moreover, the attack of the division was to be merely a straight advance, with no complicated maneuvering. One has difficulty in seeing, therefore, that the task of command would have been beyond the capacities of a colonel. Brockenbrough, indeed, can scarcely be called a temporary commander, though the record seems to indicate that he was perhaps the least fitted of the four to handle a brigade. Of Marshall and Lowrance little is known; we can only assume them to have been average senior colonels. Fry, a West Pointer, was definitely brigadier-material. He had fought with distinction in Mexico. As a filibuster, he had been a brigadier under Walker in Nicaragua, and had won renown by his desperate defense of Grenada. In the Confederate army he had been wounded three times. Though slight in build and quiet in manner, he was apparently indestructible, and was known as "a man of gunpowder reputation."

25

One of the controversies about the battle was to involve the question as to whether the troops from Heth's and Pender's divisions were inferior to those of Pickett's. In one important respect they were. Pickett's men were fresh to combat, but the others, except for Lane's brigade, had been fought out on July 1, had been granted an insufficient time to recover, and were very short of officers. But the frequent statement that they were "raw" troops would apply at most to only five regiments out of twenty-seven, and even these five had seen a good deal of service. The concentration of these five regiments into Pettigrew's and Davis's brigades did not particularly weaken those two, because they also had three veteran regiments.

Some of the Heth and Pender regiments were, in fact, colorful and famous ones. Such was the 11th Mississippi. Its men would have been ready to take on at any time, no holds barred, the 1st

Virginia or anything else that Pickett's division could supply. It included, as Company A, the University Grays, of whom you may read in Mr. William Faulkner's *Absalom, Absalom!* In spite of their white-glove origins, the men of that company prided themselves on being "always impulsive and undisciplined." It was an achievement to have such a reputation in such a regiment, of which a historian wrote, "No more disorderly mob of men have ever got together to make an army." General Whiting, in whose brigade they once were, is reported to have "cussed" whenever he thought of the 11th, but always to have concluded: "Damn 'em! I wouldn't go into battle without 'em." Being backwoodsmen, they were also famous marksmen. Someone once came to report the loss of a hog within their lines, testifying that a shot had been heard and a squeal. General Whiting replied soberly, "I am satisfied you are mistaken. When an 11th Mississippian shoots a hog, it don't squeal." The 11th had been guarding trains on July 1, and so had suffered almost no casualties.

The 26th North Carolina of Pettigrew's brigade was another notable regiment. It was recruited mostly from the Piedmont area, with two companies from the mountains. It had fought on the Peninsula, and then had been sent south for duty along the North Carolina coast. When it came to join the army again, after Chancellorsville, it had "splendid uniforms," and a band. But if anyone thought that the 26th was merely a fancy-pants regiment, the first day at Gettysburg should have set him straight. It went in with about 800 men, and it lost 549. Company E lost 18 killed and 52 wounded, and came out with only twelve men, all but two of these slightly wounded. Company F had only Sergeant Robert Hudspeth remaining! We might consider this last to be a myth, were it not that the company roll with the nature of the wounds of each man has been printed. By the re-joining of detached men Hudspeth had Company F up to a total of half a dozen on July 3.

There were many other notable regiments too, among Pickett's and Pender's as well as among Heth's. One can hardly omit from notice the 1st Virginia of Kemper's brigade, "The Old First," which had had continuous existence since 1754, and had fought its first engagement in that year, under Washington at Great Meadows. It had also fought in the Revolution, the War of 1812, and the Mexican War.

On the whole, however, it is hard to distinguish one Confederate regiment from another of the same state, since "personality" seems to have existed more in the brigade than in the regiment, in distinction from the Union army where the reverse was true.

26

As the sun rose higher, Alexander continued to place his guns, still moving them "inoffensively," so as not to attract fire. Much of this later arrangement involved Dearing's battalion, which had not got to the battlefield until that morning. Alexander must have considered it his ace. Dearing had four batteries, all Virginian. It was an efficient unit, and Major James Dearing was an artilleryman clear to the last inch of red stripe. There was not one of the obsolete howitzers in his battalion. Instead, there were twelve Napoleons, and six rifled guns, including two 20-pounders. The battalion had not yet been engaged, and so was in perfect condition.

Alexander assigned to it the best position of all, where it could fire upon the clump of trees with most deadly accuracy, and also, of course, be fired upon. This position was on that insignificant ridge between the two lines of battle, just north of where the Emmitsburg road crossed it. The guns were just below the crest of the ridge, ready to be pushed up by hand when the time came for firing. They were about a thousand yards from the clump of trees — a range well within the capacity of the Napoleons.

As the final extention of his line, Alexander placed — or had

already placed — six guns a little farther north. One of the
batteries was Virginian, of Alexander's own battalion — two
20-pounders. The other was a Georgia battery of Cabell's
battalion — two 10-pound Parrotts and two 3-inch rifles.

27

Once he had finished with his guns, Alexander so reported,
and Brigadier General Pendleton, Chief of Artillery, came to
inspect.

William Nelson Pendleton was to have an important, if nega-
tive, influence upon the momentous events of this day. Born a
Virginian in 1809 he attended West Point, and then served for
a few years as a second lieutenant of artillery. But he had soul-
searchings, and after prayer and much reading of Scripture, he
resigned from the army, and entered the ministry. In 1853, he
became Episcopalian rector in Lexington, Virginia, and there
he remained happily and quietly devoting himself to his parish,
until 1861. He was then fifty-two, and his brief military experience was almost twenty years behind. He was dedicated to his
high calling; fife and drum failed to stir him.

But patriotic members of his congregation began to tell him
that artillerists were now more in demand than preachers. Re-
luctantly he donned the gray, as captain of a locally organized
battery.

He was, however, intimately known to Davis, Lee, and many
others who had attended West Point and who were now in high
office. His age suggested that he had attained wisdom; his pro-
fession, that he was trustworthy. Almost at once he was
promoted to colonel, and before long he was a brigadier, on
Lee's staff, Chief of Artillery.

He had some capacities as an organizer, and was not without
admirers. But among many of the younger officers he seems to
have been something of a joke. "Parson Pendleton" they called

him, or even referred to him as "an old granny." When commanding his men to fire, he was said to have shouted, "Aim low,
and may God have mercy on their misguided souls!" Moxley
Sorrel disposed of him in a devastating conclusion: "A well-
meaning man, without qualities for the high post he claimed."
He still preached whenever he had the chance, putting a surplice
over his uniform.

One would not wish to deprecate a gentleman preferring to
labor at saving men's souls rather than at destroying their bodies.
Still, one must respectfully point out that on this particular
morning it was a question of salvos, not of salvation; of a cannonade, not of a canonization. Not within twenty years, if ever,
had Pendleton studied the techniques of artillery preparation,
and in the deeper levels of his consciousness, the whole matter
was probably distasteful.

28

Fortunately, the present situation — at a superficial level, at
least — offered no difficulties. Alexander was known to be an
efficient officer. There was no reason to doubt that the guns
were properly placed; as Pendleton rode along the line, he raised
no objection.

To give him credit, he made a positive suggestion. As Chief
of Artillery, he knew the disposition of the guns of Hill's corps
also. This line was so far back that its howitzers could not be
used. Nine of them had therefore been collected into a mobile
battery, and were being held in reserve behind the ridge. Pendleton offered them as a force to accompany the advance of the
infantry.

Alexander jumped at the chance. These guns, light and
maneuverable, were ideal to go forward in a hell-for-leather
charge. Swung around and quickly unlimbered, they could pour
a devastating short-range fire into the opposing infantry. Alex-

ander had been instructed to cover the right flank of Pickett's advancing troops, and with these howitzers the problem was solved. Alexander rode back, placed the guns under cover, and ordered the officer in charge to remain there until he received further orders.

29

Having remained in position behind the ridge for several hours, Pickett's brigades were advanced over the top, still shielded from view by the woods. In line of battle they came down the gentle slope, through the trees on the eastern side. Then the ragged lines of the two leading brigades broke from the edge of the woods, and were halted and dressed.

A hundred-fifty yards ahead up an easy slope, sharp against the bright sky, the men saw the crest of a low rise. Where they stood, in the swale, they were concealed from the enemy, even from the lookouts on the tops of the hills. A little to their left a rail fence zig-zagged up the slope. In front of their center they saw a farmhouse and a barn against the skyline. Just under the shelter of this low crest a line of guns was in position; it was their own artillery, Dearing's battalion. Again the men were told to lie down, and to do nothing that would attract the enemy's attention. Because of the order of the march Garnett's brigade was on the left; Kemper's, on the right. Armistead's brigade, following, had halted in the woods behind.

Thus, unknown to the Union army, Pickett's division had been skillfully placed in a position from which to launch an attack.

30

Unknown to the enemy? In a practical sense, yes. But, as it happened, on the peak of Jack's Mountain, ten miles to the south, there was a station of the Union Signal Corps. Its observers at some time sighted the two brigades that lay in the open, and then wig-wagged frantically to attract the attention of the signal-station on Little Round Top. Either some trick of light made them invisible or else Little Round Top was otherwise busy. Jack's Mountain had no response. Thus, by one of the accidents of battle, the Union artillery was not turned loose upon the men who waited within easy range.

31

By this time much of Hill's and Ewell's artillery also was in position for the cannonade.

"By this time" — yes. But what time? Nine o'clock, at least. Perhaps, ten. What, even, does this mean? Whose time are we using? There is time as marked off by the sun, and as struck by the courthouse clock. There is time as it is ticked away by the watches in the pockets of thousands of officers, and of a few privates, in each army. Most of all, there is time as it appears to the men themselves, so that to one it lingers and to another it speeds. Then, after the battle, if two men, equally qualified, write down the minute of some particular event, their opinions differ by as much as five hours!

We are not even sure that the watch-setting of the two armies was the same. This was before time-zones. Some evidence suggests that time in Lee's army was about twenty minutes faster than in Meade's army. So the moment can seldom be established with accuracy. Generally, the best that can be done is to write "about this time," or "somewhat later," hoping that it was not really "a little earlier."

But now, let us take a fresh start, for time and for other things also, and cross, as with a flag of truce, those intervening trampled fields and shot-torn pastures, thus to view the Union lines, by the clump of trees and the low stone wall with the angles in it.

PART II

Later Morning — Mostly Union

> They were a reliable army still.
> — LIEUTENANT F. A. HASKELL

GEORGE GORDON MEADE was not only a major general commanding the Army of the Potomac, but also a loving husband, and at 8.45 on this morning, he snatched a respite from military duties to write a brief note. By the time of delivery, his first sentence cannot have been of much interest to Mrs. Meade, but at the moment of its writing, Robert E. Lee could profitably have sacrificed a good regiment to capture that bit of paper and read the opening words: "All well and going on well with the Army." For — Meade not being given to unfounded optimism — this sentence would have served as plain warning to all Confederates not to cultivate over-confidence or to indulge in wishful thinking that the Union army needed only one solid punch for its knockout.

2

He was by no means a brilliant leader or a genius of war, this forty-seven-year-old Pennsylvanian (born, actually, in Cadiz, Spain), whom fate and the incapacities of Joe Hooker had elevated to his present high position. After West Point and the Old Army, he had maintained a distinguished war-time career as the commander of a brigade, a division, and then of the Fifth Corps. Suddenly placed at the head of the army, he continued the so-to-speak rearward advance toward Gettysburg, with rapidity, though with vacillation between offensive and defensive think-

49

ing. By this morning, however, he had solidly committed himself to the defensive. A counterattack to rectify the lines on
Culp's Hill was as far as his naturally cautious temperament
would go. We must always remember, however, that he was in
a position of extraordinary difficulty, having been placed in
command only three days before he was forced to fight a great
battle.

Personally, Meade was solid and capable. In appearance he
did not make what was called in those days a "fine military
figure." He wore spectacles, and these appurtenances, it may
have been, led people constantly to comparing him to a
school teacher, which on one occasion becomes a Presbyterian
minister, though we may at least be allowed to query, "Why,
Presbyterian?" His one colorful trait was the unpleasant one of
being subject to violent outbursts of temper.

During the preceding night Meade had held a council of war,
and at its end he made a remarkable prediction. Speaking to
Brigadier General John Gibbon, in temporary command of the
Second Corps, Meade said, "If Lee attacks tomorrow, it will be
in your front." Being asked why he thought so, Meade continued, "Because he has made attacks on both our flanks and
failed, and if he concludes to try it again, it will be on our
center." Gibbon remained privately skeptical about what he
called "Meade's reliance upon the doctrine of chances." Thus,
by what seems pure intuition, Meade made a prediction of which
Lee or Napoleon might have been proud. Whereupon, darkening his virtue, throughout the next day he paid little attention
to that particular sector. By and large, therefore, Meade fails
to demand much attention here. He was curiously uninvolved
in the day's chief event.

3

"Your front," Meade had said, thus designating a scant half-
mile of American hillside that would be thenceforth famous.

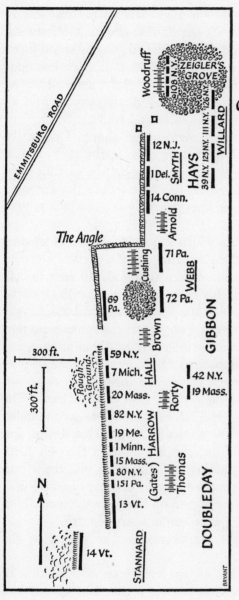

Union Position on Cemetery Ridge
(Morning, July 3)

Divisions, e.g. **HAYS**
Brigades, e.g. <u>HARROW</u>
Batteries, e.g. Thomas

⎯ One gun
〰〰〰 Stone wall
▥▥▥ Entrenchment
▬ ▬ ▬ Union troops
🌳 Woods

The order of regiments in line is presumably correct; the position of regiments in support is approximate. The length of line shown for each regiment is roughly adjusted to its strength, with allowance for men on the skirmish line. The 8th Ohio and 16th Vermont, being wholly on the skirmish line, are not shown.

EMMITTSBURG ROAD

Woodruff

ZEIGLER'S GROVE

108 N.Y.

39 N.Y. 125 N.Y. 111 N.Y. 126 N.Y.

WILLARD

HAYS

12 N.J.

SMYTH

1 Del.

14 Conn.

Arnold

The Angle

Cushing

71 Pa.

WEBB

69 Pa.

72 Pa.

GIBBON

Brown

300 ft.

300 ft.

Rough Ground

59 N.Y.

HALL

7 Mich.

42 N.Y.

20 Mass.

Rorty

19 Mass.

82 N.Y.

19 Me.

HARROW

1 Minn.

(Gates)

Thomas

15 Mass.

80 N.Y.

151 Pa.

13 Vt.

DOUBLEDAY

N

14 Vt.

STANNARD

BRYANT

Looking out from that site you might still have exclaimed, in spite of the ravages of war, "A beautiful landscape!" Westward, the gently undulating countryside stretched away — bright green pastures, yellow fields of ripened wheat. A mile off, a low ridge was crowned with the darker green of woodland, and still farther the first ridge of the mountains stood dimly purple. And all above stretched the summer sky, blue and white.

Farmhouses and big barns were dotted about. Diagonally, farther away at the left but drawing close at the right, a road extended across the view. It was lined on both sides with stout post-and-plank fences. Most of the others were the common zig-zagging rail fences, their lines generally marked by a growth of bushes and small trees.

As for the low ridge from which you are conceived as looking, in some geological age, along a narrow crevice, molten rock had pushed toward the surface and then solidified. In later millennia, as the surface eroded, this rock was left as a gentle, forested rise. Now for a hundred years the hand of man had lain heavily upon this land; the once-wooded slopes and the swales were now all plowland, treeless. Even the ridge was mostly in pasture, and so it stood out clearly, emphasized a little by the growth of trees and bushes that still crowned it here and there.

The hand of man had done more than cut the trees. The ancient rock of the ridge had so weathered that well-rounded chunks of it remained on the surface. Then, to clear a field, and also to divide one field from another, farmers through three generations had been gathering the stones, to pile them into walls. But many of the rounded chunks of rock, of convenient size to a man's hand, still remained on the ground, especially in and about the little clump of umbrella-shaped trees — a circumstance of some slight significance in the events of the day.

The walls, here, were low — two feet; three, at the most. In fact, many of them would not restrain a cow, and so they had been heightened by having a rail fence straddled over them. The result was very practical — the wall, pig-tight; the fence, cow-high.

Today there was little thought of pigs and cows, even though many hundreds of farm boys were among the soldiers who waited on that low ridge. Those men, veterans of the Second Corps, were judging it as a military position, and found it not at all a bad one. The clover-field along most of their front gave them an unobstructed field of fire. The height and the slope amounted to nothing, but at least were sufficient to let the guns have a good sweep for canister. There was a little natural cover — the low crest itself, a few rocks, some bushes and trees, including the clump of oaks. And a stone wall, even if it is only two feet high, is a remarkably comforting thing to be lying behind.

As for a name, this little rise of ground was so ill-defined and so insignificant that before the days of battle it would never have been named at all. Later, since it was a kind of appendage to Cemetery Hill, it came to be known as Cemetery Ridge, though it was scarcely a ridge and there was no cemetery on it — and could not have been, since the rock came almost to the surface.

This was Gibbon's front, and the men holding it must have been well-enough satisfied. Besides, they were the Second Corps, Hancock's men! Let the Johnnies try!

4

True, he had commanded the corps for only three weeks, but they knew him already as the major general of their First Division. Besides, it did not take long under the leadership of such a one to make you know that you were one of "Hancock's men."

Let us see him as one of the soldiers saw him, writing simply enough:

General Hancock . . . was the best looking officer in the army. He was tall and well proportioned, had a ruddy

complexion, brown hair, and he wore a mustache and a tuft
of hair upon his chin. . . . Had General Hancock worn
citizen's clothes, his orders would have been obeyed anywhere, for he had the apparance of a man born to command.

Second only to Lee, of all those who were at Gettysburg,
Hancock dominated men by his mere "presence."

His pre-war career had been ordinary enough. Born near
Philadelphia, graduated from West Point, granted the opportunity to pick up some battle-experience in Mexico, subjected
to the endless routine of army posts — through it all he proved
to be the almost ideal soldier. As one wrote, "The smoke of
battle had been in his nostrils, and he found it fragrant," and
then he continued, "While, by what might almost seem a con-
tradiction, he loved 'papers,' rejoicing in forms and regulations
and requisitions." He ended all this as a captain in command of
the quartermaster's depot in Los Angeles, where he gave the
farewell party and said his goodbyes to Armistead.

At the opening of the war, with rare perspicacity, the War
Department jumped him to brigadier general. With a mixed
brigade — Pennsylvania, New York, Wisconsin, Maine — he
fought so well at Williamsburg that McClellan telegraphed,
"Hancock was superb." The epithet stuck to him — enough to
sink a smaller man. But Hancock throve with it; after all, he
was superb! At Antietam and Fredericksburg, he so continued,
and at Chancellorsville his division held the line between defeat and disaster. When there was a vacancy just after that
battle, Hancock naturally stepped into the command of the
corps, at the age of thirty-nine. In the first two days of fighting
at Gettysburg he had managed to be even a little more superb
than usual.

He was Meade's trusted friend, but did not share Meade's
love of caution. At the council of war on the night of July 2,
he had given his opinion characteristically, "Can't wait long;
can't be idle." Indeed, the *beau idéal* of the soldier — even to

the touch of white linen at his cuffs, when the other generals on the battlefield were looking dingy; even to the occasional great burst of passion and the thunderous language that accompanied it!

Yes, they were Hancock's men, and if he told them to charge, they would charge, and if he told them to get behind a stone wall and stay there, they would stay. Doubtless, if he told them to retreat, they would retreat — but in that case they would be somewhat surprised.

5

They were also the Second Corps, and they had given that simple number a certain significance. "Clubs are trumps!" was their rallying cry, because they wore the trefoil on their shoulders as their badge. Where the Army of the Potomac had fought, there the Second Corps had fought too — no need to name the battles. One brief statistical note can sum up the record as of that morning at Gettysburg. As the Second Corps, these men had never lost to the enemy a single one of their colors, but they had captured fifteen!

Actually, very depleted ranks held the gentle slope. The First Division had been sent on the preceding afternoon to join the battle on the left, and it was still detached. Similarly, most of Carroll's brigade of the Third Division, and one regiment of the Second had been sent to bolster up the Eleventh Corps on Cemetery Hill.

Since the outcome of the battle and perhaps even the fate of the republic was to depend upon how well these troops could fight, we may properly consider what they were. Above all, we are at once forced to note, they offered much more variety, regiment by regiment, than could be found in any Confederate corps — differing in military experience, skill, and reliability, and also in national backgrounds and modes of life.

The Third Division, under Brigadier General Alexander Hays, held the right wing. . , . The First Brigade was Carroll's. Its single regiment remaining with the division was the 8th Ohio, from the northwestern part of the state, the Sandusky region. The men of Carroll's brigade seem to have had a reputation for being what an army is likely to call "fighting fools." This point need not be argued, since the record of the day fully establishes it for the 8th Ohio.

The Second Brigade was Smyth's — 14th Connecticut, 1st Delaware, 12th New Jersey, and 108th New York, with the 10th New York Battalion in the rear doing provost-guard duty. Of the four regiments in line, all except the 12th New Jersey had gained plenty of battle-experience from Antietam on. The Jerseymen had been well blooded at Chancellorsville. All four regiments were from rural parts of their states, and they were almost wholly "old-American." Nevertheless, in the 14th Connecticut was Private Joseph L. Pierce, pig-tail and all, the only Chinese in the Army of the Potomac. Of this brigade one of their officers recorded, "The men were young, well disciplined, of respectable parentage, in comfortable circumstances." The historian of the 14th Connecticut declared, "There was no question about the morals of the regiment, and it may be a joke, but it has some significance when it is said that the Colonel offered a prize of $5 for any one that heard a man swear." Nevertheless, he is ready to admit that "the 14th Wooden Nutmegs," as they sometimes called themselves, had a weakness for poker.

The Third Brigade, still generally known as Willard's, was now commanded by Colonel Eliakim Sherrill, since Willard had been killed on July 2. It was solid New York — the 39th, 111th, 125th, and 126th. In personnel, the three high-numbered, "up-state" regiments closely resembled Smyth's brigade. The 39th was different. Known as the Garibaldi Guards, the regiment had come into existence as the result of someone's brainstorm of recruiting a regiment of European refugees to fight for liberty against slavery. The plan called for three companies of Germans, three of Hungarians, and one each Italians, Swiss,

French, Spanish-Portuguese. In the end the men turned out to be mostly German, but there were enough of the other nationalities to make it difficult for the regiment to develop much *esprit de corps*. The Garibaldis might have done well enough, however, if they had not been involved in the disaster that overtook the whole brigade.

It had been part of the garrison of Harpers Ferry, when Stonewall Jackson descended upon that post in September, 1862. The men of the garrison, irresolutely commanded, had been ordered to lay down their arms before they had even been allowed to fight. Immediately paroled, the whole brigade had the chagrin of marching away from the sound of the guns of Antietam.

They were kept in parole camps for some months, and their morale suffered badly. When they got back to the army, the men of other brigades jeered at them for their surrender, though it was not their fault. The Garibaldis were the worst of all, but the other three regiments were also about as bad as can be imagined. Then they had a break of luck, and were assigned Hays as their commander. He was horrified at the condition of his troops, but he went resolutely to work — "drilled, punished, rewarded, coaxed, and stormed." Since the regiments had basically good stuff in them, their improvement was rapid.

Less than a week before Gettysburg, the brigade had joined the Second Corps, and Hays had gone to divisional command, with the brigade transferred to Colonel Willard. The men had arrived on the field of Gettysburg, still almost unblooded. Then, on July 2, they had been thrown in to stop the victorious advance of Barksdale's Mississippians. The brigade charged, shouting, "Remember Harpers Ferry!" In a few minutes both Willard and Barksdale were down, the Mississippians were in retreat, and the New Yorkers were counting heavy casualties. Never again would they have to hear the old taunt, "Harpers Ferry cowards!"

To the southward, Gibbon's division, the Second, held the line with three brigades. . . . The First was Harrow's — 1st Minnesota, 82nd New York, 15th Massachusetts, and 19th Maine. Except for this last, all the regiments had fought on the Peninsula, and ever since. If you had been looking for an easy spot, you would not, that day, have picked the sector held by Harrow's brigade.

The 1st Minnesota was a regiment with a reputation, if there ever was one. When the Union line was reeling back on July 2, Hancock had ordered it, with only seven companies in line, to attack. The Minnesotans had charged Wilcox's brigade of Alabamians, halted them, turned the tide of battle, and suffered casualties that reduced the seven companies from 262 to 47 effectives. This 82 per cent loss, with none reported missing, is generally considered to have set a record for the Union army. The next morning one of the detached companies had rejoined, and the regiment mustered, according to one of its captains, "eighty odd" — good men, but hardly numerous enough to count in a great battle.

The 82nd New York was an old organization of the city itself, an excellent and thoroughly experienced regiment. So was the 15th Massachusetts, which was from Worcester and the surrounding district. It was composed, wrote its historian, of young men from "farms, factories, mills, shops and stores." Many of its companies traced their origin to militia organizations dating from the eighteenth century. The 19th Maine, though without much experience at fighting, was of good stuff. It came from the counties between the Kennebec and the Penobscot, and was remarkable for the considerable number of college graduates in its ranks. One observer wrote that it had "the largest men in it that I ever saw."

Webb's, the Second, was known as the Philadelphia Brigade — the 69th, 71st, 72nd, and 106th Pennsylvania. This was the only brigade of either army to bear a city designation, and it did so honestly, all but a few companies being from Philadelphia.

Under a curious system of sponsorship which at first prevailed, this had first been known as the California Brigade, and its regiments as the 1st, 2nd, 4th, and 5th California. The shadowy far-western connection soon disappeared, and the regiments gladly took the designation of their own state, though to their disgust they had to assume high numbers.

The 69th carried a green regimental flag, with the insignia of the wolf-dog, round tower, and sunburst, to indicate that it was almost solidly Irish. It was not, however, fanatically Irish, and was proud to include in its ranks some others, including two fighting Quakers and several Jews. The 71st had been the 1st California, and was still called the California Regiment; it had been one of the numerous Zouave organizations, and had originally worn that fancy uniform. The 72nd had been largely recruited from the fire companies of Philadelphia, and was known as Baxter's Fire Zouaves. These men, more than others, stuck by the original uniforms, so that some of them still wore the short, cutaway jacket and baggy pants, and most of them kept the white leggings. This regiment, for some reason, carried no regimental flag, but only the national colors. The 106th was officially on Cemetery Hill, but some of its men were on the skirmish line, and others had just come in from it. These "orphans" attached themselves to the left of the 72nd.

The Philadelphia Brigade had fought in the battles from Balls Bluff onward. Yet, studying the records, one comes up with a feeling that perhaps all was not well, that beneath the surface it was suffering from some lapse of morale. Why, for instance, had Gibbon thought it necessary to put its brigadier under arrest, a few days before the battle? Then there are evidences that Webb, having just taken command, immediately had to exert himself to stiffen the discipline. He issued stern orders against straggling, with a threat of the death penalty. The officers of the 71st, he discovered, tried to look as much like

privates as possible, so as to avoid becoming targets. Webb
ordered them to wear all their insignia. Also we find a private
of Harrow's brigade writing that some of the regiments of
Webb's brigade, such as the 72nd, "never were known to stand
fire." Why, again, should a certain captain have remarked, before the battle, that the 72nd did all its fighting on the rear line?

During the evening of July 2 the 71st had managed to behave
so ambiguously that the regiment, or its commanding officer,
received unfavorable mention from two generals. Sent to support the Twelfth Corps, Colonel Smith was apparently so confused that he thought he was supporting the Eleventh Corps.
Becoming more confused by stumbling on some Confederates
in the dark, he withdrew the regiment without orders.

The 71st and the 72nd — about them, on this morning, one
senses some faint suggestion as of inward rottenness. Yet there
was nowhere any official indication that these regiments were
not of first quality. They had done their duty on many hard-
fought fields, and might reasonably be expected to do so again.

Gibbon's Third Brigade was Hall's — 19th and 20th Massachusetts, 7th Michigan, 42nd and 59th New York. Except for
the 59th New York, all the regiments had been with the army
since the Peninsula. Even the 59th had fought in everything
since Antietam.

The 19th Massachusetts was from Boston and the north-
eastern towns. At Fredericksburg, along with the 7th Michigan,
the 19th had crossed the river in pontoon boats under fire, and
established the bridgehead — a famous exploit. This exploit
also made the 7th Michigan a well-known regiment; its men
were mostly from Detroit. The 20th Massachusetts, except for
a detachment from Nantucket (How did they ever keep out of
the Navy?) was unusual in being recruited from all over the
state. It had been the first regiment to cross the bridge at Fredericksburg, and had fought to clear the streets of the town, losing
a hundred men in an advance of fifty yards. Behind this regiment

on the bridge had come the 59th, and then the 42nd New York.
The 59th was mostly German. The 42nd was almost solid
Irish; it had been recruited under the auspices of Tammany
Hall, and was known as the Tammany Regiment.

Such, for good and for bad — and mostly, as far as Confederates were concerned, for bad — were the infantrymen of these
two divisions of Hancock's corps, against which Lee was preparing his column of assault.

6

Joining the Second Corps on the left were five regiments of the
First, which shared in the same fighting.

Two of these regiments — the 80th New York and 151st
Pennsylvania — were at this particular spot mainly because they
had happened to become detached from their brigade, and had
taken a position almost at haphazard. The surviving colonel,
Theodore Gates of the New Yorkers, had assumed command of
what he grandiloquently termed a "demi-brigade." These two
regiments had suffered heavily on the first day, and were very
small. The 80th was composed of veterans. It was also known
as the 20th State Militia and the Ulster Guard, taking this name
from the county on the Hudson from which it came. The 151st
was an interesting regiment, containing several companies that
had been recruited from academies. More than a hundred
schoolteachers had enlisted in it, and its commander had been
a principal. To the honor of all egg-heads be it known that this
schoolmaster colonel took 466 of his unblooded regiment into
the first day's battle. He himself fell wounded, and the school-
boys fought so desperately that next morning they mustered only
121, under a captain.

Next in line to the left of Gates's men were three regiments of
the Second Vermont brigade under Brigadier General G. J.
Stannard — the 13th, 14th, and 16th. These were nine-months

men, and according to one of their historians they had often
been taunted by being called "nine monthlings, hatched from
two-hundred-dollar bounty eggs." (This does not sound to me,
personally, like anything that one soldier calls another, but perhaps it is the polite version.)

Not only were they nine-months men, but also their time
was within a few days of being up. They had spent it guarding
the defenses of Washington; except for one or two insignificant
skirmishes with Stuart's cavalry, they had heard no bullets until
July 2. Then they had suddenly found themselves opposed to
an advancing line. Scarcely knowing what they were doing, they
had charged, had halted the Confederates, driven them back,
and taken heavy casualties. Afterwards they had decided that
they could think very well of themselves, and that they were
maintaining the traditions of the First Vermont brigade, which
had made a reputation for itself with the Sixth Corps.

As to what kind of men they were, be it enough to say that
they were Vermonters — the stock of backwoods New England.
As to why they were there, let us quote the simple words of one
of them, words which might equally well apply to many who
were not Vermonters: "I was a soldier, not for money or office,
glory or renown, nor because I expected to enjoy the fighting or
the horrid sights and scenes of battle. I was young, single, physically able, and my country was assailed, and I felt it a personal
duty to respond, and therefore volunteered."

Though this was their first battle, these raw troops from the
far-northern hills were to be granted, and were to seize, a military opportunity such as a professional soldier might dream about
during a lifetime of fighting and never realize.

7

Also in line of battle were the five batteries of the Second Corps
— from north to south, I of the 1st United States, A of the 1st
Rhode Island, A of the 4th United States, B of the 1st Rhode

Island, and B of the 1st New York. Commonly a battery was known by its commander's name, and the five were thus, in the same order, Woodruff's, Arnold's, Cushing's, Brown's, and Rorty's. By the time of Gettysburg, the volunteer batteries had wiped out the margin that had once separated them from the Regulars, and the artillery of the Army of the Potomac was in a high state of discipline and efficiency. Woodruff's and Brown's batteries were of Napoleons; the others, of rifles. The complement of a Union battery was six guns, but Brown's and Rorty's had suffered heavily, and now could put into the line only four guns apiece, and Arnold had only five. The total of the guns was, thus, twenty-five.

8

The question of command of these two divisions, plus five regiments and the batteries, was a somewhat complicated one, and there may even have been a question at times as to who commanded whom. The uncertainty, however, seems to have caused little difficulty, probably because most of the commanders were used to working together.

By Meade's order, after the wounding of Sickles on July 2, Hancock had assumed command of the whole Union center, including the Third Corps and part of the First, as well as the Second. Gibbon thereupon succeeded to the command of the Second, at least of its two divisions which were still together. Hancock, however, remained on the ground. In theory, therefore, Gibbon commanded the corps, but he actually did not relinquish command of his own division. Brigadier General William Harrow remained with his brigade, though theoretically he should have taken the division when Gibbon assumed command of the corps.

9

No matter what he commanded, Brigadier General John Gibbon was an outstanding officer. Though born in Pennsylvania, he had been reared in North Carolina and appointed to West Point from that state. Three of his brothers were serving in the Confederate army, and had disowned him. He was thus one of those persons who had set national above state loyalty, had remained true to the oath which he had taken as an officer of the United States Army, and had therefore become one of those whom the more violent Southerners called "traitor." (On the other hand, these same people were accustomed to honor any Marylander or Kentuckian who had deserted both the old flag and his own state to fight for the Confederacy.)

At Gettysburg, Gibbon was thirty-six years old. As one of the 19th Maine described him, he "had brown hair and a reddish mustache. He was, upon the whole, a good looking officer, and never appeared nervous or excited." Another described him as "steel cold," and others emphasized his intelligence. Restrained in manner, a blunt speaker, a strict disciplinarian, he won the basic respect of his officers and men rather than their emotional enthusiasm.

Before the war, he had been an artillery captain, and his intelligence and intellect show in his *Artillerist's Manual,* a highly scientific work, replete with mathematical formulae. Early in the war, he took command of some western regiments, and from these raw recruits he soon "forged that thunderbolt of war known as the 'Iron Brigade.'"

The other divisional commander was Brigadier General Alexander Hays, forty-four years old, also a Pennsylvanian. He was the antithesis of the cold and quiet Gibbon. As one of the "Harpers Ferry" men described him, he was "a princely soldier; brave as a lion . . . one of those dashing, reckless, enthusiastic generals. . . . His old brigade, then the Third of his division,

idolized him, and we would have followed him to the death."
Hays was a thorough soldier, but he gave way to stagy, over-
exuberant enthusiasm for battle that had about it a suggestion
of adolescence. Another summed him up, "His extraordinary
vivacity in battle was united with the soundness of judgment
and firmness of temper which made him one of the most useful
officers in the service."

The troops on the left, being a part of the Third Division of
the First Corps, were under the command of Major General
Abner Doubleday. Better known now for his contributions to
the game of baseball than as a soldier, Doubleday was a reliable
but not an outstanding officer.

10

Thus composed and commanded, the Union troops along this
half-mile of gentle hillside were posted in a manner which may
be described as at once effective and conventional.

Some two hundred yards in advance, about at the bottom
of the slope, were the skirmishers, probably totaling about a
tenth of the number of troops in the front line, comprising two
whole regiments, the 8th Ohio and 16th Vermont, along with
four companies of the 19th Maine and smaller detachments
from a number of the other regiments. In the history of tactics
the skirmish line must be considered a temporary expedient,
reaching its height of usefulness under the particular conditions
of this war. Its importance sprang from the increased range of
infantry small-arms. In an attack the traditional battle line —
men advancing in two ranks, elbow to elbow — had become
almost an anachronism, and in a sense had to be protected by
skirmishers. In a static situation, unless you had a skirmish line,
the enemy's sharpshooters would work up close. The only solu-
tion was to send out skirmishers of your own to keep the enemy
at a distance, and also to protect against surprise attack.

Being within range of the Confederate skirmishers, the men in the line at the bottom of the slope had to keep themselves covered. They made use of any inequality of ground, any bush or clump of tall grass. The Emmitsburg road ran diagonally across the position — toward the south in Confederate hands; toward the north, in Union. The fences along it offered some protection, and in places the road was below the level of the ground. West of the road was a field of wheat, with the grain tall enough to give shelter to a man who lay or crouched.

All through the morning, the skirmishers played a deadly cat-and-mouse game — firing at a half-glimpsed figure or at a movement in the wheat, then dropping quickly to escape the inevitable shots at where the smoke of the discharge had revealed one's own position. Casualties mounted on both sides, the slow wastage accompanying static warfare.

In the skirmish line the function of the 8th Ohio was somewhat peculiar. In a sense, this regiment was not on the skirmish line, but was holding an advanced post. The regular orders for skirmishers, in case of a major attack, were to fire a couple of shots and then run for it. The 8th, however, had been instructed to hold the position, no matter what. These are not comfortable orders to be stuck with, but Lieutenant Colonel Franklin Sawyer, now commanding fewer than two hundred men, was taking the words literally.

Under cover of the skirmishers, Hancock's main battle line began on the north at a few acres of woodland known as Ziegler's Grove. Here were posted Woodruff's Napoleons, at the top of a little slope which afforded an excellent field of fire. Supporting the battery was the 108th New York. At their left was a little gap, with no troops in position, and there stood a small wooden house and barn. From the southeastern corner of the barn, a low stone wall ran off, south, along the slope; Smyth's brigade held this part of the line. Hays's other brigade, the "Harpers Ferry" New Yorkers, was in support, a couple of hundred yards to the rear. To the left of Smyth's brigade was Arnold's battery.

Just south of the battery, the wall kept on for about fifty feet, and was not held by any troops. Then the direction of the wall changed, at right angles, and it ran westward toward the Confederate lines. This turn is what came to be known as "the inner angle." The wall continued westward for a distance which has been established in the Pennsylvania courts as 239 feet. Then it made another right-angled turn and went off to the south again. This turn is known as "the outer angle," or more commonly "the angle." Within it, though not very close to either wall, stood the landmark clump of oaks.

The Philadelphia brigade, with Cushing's battery, defended this area. The six 3-inch rifles were in position, well-spaced, somewhat in advance of the Inner Angle, extending from the east-west wall to the clump of trees. At the opening of the battle there had also been bushes and smallish trees extending north from the clump, but they had been cut down to clear a field of fire for the guns, and these cut trees were still lying around in what was known as a slashing. (On the whole, it was a different scene from that of the now well-kept park. The ground was rougher and rockier. There was a growth of bushes north and west of the clump of trees, and among the trees was thick underbrush, largely briars. The slashing was untidy, and this effect must have been enhanced by the dead horses that always accumulated around a battery position.)

There was almost no slope in front of Cushing's guns, and therefore no infantry could be placed there. This was accepted tactics; a battery had enough fire-power to protect its own front. Nevertheless, for emergencies, some infantry was regularly kept at hand to support such a battery. Here the 71st Pennsylvania was thus assigned, and its men were lying well behind the guns. If occasion arose, they could be rushed forward. In front of the clump of trees, south of the line of fire of the battery, the 69th

Pennsylvania held the wall — isolated, with no infantry on either flank. Just as its right was held in by the fire of Cushing's rifles, so was its left by that of Brown's Napoleons. These latter were posted just to the south of the clump of trees about two hundred feet back from the wall, which at this point had been torn down, the preceding afternoon, to allow the passage of some guns. The third regiment of the brigade, the 72nd Pennsylvania, was in support, lying behind the shelter of the clump of trees.

South of Brown's battery, Hall's line began — the 59th New York, 7th Michigan, and 20th Massachusetts. A hundred yards to the rear Hall had the 42nd New York and 19th Massachusetts in support. To the south, Harrow had all four of his regiments in line. Rorty's battery was behind the right of this brigade. The slope of the hill was enough so that his four Parrotts could fire over the infantry.

South of Harrow were the 80th New York and 151st Pennsylvania. Beyond, the 13th and 14th Vermont extended the line. The 14th, however, held a position about seventy-five yards in advance, utilizing some natural cover, which they had strengthened as best they could. They were thus placed en potence, as an elegant European writer upon military affairs described it. One may doubt whether any of the Vermonters would have recognized this term, but they knew that they were better off behind cover than in the open.

11

Many references have been made, by Southerners, to strong fortifications; Northern writers have made little of them. Naturally, the point of view is of importance. To a man trying to get shelter, the fortification will seem very weak; to a man advancing against it across an open field, the same ditch or stone wall will seem much stronger.

The descriptions left by the Union soldiers indicate that little intrenching was done. On Hays's front the stone wall was "about knee-high." All that the men did here was to build the wall up in places where it had tumbled down, and to increase its height a little by laying a few rails on top. South of the Angle, on Gibbon's front, the wall amounted to little — not more than two feet high, and in places petering out to nothing more than a row of stones along the ground, over which a rail fence was straddled. The wall was so insignificant that one writer described it as "the remnants of a stone wall," and a detailed official report mentioned the fence but ignored the wall. The straddling fence had probably been pulled apart in most places and its rails laid on top of the stones.

Several soldiers of this division have left records of their attempts at fortification. The men of the 20th Massachusetts "with one shovel threw up a line of dirt about a foot in height, which might have stopped a bullet if a little weary of flight before reaching it." In the 1st Minnesota there were no tools at all, and the men "made a slight barricade of loose stones and fence rails picked up nearby, and used tin plates as shovels in scooping up sand." The same writer referred to this as "the molehill which passed for a barricade." From others comes additional testimony of lack of tools, rockiness of ground, and the ridiculous inadequacy of the result. In places the men filled their knapsacks with dirt and gravel and added them to the barricade. A soldier of the 19th Maine summed up: "Every man in our lines protected himself the best he could behind such protection as nature afforded and his own genius and labor could devise." All along the line there was nothing that would withstand the impact of a cannon shot or offer more than momentary impediment to a charging Rebel. Nevertheless, slight as they were, these low walls and shallow ditches were to prove invaluable under the particular conditions of the day.

Thus inadequately fortified and lacking much natural strength, the position as a whole displayed some definite weaknesses.

The right of the line, at Woodruff's battery, was really in the air. This worried Hays considerably. The troops of the Eleventh Corps extending the line in that direction were posted a good two hundred yards to the rear, so that any Confederates advancing there might outflank the battery and roll up the line. Besides, no one in the Second Corps had any confidence in the infantry of the Eleventh Corps, which was now holding Cemetery Hill under the command of Major General O. O. Howard.

Also, the whole situation around the Angle had elements of weakness. Because of the Angle itself, this was a kind of salient, and therefore subject to be taken in flank. Moreover, stretches of the front line, on both sides of the 69th Pennsylvania, were not held by infantry.

A third potential hazard was the rough ground in front of Hall's brigade — a few acres studded with biggish rocks and thinly overgrown with bushes and stunted trees. Though the trees had been cut down to low stumps, there was enough cover to give some protection to attackers.

The really serious weakness, however, was the lack of reserves. There was infantry to man the front line, and a little left over for support. But there was no solid body of troops, ready at call, to be thrown in to meet any major breakthrough.

Just as Hays recognized the weakness of his right flank, we can only suppose that Hancock recognized all the weaknesses. Being committed to the defensive, however, he could only make the dispositions that seemed most likely to be the best. As for the reserves, Meade was doing his best to keep the Sixth Corps ready for some supreme moment, and otherwise he had few troops available. By this time, apparently, his intuition of the previous night had faded, and he was no longer convinced that the attack would be launched against Gibbon's position.

The same kind of defensive tactics accounts for the placement of the Reserve Artillery.

13

Brigadier General Henry J. Hunt was Chief of Artillery, and a very different person from his Confederate counterpart "Parson" Pendleton. Sprung from a family of soldiers, very much Old Army, he had served with high distinction in Mexico. By 1861 he was a leading American authority on artillery. Ever since First Bull Run he had been handling Union guns to the acute discomfort of Confederates. At Malvern Hill he placed the hundred pieces that smashed Lee's attack almost without infantry aid. He commanded the artillery at Antietam and Fredericksburg, with great effect. He had had great opportunities, and he had utilized them well.

His weakness lay perhaps in his conservatism; he was just a little too much Old Army. Perhaps he never quite managed to shake off the stuffiness of the peace-time service. According to one anecdote, at the height of a battle a battery commander appealed for more ammunition. "Young man," Hunt is said to have replied, "Are you aware that every round you fire costs $2.67?" Whether he said it or not is of less importance than that it was considered a story that might be told about him, and one amusing detail is that he himself once told it, apparently considering that he had made a rather apt remark. But any man has his weaknesses, and we must always remember that Hunt was a superlatively good Chief of Artillery.

14

Like the infantry, the Union batteries had taken a pounding on the first two days of battle; again like the infantry, they still had plenty of fight left in them. Not counting the Horse Artillery, they were divided between the thirty-seven batteries assigned to individual corps, and the twenty-one of the Reserve. Hunt was in general command, though the corps-commanders might also give orders to their own batteries. There was, indeed, a twilight zone of authority which was to have its influence upon the conduct of the battle.

Like Meade, Hunt was forced to think defensively, and he could therefore assign his guns only to the most generally favorable positions or else to those where he deemed an attack most likely. His own opinion he expressed, that morning, to Major Thomas W. Osborn, Chief of Artillery of the Eleventh Corps — that Cemetery Hill and the Union left were the danger spots.

Accordingly Hunt did not reinforce the Second Corps artillery. All he did there was to extend the line a little by stationing one of the Reserve batteries behind the First Corps regiments. This was Thomas's, C of the 4th United States, six Napoleons.

Hunt moved two Reserve batteries to Cemetery Hill. Even if he had not considered this a likely objective of attack, it was an obvious point for artillery concentration — the curve of the fishhook line, flat enough at the top to afford good sites, high enough to dominate much of the field. By this massing of batteries Hunt turned the hill into a fortress. Some of the pieces could be swung about to fire either north, east, or west. Only those that could fire in this last direction could cover the front of the Second Corps, but these came to the substantial number of twenty-nine.

Three of these were big 20-pounders of Taft's battery, the 5th New York Independent. Similarly faced, arranged in two lines but so as not to interfere with one another's firing, were five other batteries — I of the 1st Ohio, A of the 1st New Hampshire, C of the 1st West Virginia, G of the 4th United States, and H of the 1st United States. By their commanders' names these were

Dilger's, Edgell's, Hill's, Bancroft's, and Eakin's. The five totaled sixteen Napoleons and ten rifles, all under the command of Major Osborn.

Well to the south of the Second Corps line Hunt ordered another concentration, under Lieutenant Colonel Freeman McGilvery of the Artillery Reserve. The position was an insignificant rise of land half way between Cemetery Hill and Little Round Top. The line of guns was built up gradually during the morning, and by noon was composed, from north to south, of Thompson's C/F Pennsylvania Light, Phillips's 5th Massachusetts, Hart's 15th New York Light, Sterling's 2nd Connecticut Light, a section of Rank's 3rd Pennsylvania Heavy, Dow's 6th Maine, and Ames's G of the 1st New York. It thus totaled thirty-three guns — fourteen Napoleons, seventeen rifles, and two 12-pound howitzers. These last, the only ones of their kind in Meade's army, were apparently dragged around with the idea that such guns might some time come in handy.

McGilvery's position was the one from which the fire of a line of guns had checked Longstreet's advance, the preceding afternoon. It was therefore a proved position from which Union gunners might fire with a sense of good augury, and it was also the place from which to crush another Confederate attack following the path of the first one. This last, or an attack farther to the south, was certainly what Hunt had in mind when he concentrated guns along this little swell of ground. Why, otherwise, would he have placed Napoleons on the left and rifles on the right? If the object had been to protect the Second Corps front, the Napoleons should have been on the right, within their effective range. Moreover, McGilvery's pieces were not well placed, as a whole, to fire on a line advancing against the Angle. They could inflict a somewhat enfilading fire, but only at fairly long range; they were too far off to use canister effectively, and most of them could not use it at all.

The Second Corps front could also count on the fire of two other batteries. Daniels's 9th Michigan, four rifles, detached from the Horse Artillery, was on McGilvery's right, where it was close at hand but probably on too low ground to be very effective. On the other hand, Rittenhouse's battery, D of the 5th U.S., six 10-pound rifles, was in a commanding position on Little Round Top, but to hit troops advancing against the Second Corps line it had to fire at a range of well over a mile.

15

Of the six brigades on Cemetery Ridge, three were commanded by generals and three by colonels. This was a better proportion of generals than the average for the army. An unfortunate military system allowed veteran regiments to shrink until they were no more than the equivalent of two or three good companies. Since few brigades at Gettysburg were larger than a full regiment, the task of command was thus not more than would normally fall to a colonel, and the creation of brigadiers for these nominal brigades was not justified. The senior colonel was often left in command — Hall of the 7th Michigan, Smyth of the 1st Delaware, and Sherrill of the 126th New York. The last was not to live long enough to prove himself; the other two were capable soldiers.

Of the brigadiers, William Harrow and George Jerrison Stannard had come up through the volunteer service. Harrow had begun as major of the 14th Indiana; Stannard, as lieutenant colonel of the 2nd Vermont. Both were good officers.

Alexander Stewart Webb was West Point '55, and a brigadier at only twenty-eight. Most of his war duty had been staff-work, and it had been rewarded with the rapid promotion that often comes to efficient staff-officers. He had the luck of being at hand and unassigned when General "Paddy" Owen, who commanded the Philadelphia Brigade, was clapped under arrest; Gibbon had eagerly seized upon Webb to take over.

Just what was Owen's offense is uncertain; being Irish, he may have taken a drop too much at the wrong time. But he had been the original colonel of the 69th, an old comrade and a popular fellow, a Pennsylvanian and an Irishman in a brigade that was wholly Pennsylvanian and largely Irish.

Obviously Webb, a non-Irish New Yorker, was in a none-too-happy situation, when he had taken command just six days earlier. To the hard-bitten veterans, he was a young whipper-snapper, and they scented dandyism in his spit-and-polish staff-officer's uniform. Besides, the implacably efficient Gibbon had undoubtedly told Webb to "ride" the brigade. Such a situation was bound to make for trouble, at least, to begin with.

The fording of Monocacy Creek came on Webb's second day. It was knee-deep, and the men naturally expected to take their shoes and socks off, since marching in wet feet meant blisters. But Webb ordered them not to halt. To set an example, he dismounted and waded too, but everybody saw his high boots, and knew that he could ride afterward. There were boos and catcalls and audible remarks — all of which the general had to pretend not to hear. The most he could do was to put one captain under arrest for walking across on a log. (Later the Assistant Surgeon trumped up an excuse that wading would have endangered the captain's health, and Webb revoked the arrest.)

Certain attempts of the new brigadier to tighten up the discipline have already been noted in connection with the presentation of the brigade itself. Such procedures could not render him popular, but a day of battle helped the situation. It made more apparent the necessity for discipline, and the brigade quickly noted, and approved, that Webb knew how to command and showed off well under fire. They began to have better feel-

ings, but still he was so new that some of his soldiers did not
even know him when they saw him.

16

But what of the men? Well commanded, well posted, well supported by artillery — all these are as nothing unless there exists
within the infantrymen themselves a deep-seated will to stand
and fight.

Lee, subtle master of the psychology of battle, was risking
heavily on his belief that they would not so stand and fight, or
at least that they would not stand very long or fight very hard.
He had good grounds. With inferior forces, he had beaten that
army shamefully, at Chancellorsville, only two months before.
Then he had outmaneuvered it, invaded the North, and finally
in two days of fighting had smashed three out of seven corps. By
all rights the Army of the Potomac should have been demoralized to a point at which the individual soldier was becoming
unreliable.

The fact was, most of that army was not feeling demoralized
at all. As for Chancellorsville, the chief impression seems to
have been a kind of puzzlement. As one officer of the Second
Corps commented about his men, they considered it "a battle
in which they had been foiled without being fought, and caused
to retreat without the consciousness of having been beaten."
An officer of the Philadelphia Brigade wrote: "the rank and
file felt they had failed; but were puzzled to know how they had
been defeated without fighting a decisive battle." Besides, the
men had a perfect scapegoat — the Eleventh Corps! If "those
Dutchmen" had not stampeded so shamelessly, the rest of the
army would have shown Bobby Lee what he was fighting against.
In fact, many of the men had never even fired a shot at Chancellorsville. The officers had another scapegoat in the person of
the now-replaced General Hooker. With Meade in command,

that gnawing uncertainty had yielded to a growing confidence.

As for the rout on the first day at Gettysburg, that also could be scored off against the Eleventh Corps. When it came to the second day, the men were by no means sure that they had been defeated. They had been driven back a mile or so, and the Third Corps had been roughly handled, and things had looked bad for a while, but in the end the Rebs had been repulsed.

This feeling of victory was strongest among the men of Gibbon's and Hays's divisions who had been engaged only in the last of the fighting, had been everywhere successful, and kept a memory of Butternut backs and red flags going rapidly to the rear. Lieutenant Frank Aretas Haskell, whom we shall meet often during the course of the day, was undoubtedly optimistic, but still his impression is of great significance. He wrote that the Confederates fled, "shattered, without organization, in utter confusion, fugitive into the woods."

Whether the men, especially the Pennsylvanians, fought harder on their own soil must be left an undecided question. The motivation of a man on the battlefield is not a surface emotion, easily to be appraised. There are not many contemporary mentions of the matter, and this would lead us to think it unimportant. On the other hand, the defense of the homeland has been a recognized cause for valor since the beginning of history, and one would not think the Union army to have been wholly insensitive.

Another occasionally mentioned matter of some importance is the feeling that this was the last chance, that the army would fight hard and give its best here at Gettysburg, but would be finished, if again defeated. This is another factor that imparts to the events of July 3 such transcendent importance. There is even the suggestion that wholesale desertions would have followed another Southern victory. One Massachusetts soldier wrote: "If the battle had gone against us, I should have made straight for Fitchburg, and I should have had lots of company."

But this is prophecy, and doubtful. As actual indices of morale, let us view the conduct, on the one hand, of a major general, and on the other, of a private. . . . Sometime that morning, south along the Baltimore Pike, the bearers carried a stretcher, accompanied by two soldiers as a guard of honor. The wounded man was General Sickles, hit on the preceding day, his leg now amputated — "grim and stoical, with his cap pulled over his eyes, his hands calmly folded across his breast, and a cigar in his mouth!" Dan Sickles — not much of a general, and in most people's books not much of a man either! But tough! His exit from the army was perhaps his greatest moment in it. How much morale may have been generated by that cigar?

As for the private, we consider A. W. McDermott of the 69th Pennsylvania. "I was adjutant clerk," he wrote, "but they took my musket away from me." Then he added, "But I filled my pockets with cartridges and picked up the first musket I saw and got in shots wherever I could." When clerks are eager to grab rifles, opposing generals may well hesitate.

Not only by morale, however, but also by discipline and even by long-time habit was the Army of the Potomac now sustained, after two years of fighting. Let us quote Lieutenant Haskell again, his words that are notable for a quiet tone of pride along with what seems an understatement: "With the elation of victory or the depression of defeat, amidst the hardest toils of the campaign, under unwelcome leadership, at all times, and under all circumstances, they were a reliable army still."

17

So, that morning, they lay behind the stone wall or worked at strengthening the little entrenchment. From dawn they had heard the sound of the fighting on Culp's Hill, at their backs and not more than a mile away. At first they were nervous, since it was almost as if their own rear were being assaulted. But as the morning wore on, everyone could tell that the Confederates were not gaining ground. Gradually a sense of confidence built up, that the Twelfth Corps was holding its own, that the Rebels were taking punishment. Still the Second Corps kept on the alert; only a few at a time were they allowed to go back from the line to where the cook-fires were burning, and make themselves coffee.

Except for those who were still too young, they were bearded men, mostly, for among civilians beards were fashionable, and even if a soldier did not care about fashion, he had little chance to shave. Though they had been marching and sleeping in the same uniforms for weeks, they still made more of a military impression than the Confederates did. They wore flat caps, and long-skirted, dark-blue blouses. Their trousers were lighter blue — unless, as generally happened, these had faded out to anything from pea-green to dust-gray.

Already, by this time, some thousands of men had been in this position for more than twenty-four hours, and the ordinary effluvia of human existence were added to the particular offensiveness of a battlefield. Their own dead they had buried or taken to the rear, but on the slope in front of the 69th Pennsylvania still lay the bodies of the Georgians who had fallen when Wright's advance was halted the evening before. (Neither side, during a battle, strained itself to bury the other's dead.) Here and there the shell-torn body of some horse displayed its nastiness.

As to what were the sanitary arrangements, no one has left even a hint — whether because of mid-century reticence in such matters, or because of a supposition that everyone would know the way such things were arranged. Yet we can only think that already a fecal odor was mingling with that of dead horses.

In any case, the men were used to such matters, and they ate with healthy appetites, if they had anything to eat. Many of them did not, and went hungry. Particularly was this true of the officers, who were supposed to supply themselves and not to eat government rations. Where there were wheat-fields, some of the officers and men rolled the heads between their palms, and chewed the still-soft grains for breakfast At Gettysburg, in fact, the stereotypes of the well-fed Yank and the starving Rebel were largely reversed.

Of all that happened during that morning, much might be written, even though it would not add up to a footnote in the history of the war or of the battle.

The men could look out and see the leisurely movement of Confederate batteries here and there. After one of these batteries got into position, it usually fired a shot or two. Since these range-finders were directed at the Second Corps line, there was something sinister about it.

The skirmish line kept busy, and a constant popping of shots came from down in the valley. The Confederate marksmen began to take a steady toll of officers and men in Hays's division. To counteract them, the 1st Company of Massachusetts Sharpshooters moved in. There were only twenty of them, but they were grim specialists. They soon got the situation under control.

Now and then the sound of firing from Culp's Hill intensified, and you knew that the yelling Butternuts were surging forward once more, and you wondered what would happen if they broke the line. Then the firing died down, and you knew that the attack had failed.

Besides, there was the Bliss barn. Enough deeds of valor were done around it, that morning, to supply material for a small epic. Once, when the sharpshooters there became too deadly, Hays sent his skirmish line forward, stiffened with a detachment from the 12th New Jersey. They took heavy losses, but captured the barn and its garrison, only to have to evacuate it later. Then Hays called on four companies of the 14th Connecticut. They too charged, and took heavy losses, and captured the barn — and burned it, since it was too close to the Confederate line to hold. (In later years the men of Connecticut and New Jersey were proud enough of these episodes to erect markers at the site of the barn. Not even a footpath leads to those markers now, and they are overgrown with poison ivy.)

At last there came another burst of firing from Culp's Hill, and then silence. Out in front the smoke still rose from where the barn had burned, but the skirmish lines were very quiet.

Then — it must have been a little after eleven — General Meade and his staff came riding from the north, inspecting the line. He looked reassuringly calm, and he talked with Hancock in tones loud enough for the staff officers to hear, and from them it filtered down to the men, as Meade must have expected — the Confederates had been repulsed at Culp's Hill, and the Twelfth Corps line was secure. Then he rode on toward Little Round Top.

About this time, the sun, which so far had been in and out of clouds, finally came out blazing hot. There was almost no breeze. It was as if both armies then decided to observe a noon hour, and to start it early. Stillness settled down over the whole battlefield.

PART III

Noon-day Lull

> While the stillness was going on.
> — Private Joseph McKeever

WITHIN the Union lines, the stillness was wholly genuine. Within the Confederate lines, preparations were continuing, and a sense of urgency was building up.

"The morning," wrote Lee, "was occupied in necessary preparations." A general who is going to order a desperate assault should not do so hastily, but after full consideration of details. If a battle is to be lost for want of a horseshoe-nail, let it not be this one!

There is a famous description of the Confederate soldier and his method of attack, written by General D. H. Hill:

> Of shoulder-to-shoulder courage, spirit of drill and discipline, he knew nothing and cared less. Hence, on the battlefield, he was more of a free-lance than a machine. Whoever saw a Confederate line advancing that was not crooked as a ram's horn? Each ragged rebel yelling on his own hook and aligning on himself.

The description enshrines an image of the Southern soldier that still is dear to the Southern heart. Even the Northerner accepts it. Of the hundreds from both sections who stand on a summer day and look out from the Angle across the fields, many undoubtedly envisage the troops advancing in this fashion.

Hill had seen a sufficient number of Confederate lines to be considered an authority. But he was not at Gettysburg, and he described the kind of tactics that could be used in charging across the narrow space of some small Virginia farm, girdled with woods. Lee and Longstreet, however, knew too much about soldiers and warfare to believe that any troops could cross a mile of artillery-swept fields in such a wild dash, and then have enough coherence and vigor left in them to break a line of firm infantry.

The assault of July 3 is thus to be considered something unique in this war. Fredericksburg comes the closest to it, but lacks the preliminary attacks to wear down and fix the enemy before the launching of the grand assault. European warfare supplies better analogies, particularly in the battles of Napoleon. One must remember that Lee, at one period of his life, had given much time to the study of Napoleonic campaigns.

This is not to say that Lee slavishly followed a model which had been outmoded by changes of weapons. In half a century the ranges of both artillery and small-arms had increased, but the latter had improved more, so that the relative effectiveness of artillery had decreased. Lee was certainly familiar with such elementary facts, but on July 3 he found himself in a tight corner. He obviously had convinced himself, in spite of Longstreet's disbelief, that the Napoleonic technique deserved a try. After all, the equation to be solved was a complicated one of many terms, and no general could be sure in advance just how all those terms were to be weighted. Besides, if the analogies of the great emperor were out-of-date, those of the lesser one were not. In 1859, only four years before Gettysburg, Napoleon III had smashed the Austrian center at Solferino by means of a heavy bombardment followed by a frontal assault.

Though now it is almost forgotten, it was in its time the great European battle; more men fought there than at Gettysburg. Rather curiously, one Confederate general had been on his way to volunteer in the French army when Solferino was fought, and he commented briefly but significantly upon that battle in a book that he wrote, immediately afterwards. This was the young and romantic Pettigrew, who had done his best to fight for the freedom of Italy. His comment was: "The invention of the Minié ball and the rifled cannon would, it was thought, abolish cavalry and reduce infantry charges within a small compass." But he added that Solferino had shown this expectation to be false. (One wonders what he would have written after Gettysburg.)

2

Lee, in his own hand, wrote careful orders for the attack, and Longstreet endorsed them. Though no full text has been preserved, some of the content is known from the testimony of officers who saw the orders. One sentence dealt with the duties of the three corps and their commanders:

> General Longstreet will make a vigorous attack on his front; General Ewell will threaten the enemy on the left, or make a vigorous attack, should circumstance justify it; General Hill will hold the center at all hazards.

We may assume that the written orders specified what divisions or brigades were shifted from Hill to Longstreet for the purposes of the assault.

This question of command calls for attention, especially since charges have been made that matters went awry, in part, because the responsibility was uncertain. Again, however, there seems to be no need to accuse Lee of such an elementary lapse of generalship as a failure to specify who was in comand of what.

Such matters as the transfer of troops from one corps-commander to another were Lee's responsibility. Once the attack was launched, he would withdraw, according to his usual practice. He thus expressed himself to the Prussian visitor, Captain Scheibert, in words which were spoken three days after Gettysburg and must therefore apply to that battle. "I plan and work with all my might, to bring the troops to the right place at the right time; with that, I have done my duty." In the same conversation he said that "it would be too bad" if he could not trust his generals, and that his own participation in the actual battle would do more harm than good.

Longstreet's responsibility would, then, be for the attack as a whole. He would not advance with the column, but would remain where he could observe. His greatest decision would be as to whether and when supports should be ordered forward.

Pickett would advance with the column. Under his orders, apparently, were all the nine brigades. This conclusion is not altogether certain but is strongly enough based on two officers' reminiscences, on our knowledge that Pickett was the senior officer with the column, and on the fact that he sent members of his staff with messages or orders to commanders outside of his own division. Pickett also probably had command over Wilcox and his two brigades, though the evidence is not wholly clear.

Hill reported himself as commanding Anderson's division and Thomas's and MacGowan's brigades of Pender's division. But all these troops were in one way or another involved in the support of the attack, and must have been at Longstreet's call. The only question would be whether he could actually send an order direct to some division or brigade or would have to send a "request" to Hill that the troops be so ordered. In effect, Hill must have been left without independent command.

No statement is extant as to the assignment of Ewell's three weak brigades — Ramseur's, Iverson's, and Doles's — which were pretty well isolated from the rest of Ewell's command. Under the circumstances they would reasonably have been put at Longstreet's call.

In any case, the haziness of our knowledge must not be taken as an indication that the assignment of command itself was left hazy; neither can the fact that under the stress of combat some errors may have been committed.

The way in which each of these nineteen brigades was to aid in the grand attack can be clearly enough determined. Nine were included in the actual column of assault. Two under Wilcox, his own and Perry's, were assigned to support this column on its right. Three brigades — Wright's, Posey's, and Mahone's — were "in readiness to move up in support." The two brigades of Hill's corps and the three of Ewell's to the southwest of the town were weak for the length of line occupied and could not do much more than hold their positions. But their very presence was a strong support to the left of the advancing column. Moreover, General Rodes, commanding Ewell's brigades, reported that he was on the lookout for some "favorable opportunity to co-operate." At least as much, then, must have been expected from Thomas and MacGowan. The orders to these five brigades would have been to support the left of the column, to make some demonstration, and to help exploit any success of the main attack.

Far then from being thrown forward in isolation, as has been often stated, the attacking force had supporting troops, in ten brigades, that totaled about as many men as its own nine brigades.

3

Lee and Longstreet were generally together on this morning, riding about and inspecting the lines. The inference would have to be that the tactical planning was a collaboration. We can deduce what the plans were, partly from scattered phrases in the reports and in reminiscences, but chiefly by observing the situation at the opening and the early phases of the advance itself — especially the positions of the troops, and their formation.

As for the positions, Heth's line was drawn up about fifty yards inside the edge of the woods, back of the crest of Seminary Ridge, with its right just north of Spangler's Woods. Pickett's line, as various reports and reminiscences make certain, was protected from Union observation, partly in and partly out of woods, and a few hundred yards behind the crest on which Dearing's artillery was posted. It therefore must have been in the low ground west and north of the Spangler house.

Of the other brigades, Wilcox's and Perry's were well in front, in support of the artillery. Wright's, Posey's, and Mahone's were in support position, sheltered behind Seminary Ridge. The other five brigades were on a good defensive line, along what was known as Long Lane, or the sunken road.

As for the formation, Pickett's division was drawn up in two lines, with Kemper and Garnett in the first and Armistead in the second. Kemper held the right; Garnett, the left. Armistead was probably behind Garnett, but since his brigade was the largest and probably had to supply no skirmishers, his line must have overlapped Kemper's considerably.

Heth's division was arranged, from left to right, that is, from north to south: Brockenbrough, Davis, Pettigrew, Archer. Some accounts of the battle work on the belief that this division was in a single line. On the contrary, Lee's own report states: "Pickett's and Heth's divisions, in two lines." Longstreet's report is equally precise: "Heth's division . . . was arranged in two lines." Further study of the reports leads to the conclusion that the division was in line of regiments, with each regiment having half its companies in the first line and half in the second. The second line was a hundred yards or more behind the first. This arrangement had a great advantage — if the second line must advance to reinforce the first, as was only to be expected, some regimental integrity would be preserved. Behind Heth's division the two brigades of Pender's formed a single line at the right. Since these two brigades were not half as large as the four that they supported, the left of Heth's division had nothing behind it.

The determination of the formation allows us to calculate the length of the various lines — each "line," naturally, being considered in the military sense of the word, that is, as consisting of two ranks with file-closers as a partial third rank. This calculation is not simple, since it demands a knowledge of the total numbers involved, of the intervals between regiments and brigades, and of the numbers of skirmishers and file-closers. It also demands knowledge that the Confederate army figured two feet of space for each man in close order. Granting that the result is only an approximation and omitting the calculations, we may state that Pickett's first line was 2500 feet long; each of Heth's, 2000. Armistead's large brigade extended 1500 feet; Pender's two small ones, 1650.

The whole front was thus not much under a mile, and some idea of the complication of the advance should thus be evident. There has been nothing more awkward under the sun that one of these long double-ranked lines, nothing more difficult to move properly from place to place, with necessary changes of direction and adjustments to the movements of other equally awkward lines — especially under battle-conditions. Simply by training his men to march like automatons, Frederick the Great overcame his enemies by mere maneuvering and won world-famous victories. No wonder that the usual Confederate line was crooked as a ram's horn! That was merely what came naturally. What would you expect of farmers and backwoodsmen and hill-billies? Their total number of hours of close-order drill was small. Yet they were excellent infantrymen, and their generals thus planned that for once, knowing the necessity and the stake, the men of these rustic brigades should emulate the Prussian grenadiers.

Even for the great Frederick, however, the attack would have raised two special problems of maneuver. . . . First, as drawn up by the necessities of terrain, the lines were not parallel with the Union line, but converged upon it, toward the north, at an angle of about 25°. This might be taken to indicate that an "oblique attack" was being planned. The Baron de Jomini in his *Art of War* was highly in favor of such attacks; he was a standard authority of the time, and Lee knew this work. But Jomini was of the Napoleonic era, and was not thinking in terms of the devastating fire-power of rifles and rifled cannon upon the advanced flank. Besides, if an oblique attack was being planned, the left of the line should have been strong, and it was not. The idea can therefore be dismissed. Instead, the problem was that of so handling the lines that they would become parallel to the Union line and thus go up to the final assault. The progress of the attack itself demonstrates that the problem was recognized and steps taken to solve it.

The second great tactical problem arose from the necessities of terrain and cover which had dictated that the troops be drawn up in two bodies. Heth's right was about a quarter-mile behind and to the left of Pickett's left. Unless the two could be united, there would be two separate and weak attacks, lacking the destructive impact of a single strong one. Again, since steps were taken to solve this problem, we can only suppose that the two generals recognized it. At some time in the morning Fry, who commanded Archer's brigade, went across and talked with Garnett and Pickett, arranging some details as to the way in which the two commands would co-operate in the advance.

The importance of having a precise objective — in this case, the clump of trees — should here become apparent. Obviously, to say that this was the objective does not mean that every Confederate soldier was instructed to march right at it. Instead, it was the point toward which the right of Heth's division would advance, and toward which, though by a more complicated route, the left of Pickett's division would direct itself.

Why Pickett did not march directly toward the clump of trees cannot be certainly determined. Most likely, he was avoiding a growth of bushes along the fence to his left. Some have assumed that Pickett started off wrong, and changed to the right direction when he came to the top of the rise and saw the clump of trees.

Such an "explanation" merely makes nincompoops out of not only Pickett but also Longstreet and Lee. Pickett may have been no mental giant, but even he would hardly have started to lead a whole division into battle without taking the trouble to ride, first, a hundred yards up the slope in advance, and take a look where he was going. Again we must assume that the plan was worked out in advance.

Once united into a single front and advancing behind its skirmishers, the column of assault would consist of three lines in its left center and of two lines on its extreme left and its right center; on its extreme right it would not be a column at all, but merely a single line. The three-line depth may indicate that the main push was expected at that point, or else it was the result of the fact that these troops had already been heavily engaged and might need an additional line to accomplish as much as Pickett's men with two lines. Both flanks were weak. Obviously, the main drive was expected to be in the center, and the extended flanks would probably serve their purpose if they spread the enemy's fire.

In addition, however, measures were devised to protect the flanks. On the right, Wilcox was held ready to advance, so as to turn the tables on any troops attempting to attack Kemper's right by in turn attacking their left. Moreover, Alexander was to advance guns to give additional protection. The left flank called for no such elaborate measures. It was not so extended, and the brigades along the sunken road gave it a considerable bolstering.

4

At some time during the morning Hill approached Lee, with the request that he be allowed to lead his whole corps to the assault. Hill was speaking in accordance with the Napoleonic dictum: "In the decisive attack the last man and the last horse should be thrown in." But Lee refused, telling Hill that what remained

The Planned Assault Column

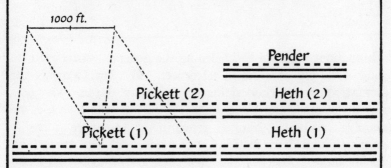

1000 ft.

Pender

Pickett (2)   Heth (2)

Pickett (1)   Heth (1)

S K I R M I S H E R S

DIRECTION OF ADVANCE

Each "line" is of two ranks, with file-closers. This represents the column as it would have appeared theoretically after the joining of the Pickett and Heth-Pender brigades, and before the skirmishers were re-absorbed.

The exact position of Pickett's second line is somewhat uncertain; it may have been more toward the right of the column (i.e., the left in the diagram). No interval is shown here between brigades and regiments.

BRYANT

of his corps was the only reserve and would be needed if the
great attack should fail.

5

Throughout much of the morning the generals were busy planning. One officer wrote in retrospect, "We saw Generals Lee,
Longstreet, and Pickett riding up and down the line, and occasionally approaching the crest of the hill to take a look at the
enemy's position." Another remembered the three riding together up and down in front of the troops, at least three times
"if not more," observing the alignment, and studying the Union
position with field-glasses. Longstreet himself wrote that after
the troops had been posted, Lee rode with him twice along the
lines to see that everything was properly arranged.

Once the plans had been settled, care was taken that they
should be explained, so that even the men in the ranks under-
stood what was expected. Again, to quote a reminiscence, "commanding officers of regiments were sent for to brigade headquarters to receive instructions that had already been given to the
brigadiers by General Lee in person." These officers returned,
assembled company officers, and carefully instructed them. The
company officers then explained the situation to the men. Far
from being unplanned, as it is sometimes represented to be, the
assault seems to have been worked out to the last detail.

6

The conclusion must be that Lee knew against what troops he
was launching his assault. In the fighting around the Bliss barn
the lines had shifted back and forth. Almost certainly the Confederates had taken some prisoners, and they would have seen
dead bodies with the trefoil shoulder-patch. Moreover, far from

trying to conceal their identity, the Second Corps and its various components were conspicuously flying their flags. Though there was not much breeze, there was probably enough to make the flags stand out occasionally, and at such moments an alert Confederate officer could have read, through his field-glasses, the plain information thus divulged. The 3rd Division, Second Corps, for instance, flew a white flag with a blue trefoil. According to a staff-officer of that division, "It needed no courier to carry to the enemy the intelligence that the Second Corps was there."

7

At noon the heat and the stillness lay heavy. Now and then some general, or two, or three, rode with their staffs along the line; when one of these generals was Lee, some of the men noted that he seemed more anxious and "ruffled" than was his custom. But if this was the time for generals to be busy and perturbed, it was the time for men in the ranks to take their ease, though some of them might well be perturbed.

They knew what they were facing; they had been told. "No disguises were used," wrote one, "nor was there any underrating of the difficult work in hand." They were informed of the strong position to be attacked and of the distance to be traversed. They were also told, by way of reassurance, that the task was not impossible, since Wright's brigade had stormed the position the day before. (This was a considerable exaggeration, but Wright had so reported.) Further to inspirit them, they were told (and this may not have been an exaggeration) that the capture of the enemy's key position would end the war. They were informed of the other bodies of troops that would advance with them. In short, the individual Confederate was treated as a man and not part of a machine, and was even encouraged to think. (The correspondent of the London *Times*, accustomed to European armies, considered this last a great mistake, and blamed some of the later troubles upon it.)

In Pickett's division, at least, the morale was high. Yet we should beware of the mistake of considering this division to be more than it really was. In later years, since its men made the grand assault, the idea arose that they were a kind of Old Guard — "the flower of Virginia." In reality, the division was available because it had been engaged in rear-guard duties, either by chance, or even because Longstreet considered that it could better be spared from the fighting-line than could either of his others. To have suggested that this division was the *corps d'élite* would have produced in Lee, we can guess from the analogy of a similar occasion, an icy silence, followed by: "And why do you consider that the other divisions of this army are less trustworthy than that of General Pickett?" To have made the suggestion to Longstreet would probably have resulted in a hearty guffaw at what could only be taken for a pleasantry. If you had said the same to a soldier of any other division, you would have had a fight on your hands, unless the whole idea would seem so fantastic as to be worth only the utterance of that short scatologism used by American soldiers to dispose of a matter not to be dignified by formal refutation.

Nevertheless the division was a good one. One of their colonels, indeed, recalled that when the men were told of the attack, "from being unusually merry and hilarious they on a sudden had become as still and thoughtful as Quakers at a love feast." Also, an artillery officer, going to visit with some of his friends in Garnett's brigade, found several officers engaged in speculating as to the chances of getting safely through the impending fight — not an occupation indicative of high morale. But such incidents can be offset by other testimony, as when a man of the same brigade recalled, "the men were in splendid spirits and confident of sweeping everything before them; . . . never was

there anything like the same enthusiasm in entering battle."
Some of Kemper's men, who were stationed near a farmhouse
under some apple trees, were so high-spirited that they indulged
in an impromptu fight, pelting each other with small green
apples. These were men of a special regiment, who could afford
a little extra swagger because they were The Old First, and came
from Richmond. We should remember that Pickett's men,
though veterans, had done no hard fighting in nearly a year, and
so should have been in fine fettle.

In the brigades of Heth's division, and in Scales's — those
which had already been fought and over-fought — there was
less of high spirits, one gathers. Not that there were not some
very tough fighting units! Still, it is not easy to be enthusiastic
about going into battle again, when you are aching with the
memory of lost comrades, and the shattering horror of devastating casualties taken only two days before. The ranks have been
built up a bit by pressing into service all the cooks and clerks
and extra-duty men, but this does not help greatly, because you
suspect that these men cannot be counted upon too much. All
the slightly wounded are back in the ranks too — men with
grimly bandaged heads, and men limping but still able to keep
up with the march. They build the numbers up, but are not
very encouraging to look at. Besides, officers have almost disappeared, especially the higher ranking ones. In camp you would
not care if officers vanished entirely, but in battle you are not
quite happy to see a regiment commanded by some young sprig
of a captain, and the brigade no longer being handled by "the
old man."

What there was to be done had been done. Colonel Marshall,
now commanding Pettigrew's brigade, had turned out the band,
and had it play the favorite tunes. This is said to have cheered
the men up, but in view of the nearly fifty per cent casualties
there might be some question whether even the sweetest rendering of "Lorena" or the liveliest of "Dixie" could do much.

8

One man has left us a simple account of his own deeply moving experience. His name was Kimble, and he bore the curiously feminine first name of June. He described himself as "a light-weight orderly sergeant of company A," of the 14th Tennessee, which was the center regiment of Archer's brigade. During the period of quiet, he walked forward to the edge of the woods, and sought to locate the point at which his regiment would reach the Union line. Struck with the frightful danger of such an advance, he was so violently moved that he found himself speaking aloud, asking the question "June Kimble, are you going to do your duty today?" As he remembered, he then answered himself back, audibly, "I'll do it, so help me God."

At that moment, all dread passed from him, and he began to act in a calm and deliberate fashion, without apprehension. When he returned to the lines, he was asked how it looked. "Boys," he replied calmly, "if we have to go, it will be hot for us, and we will have to do our best."

9

The men were in extreme physical discomfort. Some of them were in the full sun. Even those who were in the woods were almost equally oppressed, since the trees cut off the circulation of air. Because the officers did not know just when some order to change location might arrive, no one could be sent for water. Canteens which had been filled in the early morning were now empty, and many men's throats were tight and dry from thirst.

The strain of waiting was the more severe because there was nothing to do. At some time, however, various detachments were assigned as skirmishers, to a total of at least ten per cent of the men in the front line. These skirmishers advanced until

they were within fair rifle range of the Union skirmishers, and
then lay down in the wheat or otherwise made themselves inconspicuous. Like the main line, they too would conserve themselves for the final advance.

The skirmishers, or other detachments, tore down as many
fences as possible, so that the advancing lines would not be
thrown into confusion by having to climb them. The rail fences
were easily demolished; the solidly built fences along the Emmitsburg road took more work. Since the northern end of this
road was behind the line of Union skirmishers, nothing could
be done about the fences there. Many of the fences, moreover,
must have had a growth of bushes and small trees along them,
as fences are likely to have and as many of those on the battlefield
still do. Getting rid of all this tangle was rather more than the
troops could accomplish. Running up the hill along the fence
just at the left of where Garnett's brigade rested, there is, at
present, a heavy line of bushes and poison ivy. If a similar
growth was there in 1863, it would account, as has been already
suggested, for the detour that Pickett took in starting his
advance.

10

General Pendleton, in his capacity as Chief of Artillery, presently
inspected the artillery lines north of Alexander's. . . . The first
guns were five of Poague's battalion, which really extended the
left of Alexander's line. This excellent position, close to the
Point of Woods, commanded a broad field of fire at effective
range.

North of these guns the ground was lower, and there was a
quarter-mile gap. Then, almost opposite Cemetery Hill, thirty-
five guns of Poague's, Lane's, and Pegram's battalions formed a
continuous line.

The position was ideal for defense. The line was close to the
top of the rise, commanding the gently rolling terrain in front.

A stone wall allowed the guns to be placed behind its shelter. Back from the wall a belt of woodland offered cover for the caissons and horses.

"Ideal for defense," yes! But since when had the Army of Northern Virginia become defensive-minded? To pulverize the Union lines in preparation for an infantry attack, this artillery was too far away. Alexander, sensing the necessity, had pushed Dearing's guns forward until they were scarcely a thousand yards from the opposing muzzles. But this great battery of thirty-five guns could only play "long taw" at ranges of from 1300 to 1500 yards! Pendleton approved, and made no effort to shift the guns to more effective positions.

But this was not even the worst. North of the thirty-five guns, the ridge again was low for a quarter of a mile. Then came thirteen guns of Hill's and thirteen of Ewell's. These guns, of McIntosh's and Dance's battalions, averaged well over a mile from the Angle, and were not much closer to Cemetery Hill. Moreover, they had to fire over the heads of the Confederate infantry holding the sunken road, and so had received orders to use solid shot only. Thus restricted, any damage they could do to the Union army would be little more than accidental.

Nevertheless, as if trying to see how far away they could get rather than how close, the Confederates had ten rifles of Carter's battalion almost half a mile still farther north, on a high place by the railroad cut. Finally, more than two miles north of Cemetery Hill and a good two miles and a half from the clump of trees, were placed the two Whitworth rifles, the longest-range and most accurate pieces in either army. These guns would actually have no trouble in sending their projectiles so far, and could do so, theoretically, with sufficient accuracy. But there was no system of forward observers and communications for fire-control; all that the gunners could do under battle-conditions was to shoot into the smoke.

It can be said that with the terrain being what it was the Confederates could not have done any better. After the war, however, Alexander argued that they could have. But that is not really the question. What matters is that, whether or nor it could have been "better," it was not "good." With dubiously placed guns and a great deal of wishful thinking, Lee's artillerymen were preparing to open one of the great cannonades of history. One wonders. What if there had been a real master-gunner, not a pious, middle-aged clergyman?

11

During this time of enforced idleness rumor was rife. Alexander reports one tale, even giving it some credence — that the army was going to advance along the whole line in a universal attack. Another rumor sounds like something that the veterans made up to gull the recruits, that all the guns would be galloped forward to a certain line and there engage the enemy, and the infantry would double-quick after them, and then this maneuver would be repeated in a gigantic leapfrog operation. Even more widespread and persistent was the rumor which had turned up also on July 1, that the Union troops to be attacked were not the Army of the Potomac, but some local militia who could be expected to run at the first fire. Southern writers have denied the story vehemently, as if it suggested that Lee himself had gone around bolstering up his soldiers' morale by false tales. But this is obviously not the question. Rumors start in the lowest ranks, not in the highest one, and they burgeon because no one is in a position to deny the story. Through that morning many a simple Southern infantryman must have cherished that belief — or, at least, that hope — of easy victory. If it made the hours pleasanter, why should we grudge it to him?

Filtering down through staff-officers and orderlies, the story of the dissension between Lee and Longstreet also circulated among

the men in the ranks as a rumor, that Longstreet had earnestly
protested against the charge, but had been overruled by a council
of war.

12

On this bridge of rumor, we may now pass to the Union lines,
and the Southern apologist may happily learn that the Northern
soldier also was an easy victim to the many-tongued one. About
noon, the stillness was broken by some distant artillery fire, off to
the east. It was the Horse Artillery getting in a few shots, before
their main engagement of the mid-afternoon. Along the lines,
however, the word ran that the firing indicated General Couch's
advance from Harrisburg. This tale, indeed, might have been
true, since Meade had been urging Couch to do this very thing.
A more fantastic bit of wishful thinking gave rise to the report
that McClellan, still revered by the Army of the Potomac, was
advancing on Lee's rear with 40,000 men. General Webb was
credited with telling his men that if they could hold out where
they were until four o'clock of the next day, McClellan would
attack Lee from the other direction. Whether Webb was ever
an active party to such deception may be doubted. More likely,
when asked whether it was true, he merely was in no position to
deny it, and so gave credence to the tale.

13

The silence seems to have affected the men of the Second Corps
more than it did the Confederates. "It was a queer sight," one
of them wrote, "to see men look at each other without speaking;
the change was so great men seemed to go on tip-toe not knowing
how to act." "At noon," one remembered, "it became as still as
the Sabbath day." To one private, the mere absence of noise
became something positive, and he testified, "while the stillness

was going on." Naturally, as another soldier put it, "All was speculation as to what was coming next."

Some were still working at the little ditch and the pile of earth in front of it, but could not do much because of lack of tools. Besides, the hot sun discouraged all except the eagerest. More congenial occupations, to judge from several mentions, were the collection and loading of extra muskets. Some of these lay in the Union lines, and others could be picked up on the slope in front, where Wright's brigade had been repulsed.

The men of the 12th New Jersey were busy, for a while, in a special way. As already noted, these soldiers might be described as "nice boys," but this did not keep them from indulging in their own brand of total warfare. The regiment had a grievance, in that it was not armed with up-to-date rifles, but with the huge old 69-caliber smooth-bore. This antiquated weapon was ineffective at over a hundred yards, and inaccurate at any range. To compensate in some degree, it was loaded with "buck and ball," which meant that it had one bullet to fit the bore and three buckshot. At short range, therefore, you had four chances to hit someone. The Jerseymen decided to increase the odds. They opened cartridges, threw the big bullets away, and loaded new cartridges with anything from ten to twenty-five shot apiece. They thus were prepared, if the Confederates ever came up really close, to let loose a devastating blast. (This was before the days of any Geneva convention, and methods of warfare were left pretty much to the individual soldier's conscience.)

By noon it was so hot that the sun seemed for the moment, more than the Confederates, to be the enemy. A few troops had the shelter of trees. In some regiments the men sacrificed military dignity by sticking their bayoneted rifles into the ground and rigging up blankets or the halves of shelter tents on the musket butts to provide shade. But most of the men merely had to lie and take the sun.

Back from the low stone wall and the little entrenchment was the long line of stacked rifles. In front of them, just behind the wall, lay the men. The colors were rolled up and leaned against the wall, along with the extra rifles. Here and there a brigade or division flagstaff was planted in the ground, but the flags hung limp.

As to what the men did, no one has bothered to record much. The term "sweating it out" was not to be invented until a later war, but here it would have applied literally.

14

No battle-story can be complete without a tale of premonition. . . . During this time Corporal Wesley C. Sturtevant of the 14th Vermont got permission to leave the ranks and to go to speak to his cousin and boyhood playmate Ralph O. Sturtevant of the 13th. The corporal had been in the previous day's fighting, and had "not flinched or been much frightened." During the night, however, he had dreamed in such a way that he could only interpret it in terms of death. Though sad at heart, he was quiet and resigned. His cousin attempted to dispel these thoughts, but without much confidence, since he knew that the young man had been brought up by a mother who firmly believed in dreams. The two said goodbye, and the corporal walked back toward his own regiment, convinced of his fate, and therefore totally unconcerned as to the target he was offering to the enemy.

15

During this lull we should take the opportunity to bring forward three Union first lieutenants, who loom curiously large in the day's story. . . . Alonzo Hersford Cushing, a West Pointer from Wisconsin, was twenty-two years old. In June, 1861, he had been a first lieutenant in the 4th Artillery, and so he was still in July, 1863, though "for gallant and meritorious service" at Fredericksburg and at Chancellorsville, he had gained brevet rank as captain, and then as major.

This was a distinguished career, and his services at Gettysburg were spectacular. Yet, others could probably equal both. Why this one man should be made to stand out as the hero is, as often, difficult to explain. Cushing was young, and looked younger than he was — but so were and did others. He was brave, far beyond call of duty, and so were others. Perhaps men remembered Cushing because he carried with him always some special buoyancy, some debonairness. Perhaps they remembered him because of a certain happening — so terrible as to become archetypal, and thus to focus men's attention by a kind of fascination. Be it what it may, Cushing was remembered. . . .

Stephen F. Brown, twenty-one years old, from the town of Swanton, had helped organize Company K of the 13th Vermont. He was a soldier only from the promptings of duty and conscience, and he was not a happy warrior. One who knew him well declared that he suffered intensely from "apprehension of death" during the battle, though "no one showed less fear or acted more bravely." He displayed an unusual concern and even tenderness of heart toward the men entrusted to his command.

This humaneness was almost his undoing. On the evening of July 1 the regiment had arrived at Cemetery Hill, and was at once put into a position, with strict orders against leaving the ranks. The men were in agony from thirst, some of them on the verge of collapse. Lieutenant Brown, unable to endure their sufferings, collected some canteens, left his post, filled the canteens at a near-by spring, and returned. He was immediately put under arrest, and relieved of his sword.

The next morning, officers being needed for the battle, he was released from arrest, but by this time his sword had been taken to the rear. As a symbol of command all he could find was a common hatchet. Like an Indian brave with a tomahawk, he was still thus armed on July 3. . . .

Frank Aretas Haskell, though a native of Vermont, had moved west after graduating from Dartmouth, so that he too, like Cushing, was from Wisconsin. He was thirty-five. As a volunteer soldier, he had been through plenty of fighting, some of it with the Iron Brigade. He does not seem to have distinguished himself particularly, but he stood out enough to be picked by Gibbon as an aide. This in itself meant something, for in those armies there were few who had a higher conception of military proficiency than did Gibbon. So, there was Haskell at Gettysburg, over-age for a lieutenant, unknown, a mounted errand-boy for a brigadier general.

At least his case is different from Cushing's in that one can say precisely why he became famous. (1) He happened to be at the right place at the right time. (2) Thereupon, combining courage and military sense, he did the right thing. (3) Afterwards, he wrote the whole story amazingly well.

As a final comment upon Haskell, we may note that on this blistering hot day he was wearing, not only his heavy uniform, but two suits of underwear beneath it!

16

Yes, Haskell wrote about it, and we may move on by quoting from that very account, to wit, "Now it so happened that just about this time of day a very original and interesting thought occurred to General Gibbon and several of his staff; that it would be a very good thing and a very good time, to have something to eat." The time actually being close to noon suggests that even on the field of battle a man is a creature of habit. For the same thought occurred not only to General Gibbon and his staff, but apparently to the universal and communal mind of both armies.

Since we are already with Haskell, we may first consider that lunch which his own writing has made somewhat famous. First,

the food had to be got together, and since the officers did not
draw government rations, this offered difficulties. Two persons
— one of whom, apparently, was Haskell — had to ride several
miles to scrounge up the eatables, and they ended with "some
few chickens, some butter, and one huge loaf of bread." The
last was somewhat fragmentary, since a hog had run away with
it and had eaten part of it before it could be rescued. There
were also potatoes, coffee, and tea. General Gibbon, who also
described the lunch, was ungracious enough to suggest that the
poultry had been stolen, and also to remember only, "an old and
tough rooster."

The divisional headquarters apparently had some "contra-
bands" with it, since Gibbon remarks that "the servants" set
about doing the cooking. Gibbon saw fit to invite his superior
officers, and at the suggestion of lunch, the generals came flocking to the little swale behind Meade's headquarters. Even Meade
was persuaded to leave work. Hancock came; Newton, who was
commanding the First Corps; Pleasonton, Chief of Cavalry. If
a clairvoyant Confederate gunner had sent a shell into their
midst, he might have changed the course of the war. Hancock
and Gibbon sat on camp-stools, Meade had an empty cracker
box; Newton and Pleasonton made do with a roll of blankets.
The staff officers sat on the ground.

The bread, as toast, was good, and so was the butter. The
chickens were not cut off in their youth, and Haskell admitted
that they were "in good running order." But he thought them
delicious as stew. Some, after tasting the coffee, asked for tea,
and vice versa, and some of these "were so ungracious as to
suggest that the water that was used in both might have come
from near a barn" — a euphemism that those who have served
in armies may put into their own idiom.

Still, they enjoyed the meal, and then they leaned back under
the shade of a very small tree, and the generals lighted cigars and
talked of yesterday's battle and today's — or merely talked.

Meade was of the opinion that the attack would again be on the left. Newton called Gibbon a "young North Carolinian," who was becoming arrogant because he commanded a corps, and Gibbon replied that Newton was no one to talk, because he too had only commanded a corps since yesterday. So it went, and Haskell was obviously impressed at being so close to Meade and the corps-commanders. . . .

Across the way, so to speak, we do not know what Lee and Longstreet ate this noon, if indeed they ate at all. Lee had been suffering from a bad case of diarrhea the day before, and he was possibly going easy on food. As for Longstreet, his big and tough body could eat, or go without eating if the need was.

There is record, however, of a lunch involving Garnett, Wilcox, and Captain Harrison of Pickett's staff. Garnett — in his blue overcoat or his gray uniform, as you please — does not seem to have been in so much pain from his injured leg as he was at other times. (In a technical sense, perhaps none of them was feeling pain.) Wilcox, whom his troops called "old Billy Fixin'," was doubtless wearing the short jacket and battered straw hat by which he was known. The scene of this luncheon was a peach orchard, though not the Peach Orchard, close to a house, which could only have been the Spangler house. Wilcox had produced some cold mutton. The house had a well from which could be drawn, according to Harrison, "the coldest, hardest water that ever sprung out of limestone rock." The Southerners found this Pennsylvania water very distasteful until they discovered that it would mix with Pennsylvania whiskey. Of this latter renowned and redoubtable beverage, one of them had a bottle. With the problem of water thus solved, the luncheon became a highly agreeable affair. Twenty yards down the slope of the hill, their horses were standing. In the blaze of noon all was quiet. Garnett, that tragic figure — at least, it is pleasant to see him for a moment relaxed, forgetful of the ache in his leg and the ache in his heart, rendering the Yankee water drinkable by mixing it with the Yankee whiskey!

In a pocket of Garnett's uniform there was a watch. This is not mere deduction, but is attested later on in the day. The hands of the watch moved on. . . .

The men in the ranks, in both armies, ate well, or merely ate, or did not eat at all — according to the luck of campaigning. In Pickett's division, as one remembered, "the men drew out their 'corn dodgers' and bits of bacon, to make their frugal dinner." But in the Washington Artillery, that aristocratic battalion from New Orleans, the men had nothing. One of their officers found a cherry tree with some boughs hanging low, perhaps because they had been hit by bullets, and he ate some of the cherries.

In the Union lines empty stomachs were the rule. A gunner of Brown's battery remembered "almost a wolf's hunger." Most of the troops had been isued three days' rations on July 1 — salt pork, hard tack, sugar, and coffee. But they had already eaten it all, with the usual philosophy of veterans, that it was easier to carry the rations in your belly than in your haversack, and that the next day, if there was one, could take care of itself.

17

About noon, Lane's and Scales's brigades moved into position. At 12.30 a careful observer from Cemetery Hill noted that the enemy was "placing a great number of batteries." He may have seen at this time some movement of Ewell's artillery at the north end of the line. Also about this time a final shift of command was effected.

18

Major General Isaac Trimble was Virginia-born in 1802, and was thus sixty-one at Gettysburg, five years senior to Lee, and very much an old man, by the standards of either army. He graduated from West Point in 1822, spent ten years in the Army, and then resigned and passed most of his life as an engineer in Maryland, becoming one of the state's leading citizens. He went with Virginia in '61, and soon attained high rank. Age had not dulled him, and he was known as a determined fighter.

Just recovered from a wound, he rejoined the army at the beginning of the Gettysburg campaign, when no division lacked a commander. Lee told him to accompany Ewell, and he thus became a supernumerary major general. Hearing that two divisions had lost their commanders, Trimble applied for one of them, and Lee gave him Pender's. Perhaps this assignment was merely one of routine — recognizing that an unemployed major general had a right to the first vacancy. Probably there was more to it than that, especially since Trimble took command only of the two brigades about to advance. Lee, it may be, lacked confidence in Lane to push his men with sufficient vehemence. But Trimble was noted for a driving ferocity in battle. The change also allowed Lane to take immediate charge of his own brigade. Lee must have thought the last-minute shift a good idea, though it meant that the two brigades were taken over by a general who was wholly unknown to them, as they to him.

Lee immediately rode over, and he and Trimble inspected the troops together. Apparently Lee now for the first time saw Scales's shattered brigade, and noticing men with heads or hands bandaged, he said to Trimble, "Many of these poor boys should go to the rear; they are not able for duty." Then having looked more closely at the officers, he said, "I miss in this brigade the faces of many dear friends." As he was finally riding away, he again looked mournfully at the troops, and muttered, as if to himself, "The attack must succeed."

19

Napoleon declared: "In war men are nothing; one man is everything." The validity of the epigram can be argued. Still, there are times in any battle when even the most democratically minded historian, considering, can realize what Napoleon meant. Such a time was this noon-hour. The batteries were in position;

the infantry was ready. But even yet some shift in the mind of one man, and a few words spoken, could change everything.

Lee is never an easy figure to appraise. He wrote little, and lacked a Boswell — even though, eventually, he had a Freeman. We know almost nothing of what went on within his mind on this day, though there happen to be several mentions of his nervousness of manner. But there is nothing to indicate that once having made the decision he ever faltered.

During much of the afternoon he seems to withdraw from the action. Scheibert, watching, was amazed that Lee sent and received only one dispatch over a long period of time. One even has a tendency to think of him as some *roi fainéant*, leaving the conduct of affairs to an active lord of the palace; or, as some elder god, Cronus replaced by Zeus. This would be incorrect. If we wish a god-like comparison (as we may easily do with Lee), we should rather think of that conception by which a god creates a universe, sets it spinning, and then withdraws from active participation. That universe will continue along predestined lines, unless the god intervenes.

Lee did not intervene, though during those long hours, as the sun rose to meridian and hung there, he may often have hoped that a move by Meade would offer some opportunity other than the desperate one to which the Confederate army was almost committed.

So, by his unaltering decision, Lee kept his universe spinning on toward its end. At such a time, we would say that Napoleon is right, and that only "one man" can be counted. Even Longstreet, second in command, was then of little more importance than a private in the ranks.

20

Of him, throughout these hours, we know more than we do of Lee, because Longstreet wrote about himself. One way to think of it is that he played the immovable body against Lee as the irresistible force. Longstreet, as a soldier, would obey orders. But Longstreet as a lieutenant general, a mature and self-confident man, and stubborn "Old Pete," would not falter for a moment in his conviction that the attack could result in nothing but a disaster.

Throughout the morning he had been kept busy. After the preparations were completed, he had a few minutes to think. This was the time that he must have remembered when he wrote, "Never was I so depressed as upon that day."

To explain this depression, one need not call upon subtleties of psychological theory. If anyone was ever in a situation calculated to produce a depression, Longstreet was the man. Yet he was not one merely to yield to an emotion, but rather one to take some step to relieve the situation. But what step? Another protest to Lee would obviously be useless. In his depression — one could even say in his desperation — he thought of a possibility. It might be considered one which compromised a little his honor as a soldier, but he either did not consider it so, or else he thought that the end justified it. Should not a general stoop a little, to save the lives of his men from being sacrificed in what he considers a hopeless attack?

To young Alexander, in immediate command of the corps artillery, Longstreet wrote a note and dispatched it by courier. Then the general apparently felt the sense of relief that comes from having taken action. He rode back into the near-by bit of woodland, dismounted, and lay down to rest. According to one observer, he fell asleep. The Confederate cause, we should think, would be benefited from his being refreshed by a nap. His critics, however, have seen in his action a serious dereliction from duty. What did they want him to do — stand, biting his nails?

Meanwhile, the courier delivered the note to Alexander, and that officer read it, undoubtedly with increasing surprise, puzzlement, and apprehension:

If the artillery fire does not have the effect to drive off the enemy or greatly demoralize him, so as to make our effort pretty certain, I would prefer that you should not advise Gen. Pickett to make the charge. I shall rely a great deal upon your good judgment to determine the matter, and shall expect you to let Gen. Pickett know when the moment offers.

Strange! It seemed to call upon him, a mere colonel, to make the decision, not only *when* Pickett was to advance, but even *whether* he was to advance. This was what Alexander could read in the lines. But what should he read between the lines?

Alexander, highly intelligent, could be expected to pick up a linguistic implication that would be lost on a mere blood-and-guts soldier. To go a step further, he might even be expected to grasp that such a procedure was to be expected of him. Finally, he knew of Longstreet's disapproval of the attack.

Alexander, therefore, probably translated the note as we should think that it should have been translated, that is:

If you can certify that our artillery fire will not be wholly successful, this will strengthen my hand with General Lee, and I can probably have the attack cancelled.

But by what was said and by what was implied, Alexander thus found himself in a ticklish situation. Why should *he* have to assume this responsibility? Considering, he began to see "overwhelming reasons against the assault," and in his predicament he turned to a fellow-Georgian, General Wright, who happened to be standing by. He showed the note, and told his misgivings. Wright advised him to express these doubts to Longstreet. Carefully preserving the original note, Alexander then wrote a reply:

I will only be able to judge of the effect of our fire on the enemy by his return fire as his infantry is but little exposed to view, and the smoke will obscure the field. If, as I infer from your note, there is any alternative to this attack, it should be carefully considered before opening our fire, for it will take all the artillery ammunition we have left to test this one thoroughly, and if result is unfavorable we will have none left for another effort, and even if this is entirely successful, it can only be so at a very bloody cost.

Roused from his brief rest, Longstreet read the note. He could have had no doubt as to what was meant. Without saying so in sentences, Alexander had clearly expressed himself: "Sir, I must respectfully decline to accept the responsibility which you are placing upon me."

Thereupon the general, never to be lightly moved from a course of action, wrote a second time. Again, Alexander preserved the note:

The intention is to advance the infantry if the artillery has the desired effect of driving the enemy off, or having other effect such as to warrant us in making the attack. When that moment arrives, advise Gen. Pickett, and of course advance such artillery as you can use in aiding the attack.

In this note there is a small word, which should strike anyone with a solid blow. That is the word "if." The attack, then, was not irrevocably determined. "The intention is to advance the infantry *if* . . ." One wonders whether Lee would have been equally surprised to read that word. Perhaps he had said that the infantry could not advance without a considerable artillery success; that would have been reasonable. But perhaps the "if" was only Longstreet's, and he meant in effect, "Unless the artillery can be remarkably successful, I can argue Lee into countermanding the charge."

At the same time, Alexander could see, the degree of success demanded of the artillery approached the impossible. The Union guns were numerous, and the gunners were skillful and determined. When had the Confederates ever been able to drive them from the field? And what could be any other effect "such as to warrant" making the attack?

Alexander's actions on his receipt of this second note suggest that he had made a mental adjustment, and was now beginning to see himself, not as one upon whom too much responsibility has been thrust, but as a junior officer who has, strangely, been granted the opportunity to make a decision upon which may depend the fate of the battle. As far as loyalty went, he must have been divided. Like the rest of the army, he had the very highest respect for anything ordered by Lee. But he was closer to Longstreet, owed advancement to him, and had high respect for him also. Alexander, thereupon, decided to make up his mind "on the evidence," as it would seem. If the evidence seemed to indicate that the charge would be successful, he would, so to speak, support Lee; if not, Longstreet.

Considering the matter, Alexander had no confidence that his artillery could drive the Union artillery off. Possibly, he thought, the artillery of Hill's and Ewell's corps could do so, but he had little confidence in that, either. About the chance for an infantry success, he consulted two generals.

The first of these was Wright, who was still at hand. "What do you think of it?" Alexander asked, "Is it as hard to get there as it looks?"

Wright replied, "The trouble is not in going there. I went there with my brigade yesterday. There is a place where you can get breath and re-form. The trouble is to stay there after you get there, for the whole Yankee army is there in a bunch."

Alexander took this to mean that the attack would be successful if made in sufficient strength. He then rode off to see what Pickett thought. Careful to ask no leading questions or to suggest that the corps-commander was dubious, Alexander felt Pickett out. The general was not worrying — at least, he was not telling his worries to a colonel. Alexander gathered that

Pickett was "both cheerful and sanguine," and in fact, "thought himself in luck to have the chance."

Returning to his post, Alexander wrote a second note, almost curt in its brevity: "General: When our artillery fire is at its best, I will advise Gen. Pickett to advance."

Longstreet wrote no more notes to Alexander. He must have realized that he had been caught bluffing. Yet also, he must have known, even if Alexander had proved co-operative, Lee might still have remained firm.

21

So, now, even Longstreet realized that the cannonade must begin, and we may turn from the imponderables of mental states to the bronze and iron of unthinking guns. Already the order had gone out to the battery-commanders to commence firing when from the right of the line they should hear a shot, quickly followed by a second. In that line were guns assembled from the three army corps, and from about forty batteries. Pendleton reported the number as "nearly one fifty," and from summation, battery by battery, we may put the figure at probably 142.

Opposing them, in a broken line from Cemetery Hill to Little Round Top, were Union guns to the total — not of eighty, as is often stated, but of 103.

Even so, the Union artillery was heavily outgunned, though there were many batteries in reserve. The reason usually given for this anomaly is that the cramped nature of the Union line gave no room for the placement of more guns. This is not correct, as anyone can see by inspecting the ground. Even at the time, an artilleryman of Arnold's battery wondered about it: "Between our battery and Woodruff's on our right in Ziegler's Grove there was space enough for three batteries." Hunt, being at this time unsure of the point at which the Confederates would launch their attack, may have preferred to keep many of his guns as a mobile reserve. Later, he may have thought it better to let the punishment concentrate upon the batteries already in position, and then to try to rush fresh ones in at the final moment.

Thus, 103 guns opposed 142. Yet mere numbers mean little. More important is the question of how the guns were disposed, particularly in the Confederate line, which had the active role.

That line divided naturally into a center and two wings. . . . To the north, ten rifles were assigned to the task of neutralizing the twenty-nine guns on Cemetery Hill. The sixteen Union Napoleons, however, were outranged so that a more reasoned statement would be that ten Confederate rifles opposed thirteen Union rifles. Since the range was about a mile and a half, neither side was likely to do the other much harm. On the southern wing, the Confederate batteries placed to the west of the Peach Orchard numbered twenty-eight guns and were definitely overmatched by the forty-three guns opposing them. The real weight of the cannonade, however, was to fall upon the Union center. Here 102 guns were placed so that their lines of fire converged upon the batteries near the clump of trees. In addition, the two Whitworths also fired at this part of the line; though they were far to the north and lacked good visibility, they had the advantage of enfilade. Since the Union guns of this sector totaled only thirty-one, the Confederate advantage was more than three to one!

On occasion some of the guns probably shifted target. In particular, considerably more than ten guns apparently fired on Cemetery Hill at times.

22

To accomplish the work assigned, the Confederate gunners had not only several kinds of guns but also several kinds of ammunition.

Solid shot, or simply "shot," consisted of a cast-iron ball. This was the most reliable of all and the one good for the longest range. Given a mass of men, a shot could be horribly effective; at the battle of Zorndorf in 1758 one of them had caused forty-two casualties. Striking a gun, a shot would break a wheel or axle, or even dent or crack the barrel. The trouble with shot, however, was that a miss was as good as a mile. Against men in ordinary formation one of them was little more effective than a musket ball.

Alliteratively coupled with shot to make the poetic "shot and shell," a second type of ammunition consisted of a hollow projectile, filled with a bursting charge of powder, exploded by a time-fuse. Even against men in ordinary formation, a properly exploding shell could cause appalling casualties. In actuality, a large proportion of shells did not explode at all, and another large proportion exploded in the wrong place. Percussion-shells, which exploded when they struck the ground, were practical for rifled guns, but the Confederates at Gettysburg had few of them. As far as shells were concerned, therefore, the Confederate gunners merely had to trust that by the law of averages a few of them would explode effectively.

About the same can be said for the third type of ammunition, officially known as spherical case, and commonly called shrapnel. Like a shell, each of these was a hollow projectile, but it was filled with musket balls, which were scattered by a bursting charge in what was theoretically a murderous way. Unfortunately — or fortunately, if you were being shot at — only an occasional one exploded at the proper place.

The fourth type of ammunition was canister. By those who knew no better — war-correspondents, poets, and infantrymen — this was frequently called grape-shot, but it differed from true grape, which it had superseded. It consisted of a big tin can filled with cast-iron balls about an inch in diameter. On firing,

the can disintegrated, and the discharge thus became that of a
large shotgun. The chief trouble with canister was that it was
good only at short ranges. It was rarely used beyond five hundred
yards, and was not very effective over four hundred. Around 250
yards, canister commenced to be really lethal, and at 150 yards
the gunners could begin to use double canister, which was two
cans fired at one shot. The statement of the manuals that under
canister fire an infantry line could be expected to disintegrate
was generally justified, though naturally the effect would depend
upon the number of guns firing. No wonder that the soldiers
called it "canned hell-fire."

The short range of effectiveness, however, limited canister to
defensive uses. Here, in fact, was one great change which had
been effected by the use of the rifled musket. At Friedland, in
1807, the French guns had opened at four hundred yards, closed
to two hundred, and finally to one-hundred-twenty, mowing
down the Russian infantry. But to advance thus against unbroken troops in 1863 would have meant that the horses were
shot down before the guns could even get to canister range, or
if they had been lucky enough to do so, the gunners would be
killed before they could fire more than a round or two.

23

Ammunition supply would also put a limit to the duration, and
so to the effectiveness, of the cannonade. Each gun, on its
limbers and caisson, took into action four chests. Standard
practice for a Napoleon was that each chest contained twelve
shot, twelve spherical case, four shells, and four canisters. To
each of these the powder charge was "fixed" in a kind of primitive cartridge. Each Napoleon could therefore have 112 rounds
of long-range ammunition. The 3-inch rifles and 10-pound
Parrotts had a little more. In addition, during a cannonade, the

caisson could theoretically go back to the ammunition train with three empty chests, refill them, and return to the gun. Under a heavy counter-bombardment, however, such movements were highly dangerous. Moreover, the Confederates had to hoard their ammunition, being a long way from a source of supply, and not having captured any appreciable amount during the first two days of fighting. Alexander, therefore, as far as his own batteries were concerned, seems to have planned to depend upon the ammunition actually with his guns. He had ordered his battery-commanders not to do any preliminary firing, and he had been irked when Hill's artillery had become engaged in a brief, vigorous action during the fight for the Bliss barn. Hill's batteries, however, had much better shelter, and might expect to replenish their ammunition from the train without too great difficulty.

The length of the cannonade, and also its degree of saturation, would also be dependent upon the rate of fire. Except for the two Whitworths the guns were all muzzle-loaders. In an emergency, firing canister at close range with no necessity of aiming, the rate of fire could be four rounds a minute. Ordinary rapid fire, since the gun recoiled at each shot and had to be re-aimed, was about two a minute.

At moderately long range, when accuracy was of more importance than mere rapidity, the rate would be even less. Alexander could therefore expect his guns to fire for an hour and a half, or slightly more, before exhausting their "ready" ammunition. If 102 guns each fired 112 rounds, the number of projectiles that could be launched at the Union center would be over eleven thousand.

Anyone might think that so many projectiles, many of them multiplying themselves by explosion, would be enough to incapacitate thirty-one guns and their five hundred gunners, with enough left over to hack considerably at the infantry. But, even at this date, the deadliness of the weapons had forced the armies to fire at longer ranges, and thus had vastly increased the wastage of lead and iron. A Confederate ordnance officer with a liking for statistics once figured that you had to shoot 150 pounds of lead and 350 pounds of iron to kill one Yankee.

24

Just what was this cannonade expected to effect? Its primary object was to dominate the Union artillery, and in particular to knock out, or drive away, the six batteries on Cemetery Ridge. As to whether this could be accomplished, there must have been considerable doubt among Confederate artillery officers. Ordinarily, most of them would admit, the Union artillery was as good, gun for gun, as their own, and it usually could muster more guns, supplied more plentifully with ammunition. On this particular field, however, fewer Union guns than Confederate were in position. The Confederates did not need to ask the reason why they were thus given the advantage; they could merely make use of the actuality. They may, indeed, have wondered. Even where more batteries might have been placed, as north of the clump of trees, why were they lacking? Did this mean that the Union artillery had already been so badly smashed that batteries were no longer available?

Any effect the cannonade would have upon the Union infantry would be a by-product. Gunners, guns, and ammunition being fallible, most of the shots would not hit the batteries, and some of these would inflict casualties upon the near-by infantry. A Confederate officer briefly stated that the object was to "damage and dismount their guns and demoralize their troops."

25

With the cannonade about to begin, Alexander decided to check on the nine howitzers which Pendleton had assigned to him that morning and which he intended to advance with the infantry. He sent back an aide, who could not find the howitzers where they had been left, or anywhere else. Pendleton, reconsidering, had withdrawn four of them, and the officer in charge, finding himself in the line of fire of some Union guns, had moved the other five. Neither had informed Alexander.

Naturally the incident loomed large in Alexander's mind. Since he was important in fixing the story of the battle, the incident also looms large in many later accounts. But nine little howitzers could have had no decisive effect, as Alexander himself made clear in his final account. Though it has become an inescapable part of the story of Gettysburg, the matter cannot be considered of much importance, except perhaps as it is indicative of shortcomings in the Confederate artillery command.

26

The hands on the face of the courthouse clock, pointing sharply upward, approached one o'clock. The Reverend Doctor M. Jacobs, Professor of Mathematics and Chemistry in the local college, was following his established habits, in so far as was possible in a town occupied by invading troops. Like many professors, he was a taker of notes, and because of this activity he has gained a little hold on immortality by becoming the chief authority for one not-unimportant detail of July 3, and for a second such detail, the only authority.

27

At last Longstreet wrote another note. He did not address Alexander this time. Now, momentarily he seemed aware of Colonel Walton, who was actually his chief of artillery.

A courier rode off with the note. Miller's battery of the Washington Artillery had already been alerted to fire the two signal-shots.

At his dressing-station, behind the 11th Mississippi, Surgeon Joseph Holt was nervously looking at his watch. He had been told that the cannonade was to commence sharply at one-thirty; it was almost that time, but the near-by gunners showed no signs of activity.

28

About this time, an immense flock of wild pigeons flew overhead, darkening the sky. The men watched idly. No one has recorded in what direction the pigeons were flying, or what seemed to be their purpose.

29

In the Union lines, the deep calm still lingered. The men, many of them, were extremely hungry, and they were suffering intensely from the heat of the sun. That was all — for the present. Who could tell? Perhaps Bobby Lee had already had enough, and was getting ready to retreat.

About this time, looking from Little Round Top, an officer saw the long broken line of Confederate guns off to the north, the polished bronze of the Napoleons glistening in the sun. He set out to count them, and got as far as a hundred, realizing that others might be concealed in the woods. But even he could not be sure. Sometimes guns were massed to cover a retreat.

About this time, a correspondent at Meade's headquarters wrote that a silence of deep sleep had fallen upon the field of battle: "There was not wanting to the peacefulness of the scene the singing of a bird, which had a nest in the peach tree within the tiny yard of the white-washed cottage." On Cemetery Hill an artilleryman heard the hum of bees.

By now the luncheon party of generals had broken up, but

Gibbon and Hancock lingered. Gibbon was taking his ease. Hancock, the ever-active, solicitous for the welfare of his men as a good general should be, was dictating an order about supplies of fresh beef. Haskell pictured the scene: "We dozed in the heat, and lolled upon the ground, with half-open eyes. Our horses were hitched to the trees, munching some oats."

General Hunt, Chief of Artillery, was at Rittenhouse's battery on Little Round Top. From this hill an alert officer now thought that he observed some activity in the Confederate lines.

General Meade, after lunch, having ridden to Little Round Top, had now returned, and was at his headquarters.

In Harrow's brigade, someone had turned up with a copy of yesterday's *Baltimore Clipper*, and a group of men gathered round to hear a lieutenant read the news, which probably included some account of the first day's fighting at Gettysburg.

Many men were moving about behind the lines — going for water, collecting wood for fires on which to make coffee, carrying messages.

There was also activity in Cushing's battery — a highly pleasant activity. Rations had arrived, and were being passed out. A hungry Philadelphian of the 69th Pennsylvania started over toward the battery from the stone wall in front of the clump of trees, the position his regiment had now been holding for more than twenty-four hours. He had a big, non-regulation hat, and now he held this as a convenient receptacle, if he should find the artillerymen minded for a handout.

The Rhode Islanders of Brown's battery, just to the south of the trees, were suddenly delighted. They were desperately hungry, and now they saw their rations-wagon coming up from the rear with the four strong mules "on the full jump." One of their men was in a deep sleep, comfortably beneath a caisson, in the shade.

Along the few yards of the little entrenchment held by the

82nd New York, a soldier was standing, looking out toward the Confederate lines.

30

Riding to deliver Longstreet's note, the courier must have passed near Garnett, Wilcox, and Harrison, still continuing their whiskey-and-water experimentation.

In all probability, Lee was at his favorite post, and Longstreet not far off — perhaps sitting, as he often did, on the rail fence that ran from the Point of Woods toward the Union lines.

Close to the top of the rise in front of Garnett's and Kemper's brigades the long line of guns, limbers, and caissons stretched off, north and south. A little in the rear of the caissons the drivers were digging shallow grave-like holes in which they might take shelter.

Some of the Confederate infantrymen were still eating. Others were lying comfortably "in desultory chit-chat, or deep in thought." All seemed "peaceful, idle, lazy-looking, or rather sleepy — as if it were a July noon-hour siesta in the harvest field."

Then there was a sudden movement, as of preparation, among the artillerymen. *"Lie down, men!"* shouted Colonel Hunton to the 8th Virginia. The captains echoed, *"Lie down!"*

31

Longstreet's courier had found Walton sitting on horseback among some oaks near the Peach Orchard. Walton, or an aide, carefully endorsed the note, "Received 1.30 P.M." Walton read the few words, which could have offered no surprise:

> Colonel: Let the batteries open. Order great care and precision in firing. If the batteries at the Peach Orchard cannot be used against the point we intend attacking, let them open on the enemy on Rocky Hill.

This last term was one of the many by which the combatants designated the hill now known as Little Round Top.

At the same time, half a mile to the north, Surgeon Holt was no longer able to stand the suspense, and dashed toward the gunners, yelling "Half-past! Time is up!"

Walton gave the command. The alerted battery was not far off. Captain "Buck" Miller was ready. At the command the waiting gunner pulled the lanyard. The Napoleon spoke with its characteristic *spang*, and flame, white smoke, and the projectile burst from its muzzle.

PART IV

Between the Signal-shots

There she goes!

THE WATCHING SOLDIER of the 82nd New York yelled excitedly, "There she goes!"

Few on either side saw the burst of the smoke, but following the light-waves in more leisurely fashion, the sound-waves, second by second, impinged upon thousands of ear-drums of men who had been waiting.

The Confederate infantry had already been warned to lie low. The artillerymen, sure that a second shot would follow, began to stand to their guns. In the Union lines heads were cocked in sudden alertness. Men who had been walking about looked quickly at the Confederate lines, and automatically began to move toward their own posts.

Meanwhile, the order was given to fire the second gun. The gunner pulled the lanyard. A misfire! Doubtless with an expletive the officer turned to the third gun.

About this time, traveling close behind the sound-wave, the projectile hit. As to where it hit, the author (being devoted to accuracy) is happy to be able to provide no fewer than five well-authenticated testimonies — thus perhaps indicating that by some miraculous intervention in favor of the Confederacy the power of this single cannon-shot was multiplied, in mid-air.

1) Lieutenant C. H. C. Brown, commanding the section of the battery that fired the shot, stated that it struck a Union caisson and exploded it. All good gunners would agree that such

accuracy in a first shot would be in itself almost a miracle. Still, who wishes to doubt the word of this Southern gentleman?

2) Private R. O. Sturtevant of the 13th Vermont wrote that the projectile was a shell which exploded a short distance behind his regiment.

3) Colonel Arthur Devereux of the 19th Massachusetts, a distinguished officer, remembered that the projectile, apparently a round shot, struck Lieutenant S. S. Robinson of his regiment, and added as confirmatory detail, "cutting his body nearly in two, killing him instantly."

4) Captain R. S. Thompson of the 12th New Jersey declared it to be a shell which hit but did not burst in the rear of Hays's division.

5) Lieutenant J. B. G. Adams of the 19th Massachusetts, who had been wounded on July 2, stated that the projectile whistled over him where he lay behind the lines in a hospital.

The author offers no comment, except to repeat his previous observation, that much of human nature is to be learned on a battlefield.

By this time the sound of the discharge, theoretically diminished according to the square of the distance, was arriving at the farther parts of the battlefield. Even with allowance for profound sleepers many more than a hundred thousand soldiers had heard that cannon-shot.

And now, for the third time, came the command, "Fire!"

PART V

Cannonade

eine Pulververschwendung.
— CAPTAIN JUSTUS SCHEIBERT

A UNION GUNNER on Cemetery Hill remembered that after the second signal-shot the burst of smoke ran along the Confederate line from south to north: "It reminded me of the 'powder snakes' we boys used to touch off on the 4th of July." His testimony would indicate that all the gunners were ready, and that the opening of their fire depended only upon when the sound of the second discharge reached them. Most of the Union soldiers recollected only that after the second signal-shot the whole Confederate line seemed to erupt in one universal explosion.

In Gettysburg, at the sound of the guns, Professor Jacobs noted 1.07, thus establishing the most widely accepted time. Curiously, the time 1.30 is equally well established from Confederate sources.

As the guns opened, Garnett, Wilcox, and Harrison ended their long lunch-hour, and hurried down the slope toward their horses, Garnett hobbling on his bad leg.

Hancock, the superb, continued to dictate his order about fresh beef.

The private of the 69th Pennsylvania, having begged a box of hard-tack from Cushing's men, dumped it into his big hat, and hurried back to the position of his regiment behind the wall.

The newspaper-reading in Harrow's brigade came to a sudden end.

The hungry men of Brown's battery had the chagrin of seeing their approaching rations-wagon suddenly turn about and make for the rear, as the cannonade broke. The men stood to their guns. The one who had been lying beneath the caisson, was knocked out of his profound sleep by the crash of shells bursting all around. Bewildered, he ran toward where he thought his gun was located, and then was struck on the shoulder by a shell-fragment — "which had the effect of waking me up."

General Hunt was on Little Round Top. With the *sang-froid* of the professional soldier he described the scene in retrospect as being "indescribably grand." He added, "All their batteries were soon covered with smoke, through which the flashes were incessant, whilst the air seemed filled with shells, whose sharp explosions, with the hurtling of their fragments, formed a running accompaniment to the deep roar of the guns." He rode immediately toward the Artillery Reserve, to see about fresh batteries and ammunition.

Gibbon, seizing his sword, sprang to his feet, and shouted for his horse. When the orderly did not appear at once, the general set out to run up the swale toward the front, to see what was happening and to steady his men, if necessary.

Haskell mounted, and was about to follow the general, when he saw the orderly, bringing the horse, struck in the chest by a piece of shell and killed.

Strange to relate, the inhabitants of some of the farmhouses on the battlefield had still lingered in their homes. Now, terror-stricken, they rushed out, seeking some new place of shelter. Among them was one woman in labor, or close to it.

2

Throughout the Union lines, there was a sudden cry of "Down! Down!" While the shells were still hurtling toward them, the veteran troops had flung themselves upon the ground, behind

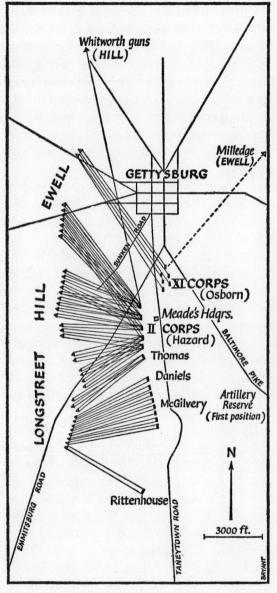

Whitworth guns
(HILL)

GETTYSBURG

EWELL

Milledge
(EWELL)

SUNKEN ROAD

XI CORPS
(Osborn)

Meade's Hdqrs.

II CORPS
(Hazard)

BALTIMORE PIKE

Thomas

Daniels

McGilvery

Artillery
Reserve
(First position)

LONGSTREET HILL

N

EMMITSBURG ROAD

TANEYTOWN ROAD

Rittenhouse

3000 ft.

BRYANT

The Cannonade

1.10 — 2.55 P.M.

Union batteries
(ca. 5 guns each)

▲▲ Confederate
batteries
(ca. 4 guns each)

Each line represents
the line of fire of
approximately two
Confederate guns.
Some of the guns
shown as firing at
II Corps fired at XI
Corps part of the
time.

the stone wall or the little berm of earth or some bit of natural cover. The men of the 111th New York rushed forward to the stone wall, and partly mingled with the men of the 12th New Jersey, who were already there. In scarcely the time that it took to draw a breath, the infantry seemed to disappear completely. To Haskell, riding up over the crest, it seemed like a magician's trick. Another officer compared it to the sudden clearing of a busy street, when a thunderstorm breaks. The battle-wise officers and men of the 19th Massachusetts, in support-position and lacking any entrenchment, "keeping their alignment, crawled to places of apparent cover. Some got behind a few large boulders, others took advantage of depressions in the ground." (In spite of the transformation of the battlefield into a park, you can still see the boulders.)

In those first few minutes, even the veteran infantrymen could do nothing but keep their noses to the ground. The Confederate fire seemed murderously accurate. Round shot hit with an earth-jarring thud, scattering gravel. Time- and percussion-shells crashed, killing and wounding. Ammunition chests were exploded in various batteries. All along the line the colors, which had been leaned against the wall, had to be laid flat, lest they should be smashed by the shot. Some of the rifles which had been stuck into the ground to support canopies were hit and went flying in all directions.

In this confusion Hancock suddenly appeared at the front. Mounted on a fine black horse, displaying alike his white cuffs and shirt-front and his imperturbable manner, with his staff behind him and his corps-flag flying, he rode slowly along the line. As a staff-officer wrote, thousands of soldiers looked at him, and "found courage longer to endure the pelting of the pitiless gale." The superb quality of the performance was marred only by the fumbling of a bit-actor, the general's horse. Though inured to battlefields, the animal found the present situation too much, thus perhaps showing a high degree of intelligence. His mount becoming unmanageable, the general was forced to halt, and to borrow the horse of an aide.

3

In this crisis, what of the Union artillery? In some accounts of the battle you will read to such an effect: "The Union artillery to the number of eighty guns immediately replied in a great artillery duel." A statement could scarcely be farther from the truth. The figure is based upon a careless reading of a statement by Hunt. Moreover, even before the firing opened, Hunt had grasped the essence of the situation — that the duty of his batteries was not to combat the opposing ones, but to reserve themselves to smash the infantry assault. His idea of not becoming involved in an artillery duel was so strong that it was almost a fixation.

His orders to his commanders were, therefore, rather to refrain from firing than to fire. Still, he left them some discretion. Accordingly, Osborn opened immediately from Cemetery Hill; he seems to have maintained an intermittent fire, thus conserving his ammunition but not permitting the Confederate batteries to take too many liberties. Rittenhouse also fired from Little Round Top, and probably Thomas's and Daniels's batteries joined in. Thus a total of about thirty-five guns replied, though not at their full rate of fire. More than sixty guns remained silent — those of the Second Corps, and all of McGilvery's long line. The gunners of these last had little temptation to fire back, since they had the comfort of a very protective ditch. Woodruff's battery had some shelter from the trees, but the others of the Second Corps were on the open ridge, exposed to the full cannonade.

At this time, a highly significant incident occurred, though no one was in a position to pay much attention to it. Cooper's battery of the First Corps artillery (B, 1st Pennsylvania, three 3-

inch rifles) came in through the cannonade and went into position at the right of McGilvery's line. Though as a reinforcement
it was insignificant, its arrival showed that Hunt still had batteries available and was able to put them into position. But the
Confederate artillery could expect no reinforcements.

4

Although the Confederate fire at first had been extremely accurate, some of the shots had gone high. As the smoke obscured
the field, the gunners had more difficulty in spotting the fall of
their projectiles, and began to overshoot badly. This inaccuracy,
curiously, brought them considerable success. The terrain was
such that any shot clearing the rise fell in the low ground beyond, and here were two roads and many of the rear-echelon elements of the Union army. Eustis's brigade of the Sixth Corps,
returning from acting as a reserve to the Twelfth Corps, was
caught under the cannonade; merely while marching through, it
lost twenty-three men, killed and wounded. At the same time
the road was full, for a few minutes, of the rag-tag of the Army,
scurrying toward the south, to get out of the line of fire or to find
some place to hole up in — skulkers, clerks, officers' servants. A
war-correspondent was amazed to see an ambulance, its driver in
a panic, going down the Taneytown road at full gallop; one of
the horses had had a leg shot off at the hock, but was still keeping
up on three legs.

The rout of these non-combatants was of no military significance, but projectiles from the guns of Alexander's battalion,
overshooting McGilvery's line, fell thickly among the parked
guns of the Artillery Reserve and the wagons of the ammunition
train. Men and horses were struck down. Three or four shells
hit among the teams of the wagons, but only one of them exploded — this furnishing a statistical datum on Confederate
ammunition. The only remedy was to move both guns and
train about half a mile southward.

Although accidental, this was a military achievement of some importance. Hunt, who visited the Reserve about this time, must have realized at once that his plans had been seriously disarranged. The time which would be necessary to allow for the movement of batteries from the Reserve to the front had been significantly increased.

The other achievement might also be called accidental, for it, too, resulted from the cramped nature of the area within the hook-shaped line. Meade had established his headquarters in a small wooden house on the Taneytown Road, a few hundred yards behind the Second Corps position. The spot was almost the mathematical center toward which the fire of a hundred Confederate guns converged. Anything that went a little high was likely to land right in Meade's lap. A shell burst in the yard among the horses, with horrible results. Another tore up the steps of the house; another carried away the supports of the porch; another smashed through a door; still another went through the garret. A solid shot barely missed Meade himself.

Because of flying splinters, the little house became more dangerous than the outside. General and staff withdrew to the yard behind, and there tried to continue their work under almost impossible conditions. Meade doubtless hoped that the cannonade would be of short duration, and he was loath to change his headquarters because of the disruption to command that might thus result.

As he was walking back and forth pondering some decision, he noticed that some of his staff had edged around to the far side of the house, though it was so flimsy that it would not stop a cannonball. In the best military tradition he then essayed the light touch.

"Gentlemen," he said, "are you trying to find a safe place? You remind me of the man who drove the ox-team which took ammunition for the heavy guns on to the field of Palo Alto. Finding himself within range, he tilted up his cart and got behind it. Just then General Taylor came along, and seeing this attempt at shelter, shouted, 'You damned fool, don't you know you are no safer there than anywhere else?' The driver replied, 'I don't suppose I am, general, but it kind o' feels so.' "

Though Meade was doubtless right, the laughter replying to his venerable anecdote may well have been as hollow and insubstantial as the house.

Before long the folly of remaining in this position became apparent. Sixteen horses had been killed. Through the full fury the general and staff moved to a barn some hundreds of yards down the road. But the cannonade reached this spot also. General Butterfield, Chief of Staff, was struck by a shell fragment; though not severely wounded, he had to be relieved of duty. After remaining in the barn for a short time, Meade was forced to shift again, this time to the Twelfth Corps headquarters on Power's Hill, near the point of the fishhook.

By the confusion resulting from two shifts of headquarters and the wounding of the chief of staff, the cannonade had accomplished a good deal. Quite possibly, also, it did even more by its almost necessary effect upon Meade himself. An axiom of war is that a man is much affected by what happens in his own vicinity. Being driven from house to barn to hill, Meade must have received a much more heightened impression of the Confederate power than if he had happened to be in a safe place from the beginning.

5

The displacement of the Artillery Reserve and of Meade cannot have been known to the Confederates, and both resulted from inaccuracy. But all their shots did not go astray. Thomas's battery was located at the southern end of Cemetery Ridge, and was thus one of the six that the Confederates had marked for destruction. Being at the southern end of the line, it was the natural target for all of the Washington Artillery, and for other batteries as well. The fire of twenty guns, or even more, all of them within effective range, must have converged upon these six Napoleons. Four ammunition chests were soon struck and exploded, with resulting casualties, destruction of ammunition, and confusion. In addition, men and horses were hit, and doubtless some of the pieces themselves were put out of action.

6

The Confederate artillerymen, after their first burst of enthusiasm, now settled to their work. The discharges of the guns increased the heat sensibly, and filled the air with acrid smoke. To carry ammunition, to ram, to swab, to drag the gun back into position after its recoil — all these were hard work. We can therefore be sure that the gunners whole-heartedly obeyed Longstreet's order to practice "great care and precision in firing." Many batteries were firing salvos, a practice which probably increased accuracy and certainly decreased the rapidity of discharge. A watching Union artilleryman decided, "The enemy served his guns very slowly." According to what statistics can be gathered, Alexander's guns were averaging about one shot a minute. The other batteries were firing more slowly. A cool-headed Union officer counted the discharges, and decided that the whole Confederate line was averaging seventy or eighty shots a minute. The gunners were not suffering much from counter-battery bombardment, since they were exposed only to the long-range fire from the two hills at the ends of the line, and from such an over-weighted battery as Thomas's.

The Confederates loaded and fired without knowing much of the results, enveloped in the smoke of their own guns. Now and then the explosion of an ammunition chest, its flash piercing through the smoke, was greeted with a Rebel yell. Osborn's policy of intermittent fire was favorably construed; with the overconfidence that marked the Confederates that day, the gunners of the ten rifles far off by the railroad cut took each cessation of fire to mean that a battery had been silenced, though actually they were not doing any appreciable damage.

The Confederate infantrymen tended to be equally optimistic about damage to the enemy, and perhaps with some reason, since they were close behind the thundering guns and were much impressed. As one of them remembered, "The earth shook."

7

Before long, the Confederate fire became very galling to the Second Corps batteries, especially since they were not permitted to fire in reply. Three chests of Cushing's had gone up in one grand explosion, killing several men. About a quarter of an hour after the opening of the cannonade, Hancock took action. Hunt might be Chief of Artillery, but Hancock was commanding the whole Union center, and he was not going to have the morale of his infantry suffer for lack of artillery support. He ordered the guns to open. From Woodruff's Napoleons on the north to Rorty's Parrotts on the south, the twenty-five guns went into action. Though Hunt was irked, the infantry was more comfortable. The whole situation, however, was not much changed. Some sixty guns now fired at the Confederates, though some of these were firing intermittently. The Confederates still maintained a better than two-to-one advantage.

8

After fifteen minutes, the cannonade became what we may call a routine, which was to last throughout most of its duration. The Confederate artillery fired deliberately but steadily. From the hill Osborn's guns fired intermittently. The batteries of the Second Corps and Thomas's (in so far as it could) undoubtedly fired rapidly, being out-gunned and suffering heavily. A little to the south, Daniels's battery (its gunners fired eighty rounds per piece this day) was joining in. From Little Round Top, Rittenhouse kept potting away at long range. But McGilvery's thirty-six guns remained silent.

The Union infantrymen were lying low, in two ranks, behind the wall or entrenchment. They were suffering few casualties, and comfortably listened to the projectiles passing overhead — "Quartermaster hunters," they called them, as if they were trying to find the rear-echelon units. The veterans, as most of them were, had about decided that this bombardment was more noisy than dangerous, though the men in the second rank, lying farther back from the protection, were nervous about their legs, and some of them drew their feet up underneath them.

Physically, they were in extreme discomfort. They were so wedged in that man was almost lying on man. The summer sun beat upon the full length of their bodies. Their crowding prevented the circulation of air. Many of them were ravenously hungry. Water was scarce. One man remembered the sweat running off his face until it formed a muddy spot on the ground beneath. Another perspired until he thought what a useful contribution to science it would have been if he could have been weighed before and after. As a veteran of Harrow's brigade put it, he wanted as much to have relief from the heat as from the cannonade, or more.

There was little to do except listen. The deep thunder of the guns themselves dominated. Against this bass came the sharper cracks of exploding shells. There were also the whirrings and whinings of the projectiles themselves, and the thuds of striking round shot. Whenever a demoniac howl filled the air, the men said, "Whitworth!" Since the Confederates had only two Whitworths, and since these guns seldom fired anything except solid bolts, the number of mentions of them is undoubtedly far out of proportion to the number of casualties they caused.

But these two guns certainly put a strain upon Union nerves.

If anyone wished to take the chance of raising his head a little, he saw something in spite of the smoke. The bursting shells flashed intensely, and then left a cottony puff of lazily drifting white smoke. You could actually see the comparatively slow-traveling, smooth-bore projectiles, but the disconcerting thing was that whenever you saw one it seemed to be coming directly at you. The more speedy projectiles from the rifles were invisible, except when they "tumbled," as they not infrequently did. But watching the cannonade was not a healthy occupation, and few indulged in the pastime, except officers who thought it their duty to walk up and down behind the line in nonchalant disregard of danger.

Most of the men were extremely tired, as would be expected after forced marches and two days of battle. Moreover, their nerves were worn down. Many of them simply settled the matter of what to do by going to sleep.

An occasional one was unlucky. Most of these died or were wounded in undistinguished ways, but a soldier of the 15th Massachusetts received more than one comment in reminiscences. As he lay in the front rank, a solid bolt from a rifled cannon struck in front of him and passed beneath him. The impact threw him into the air, whirled him around, hurled him clear over the rear rank, and dropped him ten feet back. An officer walked over to him, and with curious euphemy remarked, "He has passed over." The man had been killed by the impact, and no mark was visible on his body. A little ridge of earth marked the place where he had been lying. (In Kemper's brigade a man was killed in the same manner.)

Some Union regiments were unlucky. The 108th New York was acting as support for Woodruff's battery, but had been placed too close to the guns, just inside Ziegler's Grove. In a letter written on July 3, immediately after the battle, one of their men declared, "It was the hardest fire the 108th [a veteran regiment] ever experienced — perfectly awful — murderous." He continued, "Large limbs were torn from the trunks of the oak trees under which we lay and precipitated down upon our heads." The 126th New York, also in the grove or near it, suffered severely. The 111th New York lost seven men from the explosion of one shell.

One effect of the intensity of the cannonade and its concentration behind the front line was to discourage any panic-stricken breaking for the rear. Even a badly frightened man could see that he was safer staying where he was, lying down behind a little shelter. At a critical moment, a few men of the 108th New York started to their feet, but a lieutenant drew his sword, and they obeyed his order to return to their posts.

Thus pinned down, the infantrymen lay and wondered. Most of them probably supposed that the cannonade was preliminary to an attack. But no one was sure.

9

The Confederate infantrymen had been told what the cannonade preluded. They were, however, far from happy. They might be hopeful that their own artillery was decimating the Union artillery, but they actually knew that they themselves were taking severe punishment from the Union fire.

The situation was a simple one. After the first few minutes, the gunners on both sides tended to overshoot the opposing artillery. Since the Confederate infantry was mostly behind the guns, many of the Union projectiles fell among them, often with devastating results.

Kemper's brigade was most exposed. There had been no chance to entrench, but individually the men had collected little piles of stones, and were lying each man with his head behind his own heap. Wilcox, who was in a position to have some knowledge, estimated Kemper's casualties in the cannonade at two hundred. Such a loss, better than 15 per cent, would have been considered crippling in many armies. The loss may well have been higher. An officer of the 11th Virginia reported about ten killed or wounded out of twenty-nine in his company; he also stated that in the next company the loss was larger. Another officer reported 88 casualties in a single regiment, though it is difficult to see who could have made such an exact count under the circumstances. The other brigades also took punishment. A captain of Armistead's reported nineteen casualties out of fifty men; the fire was so terrific that when someone sang out "Wounded!" the ambulance corps would not go to his relief. R. A. Shotwell, a soldier of Garnett's brigade, who later made a study of the battle, stated, "Pickett's division lost by this cannonade, probably near five hundred men." Another estimated "not less than three hundred," probably a better figure, though there is no denying the possibility that Shotwell's may be correct.

In the other brigades, Davis reported twenty-three casualties, and Lowrance "a most galling fire." Archer's brigade suffered "considerable loss," and the wound-prone but seemingly immortal Colonel Fry was hit for the fourth time in the war, a painful wound in the shoulder from a shell-fragment. He managed to keep to his feet and retain his command. On the whole, however, Pettigrew's and Trimble's men, having the shelter of the woods, suffered much less than did Pickett's.

Statistics provide little real idea of the ordeal. Reminiscences yield a more vivid impression. . . . Sergeant Major Johnston of the 7th Virginia, trying to escape both the cannonade and the sun, lay flat beneath the shade "of a friendly apple tree." At one moment he raised his head for a breath of air, and Lieutenant Brown said to him, "You had better put your head down, or you may get it knocked off." Johnston replied, "A man had about as well die that way as to suffocate for want of air." At that moment a shell exploded near by, taking the heads off two men above the ears, and wounding three others, including Johnston and Brown.

Major Hutter of the 1st Virginia was talking with a friend, both lying on the ground. The friend made some remark, and the major asked him what he had said. Getting no reply, he looked, and found that his friend was dead.

On the front of the 11th Mississippi a shell burst near "Jere" Gage of the University Grays, and he was carried back with his left arm almost severed, and the front of his abdomen torn away together with the bladder, much of the intestine, and part of the pelvis. In great pain, he asked for something to ease it. The surgeon started to give him some opium, and then asked if he had any message. The wounded man cried, "My mother, O, my darling mother! How could I have forgotten you?" With a comrade's help he then wrote a note of farewell to mother and sisters, and "my dying release to Miss Mary . . . you know who." With the melodramatic sentimentality of the time, he touched the letter to his side, and ended, "This letter is stained with my blood." He then took the opium.

10

The skirmishers of both sides, for a welcome change, had an easy time of it. With so much going on, no one expected them to bother each other. Since they were on low ground, about half way between the two lines, the projectiles arched high overhead. Except for a premature explosion or an unusually wild shot, there was nothing to worry about. "All we had to do" wrote a soldier of the 19th Maine, "was to flatten out a little thinner, and our empty stomachs did not prevent that."

After a while the skirmishers did not even bother to lie flat. One who saw them compared them to two rows of posts in the field, a butternut row on one side and a blue row on the other.

11

By military usage a white light plays about the heads of generals, and we may therefore fittingly record what some of them were doing.

Meade, having been driven out of two headquarters, stayed put for a while in his third.

Hancock ranged about widely. About a quarter of two, he suddenly appeared at the right of McGilvery's line, ordering the battery-commanders to open fire. Not wanting to argue with a major general, they obeyed, and three batteries went into action. Hancock then rode on, and McGilvery, reverting to Hunt's instructions, ordered the guns to cease fire. One of the artillery captains commented scathingly that Hancock's order merely showed "how little an infantry officer knows about artillery." But the point can be argued. (And even after the war, it was.)

Like Hancock, Hunt ranged widely, turning up now on Cemetery Hill; again, at other parts of the line.

Gibbon, having gone up to the front and found his men steady, went back to the other side of the crest, and sat down in a comparatively safe place. He had experienced plenty of combat, and had developed a common-sense attitude. In previous conflicts he had proved his courage, and he did not need to go about proving it further to other men or to himself. He also was a good-enough soldier to know that the life of a general is not to be needlessly endangered.

Since Gibbon was thus stationary, the general taken to be Gibbon by a captain of one of the First Corps regiments was probably Harrow. This officer "with folded arms and in cool dignity walked up and down in front of the line, apparently indifferent to the rain of shot and shell." The captain was struck by a disturbing idea: "I thought as I saw him that the force of his example might be lost and it even prove disheartening if, as seemed probable, he should be struck down while teaching us to despise the danger. Fortunately for him and perhaps for the men, nothing of the kind happened and he paraded slowly back and forth along the line several times, uninjured and admired."

Hays worked toward a similar end, but in characteristically different manner. Combat affected him with an almost sexual excitement. Again a soldier reports: "Most of the time he was riding up and down the lines in front of us, exhorting the 'boys' to stand fast and fight like men. . . . Once he rode by and said, 'Boys, don't let 'em touch these pieces,' and in a few minutes he rode back again laughing, sung out, 'Hurrah, boys, we're giving them hell,' and he dashed up to the brow of the hill and cheered our skirmishers."

Under all his exuberance Hays kept a level head, and never forgot that he was a general. He was convinced that the attack would be on the Second Corps line, and he was still worried about the gap on his right. He kept the 126th New York ready to rush into it. He was also concerned about Webb's situation around the Angle, which looked weak. Once he sent his young aide, Lieutenant David Shields, to talk to Webb about the matter.

Webb himself practiced still another technique. He merely stood in the most conspicuous and exposed place, leaning on his sword and smoking a cigar. In vain the men appealed to him to take shelter: "He stood like a statue watching the movement of the enemy."

Doubleday too had his moment. He was eating a sandwich when a shot struck near-by and scattered gravel on the bread. Rising to a touch of military humor, he said, "That sandwich will need no pepper!"

On Cemetery Hill, Howard imperturbably settled himself to observe what was happening. Taking position down the hill from one of the batteries, he had his aides pile up cracker boxes to protect him from the flying debris that came from his own guns. Sitting in front of these boxes, he was completely exposed to the Confederate fire, but had a good view. (Historians have deprecated Howard's generalship, but never his courage.) After a while he sent off a calm note to Meade: "The fire has been concentrated upon this point about an hour with no great effect. The batteries on our right do not reach us, and in center invariably overshoot us."

12

Of Confederate generals less detail is preserved, but their conduct also seems to have been exemplary.

Lee apparently spent most of his time at his favorite position. The concentration of fire there was probably not heavy. Once he rode in front of Pickett's line. His appearance there both inspired and horrified the men, and they shouted at him to take shelter. He took off his hat in acknowledgment, and then rode on without quickening Traveller's pace.

Longstreet seems to have kept near his fence. He also several times made the dangerous ride along the lines. So, too, did Pickett.

The brigadiers were equally courageous. Garnett rode back and forth until finally induced to dismount. Armistead kept to his feet, but exposed himself equally. One of his men rose in protest, and Armistead ordered him down. The soldier argued the general's example, but was told "Yes, but never mind me; we want men with guns in their hands."

13

Of Pickett, we have another anecdote, of more military significance. . . . Captain Robert A. Bright was one of Pickett's four aides. When he returned from performing some duty, he found his general talking to a strange officer, a big man with red whiskers. Pickett made the introduction, saying: "This is Colonel Gordon, once opposed to me in the San Juan affair, but now on our side."

Thus knowing the stranger to be British, we can identify him as Lieutenant Colonel G. T. Gordon of the 34th North Carolina, in Scales's brigade. One of the two field officers left in that brigade, he had for a short time been in command of it. He was one of a number of foreigners serving as officers with Lee's army. He was also notorious as a gambler.

Bright had come in on the middle of a conversation, and the two senior officers did not bother to inform him of what had gone before. He was therefore definitely shocked when he heard Gordon saying (at least these were the words that Bright years later remembered): "Pickett, my men are not going up today."

"But, Gordon, they must go up; you must make them go up."

Gordon's reply was even more shocking than the first sentence: "You know, Pickett, I will go as far with you as any other man, if only for old acquaintance sake, but my men have until lately been down at the seashore, only under the fire of heavy guns from ships, but for the last day or two they have lost heavily under infantry fire and are very sore, and they will not go up today."

Now, obviously, Bright did not remember the conversation exactly. Gordon was in Scales's brigade, and the only brigades to which the description of having been "down at the seashore" would apply were Pettigrew's and Davis's. Yet there is no reason to suppose that Bright invented the story. In fact, it is highly circumstantial, even though confused in places.

About what can be made out of it is that in some brigade that had been in the heaviest fighting on July 1, some of the men were saying that they would not advance when ordered.

14

Meanwhile, the cannonade pounded on, both sides continuing to shoot high. According to one Confederate, the gunners in front of Heth's division were cutting their fuzes for a mile and a quarter, which would be a good quarter-mile too much. Because of such bad judgment and their faulty ammunition, the Confederates were spraying nearly the whole Union position, in spite of their good intentions of concentrating upon the Second Corps line. Carr's brigade of the Third Corps, lying in column of battalions closed in mass, suffered severely from shells dropping into its dense formation. Clear over near the point of the fishhook, the men of the Twelfth Corps grew nervous at being bombarded from the rear. An unlucky regiment of the Eleventh Corps had twenty-seven casualties from one shell. But these losses in scattered commands were of no military significance.

Threatening to be more serious was the sudden outburst of firing that struck Cemetery Hill from a new direction. Three guns of Milledge's Georgia Regular Battery had gone into position on a ridge to the northeast, and had opened a fire that was surprisingly accurate from the very beginning. As Osborn commented later, "It was admirable shooting. They raked the whole line of batteries, killed and wounded the men and horses, and blew up the caissons rapidly. I saw one shell go through six horses standing broadside." But he swung Taft's 20-pounders to meet the new threat. These big guns quickly got the range, and the Confederates ceased firing.

It was a mere pinprick, considered in the light of the whole cannonade. Much, however, has been made of it, and some Confederate writers, Alexander particularly, have expressed the opinion that the tide might have been turned if a large number of Ewell's guns had thus joined in the cannonade from the north and northeast. To consider what might have happened, and did not, is not the conception of history under which this book is being written. Certainly, however, if the Confederates had opened fire from this new direction, they would have been opposed and probably neutralized by the Union batteries on East Cemetery Hill, and by others which could have been sent into that position from the Reserve.

Illustrations

The pictures of the battlefield are all
from original photographs by the author,
taken in the summer of 1957

LEE

MEADE

OPPOSITE NUMBERS–1

LONGSTREET

HANCOCK

PICKETT · GIBBON

LEE (A. L. Long, *Memoirs of R. E. Lee*, Frontispiece). Since this is an engraving based upon a post-war painting, it is far removed from the original, and is therefore useful not so much for showing the actual Lee as for showing the image that he projected upon his Confederate contemporaries. Note the sorrowful face which seems to be carrying all the woes of his soldiers. This image of Lee probably began to appear for the first time after the repulse of Pickett's Charge.

MEADE (from a sketch by a soldier, perhaps based on a photograph, Jacob Hoke, *The Great Invasion of 1863*, p. 241). Note that the schoolmaster-ish quality of the general comes out strikingly as he is portrayed by the unskillful hand of one of the soldiers.

LONGSTREET (from Jefferson Davis, *Rise and Fall of the Confederate Government*, p. 442). Hair and beard are longer than in most portraits of Longstreet, and thus produce a somewhat

venerable appearance, though this is belied by the dark hair and smooth skin. HANCOCK (*Battles and Leaders* iii, p. 286). Note, as always, the shining white collar.

PICKETT (*Battles and Leaders*, iii, p. 350). In this standard portrait the hair, though obviously curled, is not nearly so long as it is described by Sorrel. It is, in fact, not much longer than Longstreet's. The portrait suggests a certain self-conscious complacency.

GIBBON (*Battles and Leaders*, iv, p. 572). With his half-grown beard and unruly hair, Gibbon presents a striking contrast to his opposite number, the meticulously and consciously groomed Pickett. He seems uncertain and uncomfortable, not complacent. Though described by one observer as "steel-cold," Gibbon scarcely lives up to these words, as he presents himself in this portrait and in his own writings, which sometimes display him as emotional rather than cold.

PENDLETON

HUNT

OPPOSITE NUMBERS–2

PETTIGREW

HAYS

ARMISTEAD   WEBB

PENDLETON (*Battles and Leaders*, iii, p. 329). He here manages to make a good military appearance, without much suggestion of the clergyman. He resembled Lee so much that the two were sometimes mistaken for each other.

HUNT (*Battles and Leaders*, iii, p. 320). Hunt displays a fine, intelligent face, but no great individuality. The portrait might almost be labeled, "Idealized Union general."

PETTIGREW (*Battles and Leaders*, iii, p. 429). Note the meticulously pointed mustache, fastidiously groomed beard, and careful display of the collar insignia. The slightly knit brows and piercing gaze produce the suggestion of military ferocity. Pettigrew, whom his friends called a genius, apparently set himself to make the proper appearance for whatever part he must play in peace or war.

HAYS (Walker, *Second Corps*, p. 474). With his full and handsome beard, not overlong, Hays may even be said to make the most thoroughly military appearance of any in this gallery. He seems here to have been caught in a relaxed mood, and displays nothing of the excitability for which he was noted on the battlefield.

ARMISTEAD (*Battles and Leaders*, iii, p. 347). He fails to make a handsome appearance in this portrait, but looks like a leader whom men would follow. The unbuttoned jacket was an affectation of military informality which may be seen in portraits of other Civil War generals as well.

WEBB (*Battles and Leaders*, iv, p. 122). A handsome youth of twenty-eight at Gettysburg, he was eighteen years younger than his opposite number Armistead. In meticulosity of appearance he rivals Pettigrew.

ALEXANDER

BROWN

LESSER CHARACTERS

HASKELL

SCULLY

| UNION SOLDIER | CONFEDERATE SOLDIERS (PRISONERS) |

ALEXANDER (his own memoirs, frontispiece). As mentioned in the text, Alexander had an undistinguished face, but was really an individualist. He is wearing colonel's insignia, but a highly unmilitary striped shirt.

BROWN (R. O. Sturtevant, *13th Reg. Vt. Vols.*, p. 401). This is one of the many thousands of soldiers' photographs, generally taken before leaving for the front.

HASKELL (photograph supplied by the Wisconsin State Historical Society). Haskell shows his age, which was well past that usual for a lieutenant.

SCULLY (Sturtevant, *op. cit.*, p. 84). The young "pivotal" sergeant here appears with cap and tie jauntily awry, as yet unblooded.

UNION SOLDIER (Sturtevant, *op. cit.*, p. 102). This is actually Corporal R. O. Bushnell, 13th Vermont. Like Brown's picture, this is a studio portrait, doubtless taken before leaving home. It displays the standard uniform, as described in the text. He may well have worn these same clothes at Gettysburg, though they would have been sadly faded, dirtied, and shredded by that time. Although the slender figure suggests height, the bayoneted rifle, apparently a Springfield, is taller than he is. He also displays his bayonet-sheath and ammunition pouch.

CONFEDERATE PRISONERS (*Battles and Leaders*, iii, p. 433, from a photograph). This is one of the few authentic pictures of Confederates at Gettysburg. As prisoners they are without weapons. Confederate infantry normally marched light, and the amount of miscellaneous material with which these three are laden suggests that they have been picking up a few things on the battlefield to take with them as comforts in captivity. Note the lack of uniform. One is in a dark, perhaps gray material. The other two in some light-colored cloth, perhaps butternut. Each is wearing a different kind of hat.

Cushing's Position (looking west)

The Angle is at right, beyond 71st Pa. monument. Woods mark line of Seminary Ridge; South Mountain beyond. Point of Woods is left of white spot (Lee monument). Car is on Emmitsburg road. The gun is a 3-inch rifle. Note generally level terrain.

Lee Monument (looking east)

Cemetery Ridge is marked by scattered trees in distance. The clump of trees is right of center. Archer's brigade was in position just behind where picture was taken. Kimble (see Pt III, #8) looked out from about here.

Hay's Position (looking south)

Bryan barn is at right; 111th N.Y. monument at left; 12th N.J., beyond. Tree near center marks Angle. Pettigrew's men advanced against Union line (posted this side of the stone wall) across the almost level field in front. Note bare rock in foreground.

Hall-Harrow Line (looking north)

The line of the entrenchment shows slightly. From here troops rushed to the clump of trees (on skyline). Single tree in center marks Angle. Small trees at left mark the rough ground; the trees here had been cut down at time of the battle.

Front of Spangler's Woods (looking south)

Because of the slope up to the left, this area was sheltered from observation, and Garnett's and Armistead's brigades were drawn up here
before the advance.

Slope in Front of Spangler's Woods (looking east)

Pickett's division advanced up this slope; at this point they came
under observation from Round Top. Note fence-line growth, which
may have prevented Pickett from advancing directly. Confederate
guns were on the crest here.

Tree near Spangler House (looking south)

This is the top of the rise, just about where Pickett began his left-oblique. The tree has been badly injured when young, and may be a casualty of the cannonade. (It also shows in the preceding picture.)

McGilvery's Line (looking northwest)

In foreground are two Napoleons (for Hart's battery); beyond, two 3-inch (for Phillips's battery). Codori barn is in distance. Kemper's brigade passed left to right this side of the barn, exposed to fire from these batteries. The trees were probably not there in 1863.

Webb's Line (looking west of north)

69th Pa. monument is at left. Cushing's guns were at the wall, just about at center of picture. Armistead crossed about at 72nd Pa. monument, just to right of center. Angle is beyond 71st Pa. monument, at tree.

The Angle (looking northwest)

The clump of trees is just off the picture at the left. 72nd and 71st Pa. monuments show. Small monument at right marks, probably with considerable accuracy, the spot at which Armistead fell. The line of the 106th Pa. was about at where the picture was taken. At the time of the battle his area was largely filled with "slashing."

15

In spite of dispersion of fire, the Confederates were managing to make things very grim for the Second Corps batteries. Woodruff and Arnold suffered the least. But Cushing had had caissons exploded and one or two guns put out of action. He himself was wounded by a bullet that carried away his shoulder strap, but he stayed with his guns.

Brown's battery, just to the south of the clump of trees, was in even worse condition. From the beginning, because of losses on the preceding day, these Rhode Islanders had been able to man only four pieces. Now, as they were loading a gun, Private Jones, Number One, stood with his rammer ready, and Private Gardner, Number Two (they called him "old man Gardner"), was just about to insert the charge. At that moment a shell struck the muzzle of the gun, exploding. Jones was killed immediately, part of his head carried away. Gardner's left arm was almost torn off at the shoulder. He was a religious man; as he lay bleeding, he shouted, "Glory to God! I am happy! Hallelujah!" He died murmuring that they should tell his wife that he died happy, and send her his Bible. Only Sergeant Straight and Corporal Dye remained of the gun crew. While Dye thumbed vent (necessary to prevent a premature explosion), Straight tried to load. But the barrel had been dented by being struck, and he could not ram the shot down. Dye tore off a piece of his shirt, wadded it, and put it on the vent, holding it down with a stone laid on top. He then went to help Straight, but the two of them still could not get the shot down. Someone came with an ax, and was about to try to drive it in, when another shell struck the side of the gun and exploded, causing no casualties, but wrecking a wheel. The gun tipped over to one side, unusable. The shot remained, partly sticking out of the end of the gun; when the barrel cooled, it clamped down securely. (The gun is still preserved in the Statehouse at Providence, one of the few authentic relics of

Pickett's Charge. Legend has built up about it, and it is frequently said that the shot was a Confederate one which lodged in the muzzle.)

South of Brown's battery was Rorty's. Of its fight *in extremis* a staff-officer has left a description.

> The men, begrimed with powder and smoke, loaded with precision and speed, sighting and firing their guns as if the fate of the nation depended upon their exertions. . . . With guns dismounted, caissons blown up, and rapidly losing men and horses, the intrepid commander moved from gun to gun as coolly as if at a West Point review. While bringing up ammunition, some of the men, to lessen their exposure, dismounted before reaching the battery; but this the stern disciplinarian would not permit, and ordered them to remount and ride into position.

Indeed, discipline in the Union artillery was almost Prussian. Even at the height of the cannonade the guns were discharged by command — "Number 1 — *Fire!* . . . Number 2 — *Fire!*" resounding "monotonously" from right to left of each battery.

Before long Rorty's men suffered so many casualties that their commander found himself unable to work his two remaining guns. So, as often happened in such circumstances, he sent to the nearest infantry regiment, the 19th Massachusetts, with a request for volunteers. The incident supplied a bit of grim humor when Captain Mahoney cried out to Company B, "Volunteers are wanted to man the battery. Every man is to go of his own free will and accord. Come out here, John Dougherty, McGiveran, and you Corrigan, and work those guns." In one way and another, twenty men volunteered for the dangerous service. Among them was Lieutenant Shackley, who called out to the color-sergeant, "Come, Jelison, let's go and help; we might just as well get killed there as here." The volunteers replaced some broken wheels, brought ammunition up from the limbers and re-opened fire.

Worst of all was Thomas's battery. It was now little more than a wreck. There was nothing to do but to retire, and what was left of it went to the rear. This might be called the first solid success of the cannonade, but no Confederate seems to have seen, or at least to have mentioned, the withdrawal.

Actually, the loss was of little significance, for in a few minutes, Cowan's 1st New York Independent, six 3-inch rifles, a Sixth Corps battery, came hurrying in as a replacement.

(Young Andrew Cowan, riding with his guns through that iron-streaked air, would probably have sold out his life-expectancy at a very easy figure. He would have been surprised to know that fifty years later, lacking only one day, he would be writing a description of the battle on a machine called a typewriter.)

Going into what had proved a very exposed position, the boys from Cayuga County must have felt some apprehension. Perhaps, however, the smoke concealed what was happening, or else the Confederates had lost the range. The battery suffered only moderate losses.

16

By this time the infantry along Cemetery Ridge had concluded that they could last through, and had settled down. "This soon became monotonous," wrote one of them. Colonel Gates of the 80th New York noted the contrast between his own veterans, who were "smoking and joking," and the Vermonters of Stannard's brigade, who were obviously suffering. Heat was still an active enemy; here and there a man quietly collapsed from prostration.

Thirst was almost as bad as heat. The location of various water-supplies was known, but they were several hundred yards away, and any man going there had to walk, fully exposed, through the rain of projectiles. A few men became heroes (temporary rank) by taking canteens and going for water. Coming back, having had a round shot strike between his feet, one of them joked bravely, "The water is cold enough, boys; but it's devilish hot around the spring."

17

Even nature was disturbed, one soldier noting that the small birds flew about in confusion. Over much of the field the rising smoke obscured the sun, which undoubtedly appeared like a pasted red wafer, though no Kipling or Crane was there to use the words.

The column of hot smoke rose high. Miles away, beyond the sound of the cannonading, looking out from the villages of Pennsylvania and Maryland, the people saw a strange gray cloud, high in the burning air of that summer day.

The sound of the cannonade enveloped the town of Gettysburg, but was scarcely heard at Chambersburg, twenty-five miles away across South Mountain. By the tricks of sound-transmission, however, it was clearly audible at various points as much as 150 miles to the west and north.

All, on both sides, who experienced the cannonade declared that it surpassed those of Malvern Hill and Fredericksburg. Hancock, a good judge, expressed his doubt as to whether in any battle of history more guns had concentrated on one point at one time — "a most terrific and appalling cannonade — one possibly hardly even paralleled."

18

Of all those on that field, there were few who were more battle-tested than Gibbon. He had the supreme courage to admit that he was afraid, and yet to go about doing his duty so calmly that no one would ever guess his inner feelings. He and Haskell, though they had retired to sit just behind the crest of the ridge in a comparatively sheltered spot, were far from being in a bombproof, and shells were striking close around. The observant Haskell saw and noted many details.

A soldier came walking up from the rear, unconcerned at the bombardment, with a full knapsack on his back, holding several canteens by the straps. A shot struck his knapsack, which disintegrated. The soldier stopped, looked puzzled, put up a hand to be sure that the knapsack was really not there, and then walked calmly on. . . . Near-by, a man crouched behind a small rock, "about the size of a common water bucket." He was bent before it, face to the ground, like "a Pagan worshipper before his idol." Haskell went across and spoke to him, "Do not lie there like a toad. Why not go to your regiment and be a man?" The soldier looked up, uncomprehending and terrified, and then turned his nose to the ground again. Shortly after, a shot struck the stone, smashing it to fragments but leaving the man unharmed. . . . A shell struck among a group of orderlies, who were sitting on the ground, holding horses. Two men and a horse were killed. . . . Stray shots struck down riderless horses which had been galloping madly through the fields; mules, bringing ammunition up from the rear. . . . Yet, the general and his aide had the satisfaction of hearing and seeing their own artillerymen on the crest sending back what Haskell described as "globe, and cone, and bolt, hollow or solid, an iron greeting to the rebellion, the compliments of the wrathful Republic." After they had sat there for about an hour, Gibbon had an idea. Noting that most of the fire passed overhead, he concluded that he would walk farther to the front since this "would be safer." Actually, the walk that Gibbon and Haskell took is not suggestive of a healthful stroll.

Hardly had they started when some ammunition chests blew up, almost in their faces. From afar, they heard the yells celebrating this triumph.

The two walked on calmly. There was a close relationship between them. Though they were almost of an age, the difference in rank made the bond seem almost that of father and son.

They passed the clump of trees, and came to where the men were lying behind the low stone wall. These would most likely have been men of the 69th Pennsylvania, who had been in that spot for so long that they were beginning to believe they had squatters' rights.

"What do you think of this?" said the general. The Irishmen (and Quakers, Jews and others) were not suffering much and they replied in the manner of veterans, "Oh, this is bully," or "We are getting to like it," or "Oh, we don't mind this."

General and aide went on, beyond the wall and down the slope. They made themselves comfortable seats beneath the shade of some trees, which Haskell was observant enough to note were elms. The view was surprisingly good, because they were beneath the smoke. They saw the skirmishers, and the two lines of guns sending out tongues of flame and bursts of smoke; the projectiles passed high overhead.

From the infantry line two men came down, apparently sharing the general's idea that it would be safer out in front. Gibbon spoke to them, more in a kind of fatherly exhortation than in command, "My men, do not leave your ranks to try to get shelter here. All these matters are in the hands of God, and nothing that you can do will make you safer in one place than in another." The men went quietly back.

Then, as if thinking that his speech needed some explanation, he remarked to his aide, "I am not a member of any church, but I have always had a strong religious feeling; and so in all these battles I have always believed that I was in the hands of God, and that I should be unharmed or not, according to His will. For this reason, I think it is, I am always ready to go where duty calls, no matter how great the danger."

They continued to sit and to watch the battle.

19

At last McGilvery gave the command, and his guns opened fire. By this time he could be sure that the Confederates were beginning to get low on ammunition, and so would have to make their infantry attack (if they made it) well before his own gunners could exhaust their chests. He ordered a slow and carefully aimed fire, concentrated upon a few of the enemy's batteries that were best in view. With the additional fire of these thirty-six guns, the cannonade reached its climax, though already under the severe punishment, the fire of the Second Corps batteries was falling off. McGilvery claimed that several of the Confederate batteries were broken up by his fire, and the concentration of so many guns should certainly have been able to accomplish something. Throughout the engagement, however, there is remarkably little Confederate reference to McGilvery's batteries, though this may be merely because no official reports are preserved from the batteries against which his fire was directed.

20

Haskell, as a good staff-officer should, seems to have kept some track of the time, although even he is not altogether to be trusted. Still, his statement that at half-past two the cannonade had not in the least abated, seems to be confirmed by other evidence. Shortly after this time, Haskell noted some slackening of fire, and with this slackening we may consider that the cannonade entered its final phase. To this point it can be considered little dependent upon the decisions of generals, who wandered about through the smoke, almost as spectators. But now the time of commands was approaching.

Pendleton, as it happened, had already given a command, and had succeeded in creating a complication by moving the ammunition train of Longstreet's artillery farther to the rear. This may have been necessary to get it out of range of the Union guns, but the removal increased the time for caissons to bring up fresh supplies of ammunition. In addition, Pendleton had caused confusion by not informing the artillery officers what he had done, so that the men with the caissons lost much time in locating the wagons.

The necessity for a decision was now becoming particularly urgent for Alexander. Twice Pickett had sent an aide to ask if it was time to advance. Alexander had taken his position where he could best observe the fire. Observing it, he was not happy. In spite of the long-continued bombardment, the whole Union line, he saw, "was blazing like a volcano." About two hours previously, having talked with Wright and Pickett, he had decided that the attack would be advisable, thus going pro-Lee and anti-Longstreet. Now, he was having very long second thoughts. As he wrote in his memoirs, "It seemed madness to order a column in the middle of a hot July day to undertake an advance of three-fourths of a mile over open ground against the center of that line." Besides, he still could not locate the lost howitzers, and this was very much on his mind, even on his conscience. Without the howitzers, he would, at the last moment, have to select some other guns, and to order the weary gunners forward for a new effort.

21

Within the Union lines, also, a time for decision was approaching. At the height of the firing, Hunt came to Cemetery Hill, and there talked with Osborn, who is the authority for the conversation.

Osborn asked, "Does Meade consider an attack of the enemy desirable?"

"General Meade expressed the hope that the enemy would attack, and he had no fear of the result."

"If this is so, why not let them out while we are all in good condition? I would cease firing at once, and the enemy could reach but one conclusion, that of our being driven from the hill."

Osborn then asked to be allowed to see Meade, and to get authorization for such an order. Hunt in turn asked if the men could be controlled when firing ceased. Osborn said that they could be. Hunt then decided that the idea was a good one; the enemy should be encouraged to attack as soon as possible. Hunt gave the order, and Osborn passed it on. One by one, as the word reached them, the batteries on Cemetery Hill ceased fire.

In his own report Hunt merely stated that he gave the order because ammunition was running low. Meade testified before the Committee on the Conduct of the War that he had had the idea of deceiving the enemy and had sent orders to cease fire, only to find that Hunt had already so acted. According to others, General Warren, Chief Signal Officer, also saw the opportunity.

The idea that the cease-fire was made gradual in order to "lure" the Confederates seems to have originated later. The gradual cessation must, rather, have been the natural result of the fact that batteries extending over a mile of front could not receive their orders simultaneously.

But what is important in the history of the United States is that the decision to cease fire was made, and that it actually occurred in such a way as to insure a decisive reaction.

22

While Hunt and Osborn were talking, Alexander had continued to watch carefully. The Union line still blazed. His own gunners, he knew, were scraping the bottoms of the chests. Imperatively, the attack must be made while the Confederate artillery still had ammunition with which to support it. A third time one of Pickett's aides came to inquire, and in a mood little short of desperation, beginning his note with an "if," Alexander wrote:

> If you are to advance at all, you must come at once, or we will not be able to support you as we ought. But the enemy's fire has not slackened materially and there are still 18 guns firing from the cemetery.

In this note we should mark not only the "if," but also a "but." As for the mention of "the cemetery," this is merely another indication of uncertainty about place names, a minor difficulty that plagued the Confederates. Alexander meant the position by the clump of trees. Thus considered, his estimate of eighteen guns was correct enough.

23

Just about the time that the note went off to Pickett, Hunt must have made his own decision. Having finished with Osborn, he rode southward, to give the orders along the line. This would mean that, battery by battery, from north to south, the Union guns would grow silent.

Probably it did not work out with that exactitude. In the Second Corps batteries, particularly, there is a difficulty that cannot be easily explained. According to Captain Hazard, the corps Chief of Artillery, his batteries ceased fire, not because they were so ordered, but because they had exhausted their long-range ammunition. The explanation may be that Hunt, finding these batteries badly broken and down to their last rounds, told them to continue firing as long as they could, since he intended to replace them with fresh batteries from the Reserve. Though Hunt may not have so realized, if the firing thus ceased in irregular fashion, the effect on the Confederates would be all the better.

24

Hunt now found all of these batteries hard hit and some of them really fought out. Cushing had had several chests exploded; apparently but three guns were left workable, and men enough to work only two of them. Cushing himself had been hit again. A piece of an exploding shell had struck him in the crotch, horribly wounding the thighs and the genitals. In an agony of pain, he still retained command.

When Hunt came to Brown's battery, just south of the clump of trees, he found it a wreck. All the officers were killed or wounded, and there were hardly enough men to work the three guns that remained. Probably the ammunition was nearly exhausted. To keep the battery in position any longer was to cause useless casualties. The only thing to do was to withdraw it.

Orders went back to where the teams were waiting. Fortunately, there were still enough horses to pull the guns. The battery, which had fought magnificently on two days, failed to make a dignified exit. With no officers left, there was no one to see that military procedure was followed, and each gun was limbered up and got to the rear as fast as possible. As a staff officer with an inexact knowledge of Shakespeare commented, "it stopped not upon the order of its going."

Yet, as Samson in his death killed more Philistines than in his life, so Brown's battery by its leaving destroyed more Confederates than it had ever done by its firing.

25

About this time, when the Union fire was beginning to slacken a little, Longstreet again passed in front of Pickett's division, accompanied by a staff-officer. He must have ridden along the skyline, for he was exposed to fire from the Union skirmishers as well as from their artillery. Rifle balls whizzed by, and once a round shot plowed up the ground just in front of the horse's nose. The general quieted his startled mount, and rode on. Men called out to him: "You'll get your old fool head knocked off! . . . We'll fight without your leading us!" But, as an officer put it, "He was as quiet as an old farmer riding over his plantation on a Sunday morning, and looked neither to the right or left."

26

Alexander, his note sent off to Pickett, still kept his eyes on the Union lines. He was ready to snatch at straws, quick to interpret wishfully anything that he might observe. But first, doubtless, he could hardly believe what he saw or seemed to see. Now at this critical moment, by what would appear to be a scarcely credible coincidence, the Union fire seemed to be slackening. As a minute or two passed, he became convinced. There could be no doubt of it! And, gazing uncertainly through the smoke, he saw, in confirmation, a welcome sight. Union guns going to the rear!

All he could have seen were Brown's three. Union records show that no other battery retired at this time. But he had actually seen some guns leaving, and now the firing ceased. Alexander jumped to the conclusion that under cover of the smoke all the guns had retired from "the cemetery." With sudden relief at heart, and with hands that must have trembled in excitement, he wrote again to Pickett, only about five minutes after he had dispatched his first note: "The 18 guns have been driven off. For God's sake, come quick, or we cannot support you. Ammunition nearly out."

27

We may consider that the great cannonade now began to end. The Union batteries, by order, were ceasing; the Confederate fire, also, was petering out.

The usual explanation is that the Confederates had exhausted their ammunition. As far as the guns under Alexander's immediate command were concerned, this was approximately true. Even those that still had a few rounds probably considered it best to cease fire, so that they would have something for an emergency. But many of Hill's and Ewell's guns had not participated so vigorously. Poague's battalion with ten guns in action fired 657 rounds, or only about half the contents of the chests, and these guns occupied some of the best positions on the field.

The cannonade, thus, began with a great general explosion, but faded in a diminuendo, and then ceased. How long did it last, and what did it accomplish?

By some quirk, Alexander mentally telescoped the whole cannonade into little more than half an hour, and he so stated in his official report and in his reminiscences, though his batteries could not have exhausted their ammunition in such a short time. Meade, Pendleton, Gibbon, and others gave the figure as two hours, more or less, obviously a round number. Hancock, devoted to accuracy, reported the time as "an hour and forty-five minutes." In strong corroboration, General A. P. Howe, of the Sixth Corps, testified under oath that he looked at his watch at the beginning of the cannonade and that the entire duration was "a little over an hour and forty-five minutes."

We may therefore conclude that it ended about five minutes before three o'clock. This may be considered to mark the first moment of silence. There may have been desultory firing after that time.

The results of the cannonade loomed large in Southern minds. Major Eshleman, commanding the Washington Artillery, reported that his fire had "caused immense slaughter to the enemy." Captain Ross, the Austrian observer, wrote that the fire "had done tremendous execution." This was apparently the general conclusion among the Confederates, since they them-

selves were overawed by the great bombardment and assumed
that the results must have been comparable to the expenditure
of ammunition. A Southern historian could write, "The Yankees
were closely crowded on the hills and devoured by our artillery
fire."

There was, however, at least one judicious observer among the
Confederates, and this was the Prussian, Captain Scheibert. In
his polysyllabic language he described the cannonade in one
word, as a "Pulververschwendung." This may be translated as a
"waste of powder." Some Union officers agreed with Scheibert.
Thus Captain C. A. Phillips wrote in a letter of July 6th, 1863:
"Viewed as a display of fireworks, the rebel practice was entirely
successful, but as a military demonstration, it was the biggest
humbug of the season." Phillips, however, commanded a battery
in McGilvery's line and was not at the point of Confederate
concentration. No one from any of the batteries on Cemetery
Ridge could have so written.

There the effect of the fire had been devastating. Two batteries had been forced to withdraw, and only one of these had
been replaced. Cushing had been reduced apparently to three
guns; Rorty, to two. The batteries had been forced to expend all
their long-range ammunition without being able to replace it.
So many officers and men had been killed and wounded that the
remaining guns could not all be kept in action. Even some of
them that were still manned were being served largely by infantrymen, not by skilled cannoneers.

By thus crippling these essential batteries, as well as by forcing
Meade from his headquarters and causing the Artillery Reserve
to withdraw farther from the line, the bombardment had yielded
substantial results.

In other respects it had failed. It had apparently not put out
of action a single gun of those that were prepared to fire from the
flanking positions — Cemetery Hill, McGilvery's line, and Little
Round Top. It had completely failed to demoralize the infantry.

Why should they be terrified, when they had suffered only slight casualties? Webb, whose brigade held the area of greatest concentration of fire, gave his losses as about fifty. Total casualties among the infantry holding the position probably did not exceed two hundred.

On the other side, the Confederate artillery had suffered little, except for a considerable slaughter of horses. Apparently the out-gunned batteries of the Second Corps line had not been able to fire effectively, and the other Union batteries had done rather little firing. The Confederate infantry, however, had suffered as many as 350 casualties, possibly more, and some regiments of Kemper's brigade must have been significantly reduced in fighting efficiency.

Successful or not, the cannonade had ground to a stop. The loud-mouthed guns had had their chance. As on most battlefields, the decision would rest with the foot soldiers.

PART VI

Second Lull

I do not want to make this charge.
— GENERAL JAMES LONGSTREET

AGAIN the stillness rolled over the battlefield, impressing men
not so much as the absence of sound as something in itself.
Major Osborn wrote, "a singularly depressing silence." Also,
in this silence that signaled the end of the cannonade, the men
on Cemetery Ridge indulged in a very human gesture — they
stood up and stretched!

In the town Professor Jacobs, that taker of notes, was not
rendered forgetful by the battle. He looked at his thermometer
and recorded the three-o'clock temperature as 87°, thus providing the only testimony upon that detail. Since the weather was
working up for a rain, the humidity must have been high. The
distress of the men on the battlefield is thus understandable.

2

Some guns, doubtless, had still been firing, when Alexander's
final note came to Pickett. At that time, we are told, he was
writing a letter to LaSalle Corbell, the young Virginia girl who
was to be his wife. That he was thus employed seems likely
enough, but the text purporting to be that letter can be nothing
but a clumsy fabrication, since Pickett's published "letters"
from Gettysburg contain references to matters that he could
not have known at that time, and are written in a high-flown
sentimental style, unlike the authentic letters that he wrote to
his fiancée.

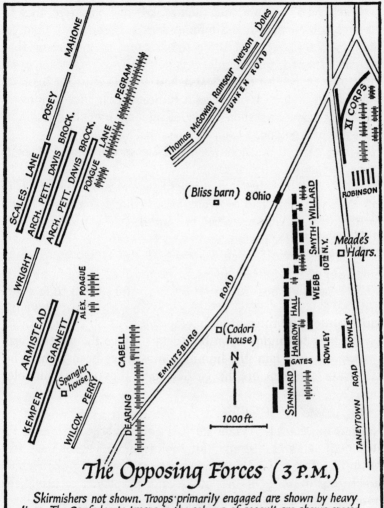

MAHONE

POSEY

SCALES. LANE

ARCH. PETT. DAVIS BROCK.

ARCH. PETT. DAVIS BROCK.

PEGRAM

POAGUE LANE

WRIGHT

ALEX. POAGUE

ARMISTEAD

GARNETT

KEMPER

(Spangler house)

WILCOX   PERRY

CABELL

DEARING

Thomas McGowan Ramseur Iverson Doles

SUNKEN ROAD

XI CORPS

ROBINSON

(Bliss barn)   8 Ohio

SMYTH-WILLARD

10TH N.Y.

Meade's Hdqrs.

WEBB

ROAD

HARROW HALL

ROWLEY

ROWLEY

(Codori house)

N

GATES

STANNARD

EMMITSBURG

TANEYTOWN ROAD

1000 ft.

The Opposing Forces (3 P.M.)

Skirmishers not shown. Troops primarily engaged are shown by heavy
lines. The Confederate troops in the column of assault are shown spaced
as they were in the first part of the advance. For lack of space the names
of Union batteries are omitted. Confederate artillery is identified by name
of battalion commander. The position of Cabell's guns is uncertain; they
may have been in line with Poague's and Alexander's in front of Garnett's
brigade.

BRYANT

Pickett read the note, and then took it to Longstreet, thus to play his part in one of the famous scenes of the day. That he went to Longstreet is of some significance. It may show that the part assigned to Alexander was not really as important as he thought it to be and that Pickett had been told to get his final orders from higher up. Or else it indicates that Pickett himself would not take the responsibility of moving a whole division at the word of a colonel.

Pickett handed the note over, and Longstreet read it. Pickett said, "General, shall I advance?"

To "Old Pete," the final moment had arrived. As he wrote later, "My feelings had so overcome me that I could not speak, for fear of betraying my want of confidence to him."

So, instead of speaking, he bowed his head.

During later years much was made of this failure to speak, as indicating a shoddy refusal to take responsibility, or some subtle kind of treason. But can we not also say that in all time a gesture has been as decisive as a word? "At the nod of Zeus high Olympus shakes." Certainly, Longstreet never attempted to escape the responsibility. In his official report he stated, "I gave the order to General Pickett to advance."

Pickett said, "I shall lead my division forward, sir." He started to leave.

But the scene, if we can trust Mrs. Pickett's reminiscences, was not quite over. When he had gone only a few yards, he swung around and returned. He took from his pocket the letter to his fiancée, and on its outside wrote in pencil, "If Old Peter's nod means death, good-bye, and God bless you, little one!" He entrusted the letter to Longstreet, turned, and rode off.

This incident has been accepted as authentic, and there is no good reason to doubt it, especially since it seems in harmony with character. It has undoubtedly brought tears to many an eye. The conclusion has seemed to be that Pickett was acting as a Southern gentleman should. Yet, how many seconds — half a minute, perhaps — were thus consumed? During that time a courier, sent to order up the Union reserve batteries, could have ridden a long quarter of a mile.

3

At this very time, along Cemetery Ridge, the Union troops were making use of every minute allowed them to recover from the confusion created by the cannonade and to prepare against attack.

Gibbon and Haskell, having walked around by the southern end of the line, were now returning north behind the line. Gibbon still inclined to the belief that the enemy was about to retreat; Haskell, that there would be an attack, and very shortly.

The smoke was drifting off. You could look out and see the now-silent Confederate guns, and also see, as yet, no infantry advancing. But no one, for a few minutes at least, spent much time looking, while the officers pushed preparations. As a soldier wrote, "All the officers on our lines, from the generals down, set themselves to work repairing the damage caused by the cannonade, reforming ranks, replacing dismantled guns, rectifying positions, exhorting the men to stand firm, and, in short, themselves offering the best examples of coolness and soldierly conduct."

The irrepressible Hays expected an attack. He called to his men, "Now, boys, look out; you will see some fun!"

He also disposed his troops to meet the attack. The 126th New York he moved to the right, to cover the gap which had worried him all day, and for which Meade had sent no reinforcements. The regiment passed near the 108th, and Captain Scott linked arms with his friend Lieutenant Colonel Pierce, commanding that regiment, and the two walked together for a moment. They had been classmates at Rochester University. "Well, Scott," said Pierce, "we have sat beside each other in the classroom many a day — but this is a new experience. This

isn't much like digging out Greek roots." (Truly, there were
men of many different kinds in those citizen armies, and their
thoughts on the battlefield were various.)

The 108th itself shifted out of the grove and a few yards
forward, so that it was in line with the rest of the brigade. The
39th and 125th New York moved up from support position to
the wall, going in just behind the New Jersey, Delaware, and
Connecticut regiments, so that along much of the line the men
were four-deep.

Hays was thus employing unorthodox tactics. He was mixing
up his two brigades, really fighting them as one unit. Doubling
the strength of much of the line would also come close to doubling its fire-power.

In Gibbon's division Webb made adjustments. Still holding
the 72nd Pennsylvania in support behind the trees, he sent the
71st forward to plug the gap that Cushing's wrecked battery
could no longer defend. Two of the companies went in at the
Inner Angle, to fill the little space just south of Arnold's guns.
The other eight companies went to the line of the low stone
wall at the Angle and south from it. By this shift at a critical
moment, most of the regiment was sent into a position with
which it was unfamiliar. In such a situation, troops were likely
to be nervous.

Farther south in Gibbon's line, where Hall's and Harrow's
brigades held the little entrenchment, no shifts occurred, except
that the two regiments in support moved forward a little to be
closer to the front line.

While these adjustments were being made in the infantry,
the artillerymen were even busier. The guns had now grown moderately cool. They were swabbed out, and cleansed of the foul-
ing that had built up during the long-continued firing. The only
remaining ammunition, the canister, was brought up from the
chests and piled handy. Then the gunners carefully loaded each
piece with canister.

There was a shifting of guns also. Two of Woodruff's Napoleons were rolled down to stand in line along with the infantrymen of the 108th New York. The other four, remaining on the high ground behind, could fire their canister at longer ranges, but could not, if the enemy came closer, because they would then hit their own infantry. But the two guns in front could fire until the charging Rebs came right to the muzzles. Arnold's guns, for the same reason, were rolled down even with the infantry line.

At the Angle, Cushing's guns were now masked by the 71st in its new position. Twice wounded and in great pain, Cushing himself still refused to leave the field. Perhaps, with a soldier's fixation on manhood, he no longer wished to live, and was merely seeking his bullet.

He had probably no more than three guns left workable — it must be "probably," because the tension was such that no one, in later years, could remember for certain. Since the battery had only enough men left to work two guns, some of the infantrymen of the 71st grabbed the third one and rolled it down to the Angle, to let the Rebs have one shot from it at close range. They loaded it with whatever they could find lying around handy, including a bayonet.

Cushing limped across to Webb. He had one hand pressed to his crotch, holding himself together and trying to ease the pain. But his request was not to be allowed to go to the rear, but to move his guns forward. He would put them in between the 71st and the 69th, pile the canister behind them, and fight there to the finish. As he spoke, the blood dripped from between his fingers. Webb granted the request.

4

While all this was happening, no Confederate infantry appeared. Though the time thus afforded to the Union troops was invaluable, no one should be hasty to criticize the Confederates for unnecessary delay. One did not launch nine brigades by saying "Come on, boys!" Orders had to be sent to the brigadiers, and passed on to the colonels. Especial care must be taken that Pettigrew and Trimble were informed, so as to time their advance with Pickett's. Quite possibly, indeed — as with Pickett's note — the tradition of a leisurely Southern gentility may have slowed

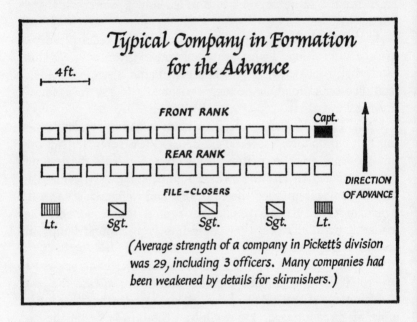

Typical Company in Formation for the Advance

4 ft.

FRONT RANK   Capt.

REAR RANK

DIRECTION OF ADVANCE

FILE–CLOSERS

Lt.   Sgt.   Sgt.   Sgt.   Lt.

(Average strength of a company in Pickett's division was 29, including 3 officers. Many companies had been weakened by details for skirmishers.)

matters a bit. Curt orders were not the practice in Lee's army; one presented compliments, and so forth. Possibly, before having a chance to deliver his message, an aide had to answer a polite question about Cousin Sue and the old Judge's rheumatism.

As a matter of record, one of Pickett's aides consumed some time with Colonel Williams of the 1st Virginia, about whether Williams, who was ill, could violate Pickett's order that officers should advance on foot. The colonel raised a sentimental argument; thus assailed, the aide replied, "Mount your mare, I will make an excuse for you." Garnett, because of his bad leg, and Colonel Hunton, because of his fistula, were granted permission to ride. Kemper also kept his horse.

5

So the orders were shouted, and in their long lines, where they had lain during the cannonade, Pickett's men rose to their feet. But a considerable number did not rise, and Captain Dooley of the 1st Virginia has catalogued these as of four classes: "There are the gallant dead, who will never charge again; the helpless wounded; . . . the men who have charged on many a battlefield but are now helpless from the heat of the sun; and the men in whom there is not sufficient courage to enable them to rise, — but of these last there are but a few."

Those who had been in the woods now advanced to the open swale, and the officers dressed all the lines. Since in their double-ranked formation the two-brigade front with the usual intervals between regiments and brigades stretched off for about half a mile, this dressing would take some time. At almost regular intervals, about a hundred yards apart, the single flag of each regiment stood above the line. These were not the flaming red of the Confederate flag, but were the blue flags of Virginia.

(And let no one think these flags to be useless ornaments, anachronistic survivals of the Middle Ages. Each was, rather, the soul of its regiment. Where the flag, there the regiment! Let it go forward, and all good men must go too, even though the colonel was down and the lines broken. Let it go rearward, and a man might retreat with honor. "Rally round the flag!" was no chauvinistic or humorous phrase, but the quite practical, even if desperate, words that a man in the smoke and blood and confusion would hear and heed — and to many a man the last words that he would ever hear.)

After the lines had been dressed, as one remembered, one of the captains led in a hymn, and a white-haired chaplain offered prayer, as if it might have been the army of the Covenanters, or of Cromwell or the great Gustavus, for there were many God-fearing men in those regiments, and they wished to go into the fight at peace with their Maker.

Close afterwards came the inevitable touch of humor, when a rabbit, which had been sheltered in a bush, leaped rapidly to the rear. A gaunt private cried out, in words which we may express in his idiom, "Run, you little ol' rabbit! If I was a little ol' rabbit, I'd run too!"

Then the instructions were given. . . . *Advance slowly, with arms at will. No cheering, no firing, no breaking from common to quick step. Dress on the center.*

Pickett rode to the front of the division, and made what has been described as "a brief, animated address." He ended, "Charge the enemy, and remember old Virginia!" Unfortunately, the length of the line was too much for the general's vocal powers, and one man at the left, nearly a quarter-mile away, reported that he heard not a word of it.

The brigadiers also addressed their men. Armistead made his customary brief exhortation: "Men, remember your wives, your mothers, your sisters and your sweethearts."

At the same time, a different kind of activity was proceeding among the file-closers. Some of these lacked confidence that all their men would bravely march forward because of an appeal to their female kinfolks and loved ones. Among these was Sergeant D. B. Easley, Company H, 14th Virginia. His captain had specified three or four men who were habitual "play-outs," and instructed the file-closers to take them into the fight or kill them. The captain declared that he did not care which; if the men were killed, he would be responsible. Easley selected an old school-mate, "as he had done more talking and less fighting than any-one in the company."

Easley's reminiscence supplies us with some valuable statistics. The average size of companies in the division was thirty men, and in the 14th, an old and battle-scarred regiment, they were probably not larger than the average. Easley specifies that his company was a good one, and yet that it had three or four "play-outs." Assuming that an average company would have had four such men, and knowing that Pickett's division contained 150 companies, simple multiplication assures us that six hundred men, the equivalent of two regiments, were not going to do any more fighting than they could be forced into doing.

Viewed from the other direction, these statistics are neither incredible nor shameful. They mean that about nine men out of ten were reliable. This is a high percentage, and would probably not be exceeded except among troops who were under such iron discipline that to leave the ranks was more dangerous than to go forward.

The brigades were now poised, ready to advance. Even at this moment, however, one seems to feel a certain leisurely approach — a sense that things should be done in gentlemanly fashion even if this meant they would not be done quite so quickly. Kemper, for instance, rode over from his end of the line to give some message to Armistead. As Kemper was riding off, Armistead pointed to the brigade, and said: "Did you ever see a more perfect line than that on dress parade?"

In Pettigrew's and Trimble's command there also were speeches, but fewer reminiscences have been preserved. Pettigrew, addressing the new commander of his own brigade of North Carolinians, cried out, "Now, colonel, for the honor of the good old North State, forward!"

6

Also among those who mustered, in the ranks of the 1st Tennessee, was Private George Stewart. There were, to my knowledge, none of my kin in that battle, but doubtless in ancient days his forefathers and mine drew claymore in same clan and charged to the same slogan. Across the uncertain bridge of a name, I salute you, Private George Stewart.

7

About this time, a few minutes after three o'clock, closing prices of the New York Stock Exchange were reported. "The news came slowly over the wires, but the prevailing belief appeared to be that the second engagement at Gettysburg, on Thursday, had resulted favorably for General Meade." The market was bullish, especially for the railroads. New York Central had gained 1¼.

8

And now they were almost ready, those about to advance and those others waiting across the fields. Let us pause to consider their numbers and the weapons with which they must fight for the great decision.

Pickett's division mustered for the advance just about 4300 officers and men. The brigades were approximately: Kemper's, 1325; Garnett's, 1405; Armistead's, 1570. In these figures allowance is made for losses in the cannonade.

Heth himself put the strength of his own division on July 3 at 4300 "muskets." To this figure must be added the officers, which can usually be reckoned at ten per cent of the number of men. But this division had suffered very heavy losses of officers on July 1, and so we may consider that these numbered about 300 on July 3. Again with some allowance for losses in the cannonade, the full strength of the division may be set at 4500. Its brigades differed greatly in strength. Brockenbrough's, reduced by losses at Chancellorsville and on July 1, went in at about 600. Archer's had apparently suffered less on July 1 than is usually supposed, and we may put it at 900. Pettigrew's and Davis's each mustered about 1500.

The two other brigades totalled 1700. Scales's, having suffered badly on July 1, took only about 500 into the fight; Lane's, about 1200.

The total number of troops in the assaulting column, therefore, may be put at 10,500. This figure is much smaller than the conventional "fifteen thousand." Even if we add the 1400 men of Wilcox's and Perry's brigades, the total still remains far below the usually stated figure. Actually, the "fifteen thousand" seems to derive from Longstreet's original statement early in the day, before the troops to make the assault had been assigned. He supposed that he was to have three divisions, and by rule of thumb he apparently figured a division at 5000. The advance was finally made with only two divisions and half of another, all of them more or less under strength.

The Union infantry that was to withstand the assault consisted of six brigades, plus three small regiments. The determination of their strength is a problem of great complexity. Most of these brigades had already suffered heavy losses in the battle, and these can be separated from the total losses only with difficulty. Yet, by a careful study of official reports, regimental histories, and battlefield markers fairly accurate figures can be obtained, again with allowance made for casualties in the cannonade.

In Gibbon's division, Harrow's brigade may be put at 700; Webb's, 880; Hall's, 570. This gives a total for the division of 2150. In Hays's division, Smyth's brigade mustered about 830; Willard's, 930. In addition, the 8th Ohio had about 160 men. The total for Hays's division is thus 1920.

Stannard's brigade consisted of only three regiments, all of them comparatively large, adding up to about 1400. Gates's two fragmentary regiments totaled very close to 235. Finally we may add a few dozen to include the company of Massachusetts Sharpshooters, and the divisional and brigade staffs.

We may conclude, then, that the total number of the infantry awaiting the assault on Cemetery Ridge was about 5750. A few other regiments did a little long-range shooting. These, however, cannot be considered as seriously engaged, any more than were some Confederate skirmishers from other brigades who also did a little shooting. The defenders, thus were not much more than half as strong as the attackers.

There were also rather fewer than five hundred Union artillery-men, with about twenty-three workable guns, only six of which had long-range ammunition. Rather than being added to the infantry, however, this force should be considered a part of the large artillery forces engaged on both sides.

Some interesting confirmation of the figures for the Union in-fantry may be derived from the length of front occupied. Harrow's brigade, for instance, held 350 feet, into which 700 men in two ranks might just be squeezed.

On both sides these figures are more likely to be high than low, because there is no good way of estimating the number of skulkers and non-combatants. All of the Union troops and five of the Confederate brigades had already been in heavy fighting in the battle. Not only were stretcher-bearers and teamsters sometimes included in the count, but also we can make no good estimate of the cowardly and panic-stricken who had run away, as well as of those who had merely become lost in the confusion. We have actual accounts of two soldiers of the 13th Vermont who scuttled to the rear on July 2 and did not reappear until after the fighting was over.

9

The number of troops supplied by various states has been a question for argument. On the Confederate side the numbers were approximately: Virginia, 4900; North Carolina, 3600; Mississippi, 1100; Tennessee, 550; Alabama, 350. Represented in the artillery or the supporting troops were South Carolina, Florida, and Louisiana. All of the states of the Confederacy thus participated, except for Arkansas and Texas.

The Northern states most heavily engaged were: New York, 1600; Vermont, 1400; Pennsylvania, 1000; Massachusetts, 475. Represented by single regiments were Maine, Connecticut, New Jersey, Delaware, Ohio, Michigan, and Minnesota. In addition, the artillery included batteries from New Hampshire, Rhode Island, West Virginia, and the Regular Army. All of the eastern states thus participated, plus two border states, and three which counted as western.

10

No matter from what state an infantryman came, whether North or South, he was likely to have the same weapons. In the remaining work of the day the artillery would still do much, but the chief responsibility would now rest upon the infantrymen and upon the rifled muskets that most of them carried.

On both sides, indeed, there were a few troops that still used the old smooth-bore, shooting "ball and buck," but these did not affect the situation seriously. A very few individual Union soldiers had breech-loading rifles, which were as much superior to the rifled musket as that was superior to the smooth-bore. These breech-loaders were in the hands of some men of the 14th Connecticut — a state noted for the manufacture of fire-arms. The men thus armed had teamed up in pairs, using two rifles, one man to load and one to fire.

The standard rifled muskets were of different models, which varied slightly in such details as length of barrel and size of bore. The "rifled gun" itself was no new invention. Some of the finest fighting in the Revolutionary War had been done by American riflemen — by Morgan's Virginians, for instance, at

Saratoga. But technical difficulties beset the development of a fool-proof rifle that could be placed in the hands of the ordinary infantryman.

Early in the nineteenth century an American named Joshua Shaw had invented the percussion cap, and in 1849 came the perfection of an almost ideal bullet for the military rifle —known to Civil War soldiers as the "Minnie ball." It was, indeed, neither a ball nor connected in any way with a girl named Minnie. Its inventor was Captain Minié of the French army, and it was, in shape, elongated and pointed, so as to be, technically, cylindro-ogival. The combination of the rifled barrel, Minié's bullet, and Shaw's percussion cap revolutionized warfare. The manipulation of the new weapon was far from simple, but with drill and practice anyone with intelligence a little better than the village idiot's could use it.

Its shots were dangerous. The big lead slug, close to two-thirds of an inch in diameter, an ounce in weight, was a killer and a crippler. The rifle was dangerous at more than half a mile, though of course you could not expect to hit much with it at that distance. Most infantry commanders did not want their men to open fire until the range had closed to under 300 yards. The rifled muskets also had their disadvantages, which would soon lead to their replacement by breech-loaders. Their rate of fire was slow, about two a minute. In addition, a man had to stand up to load quickly, and this made him an easy mark.

Nevertheless, not only had the rifled musket made the Napoleonic artillery tactics highly questionable, but also it had just about outmoded the bayonet charge. In the time it took a line to advance from 300 yards to close quarters the defenders could fire five or six shots apiece, each one at shorter range and more deadly. Flesh and blood could seldom go in with the bayonet against such a fire. Instead, the men stopped and fired back. If the attackers were reinforced or for some other reason were able to advance again, they could expect that by this time their opponents would either run or surrender.

The volunteer soldier, who was likely to remain a thinking man, thus came to consider the bayonet as a useless weight upon his already overweighted body. The Union soldier, restrained by discipline, continued to carry his bayonet, even though he found no chance to use it. The Confederate soldier often "lost" his, so that in some brigades bayonets were rarities.

There is no precise evidence as to the troops advancing in the charge. Many descriptions mention "gleaming bayonets," and the numerous drawings show stern-faced soldiers pressing forward at close quarters with points advanced. But most of these descriptions were written, and probably all of these drawings were drawn, by people who were not there; in any case, the conventions of literature and art demanded the bayonet. Still, there is enough testimony for Pickett's division to make it seem likely that his men had bayonets and advanced with them fixed.

11

But now that the lines stood ready, the decision still hung in the balance.

Having nodded his head to Pickett, Longstreet had ridden forward, to find Alexander. The latter was on the left flank of Dearing's guns, on the top of the rise in front of Pickett's division. Alexander explained the situation, saying that he was somewhat more hopeful than he had been, but was fearful that the ammunition was too low for proper support of the infantry.

At this word about the ammunition, Longstreet apparently realized that he had a last chance. He snapped out, "Go and stop Pickett where he is, and replenish your ammunition!"

Alexander could only reply, "We can't do that, sir. The train has but little. It would take an hour to distribute it, and meanwhile the enemy would improve the time."

Longstreet was silent for a moment, seeming uncertain. Then he spoke slowly, almost overcome with emotion: "I do not want to make this charge. I do not see how it can succeed. I would not make it now but that General Lee has ordered it and is expecting it."

Again there was a pause, and Alexander thought that if he could raise some objection, Longstreet would still countermand the charge. But the corps-commander was not exercising an independent command; the whole operation was immediately under Lee's eyes. This was the defense that Longstreet gave in later years, for not having countermanded the charge at this last moment.

12

The Confederates had expended, in one way or another, about a quarter of an hour since the cannonading had ceased. The time was about ten minutes past three. Now the lines had been dressed and the speeches made. The command rang out, *"Forward! Guide center! March!"* The ten blue flags of the first line moved ahead; the men kept strict formation as they moved up the slope.

Longstreet was still thinking of what he might do, when — with a coincidence of timing that suggests a melodrama rather than a battle — the advancing line came into view.

PART VII

Advance

Terrible as an army with banners.
— Song of Solomon

Along the Union line, you may read, ran a universal exclamation, "Here they come! Here comes the Johnnies!" But this is rather, we must think, a part of the legend.

Pickett began his advance from the bottom of a swale, and for several minutes his lines moved forward without anyone on Cemetery Ridge being able to see them. Almost at once, however, his two front brigades came under observation from Little Round Top, and the alert men of the Signal Corps sprang into action. The Vermonters of Stannard's brigade, occupying low ground, knew that the attack was launched before they saw a Confederate flag or soldier.

On the other wing, Heth's division had only to advance fifty yards before breaking from the woods, in full view for Hays's division — and for Osborn's gunners on Cemetery Hill. The smoke of the cannonade, which would have offered some concealment, had now drifted off. One of Pettigrew's aides remembered the sudden break from the shady woods into the "beautifully clear" sunshine — "Before us lay bright fields and fair landscape."

Pettigrew himself, riding in advance with his staff, looked back, and was horror-stricken to see, instead of four brigades, only the two forming his right, Archer's and his own. His immediate reaction was that Davis, because of the thickness of the woods, had not noticed that the brigade on his right had advanced — a charitable but not likely explanation, especially since Davis had been specifically cautioned against this very error. At this moment, then, we might do well to remember the story that Gordon had told Pickett, that some brigades were not going to advance.

Just what happened there in the woods is lost in the dark of the past. Perhaps, to start the advance, the officers and the color-guards had to begin moving, and then the fighting spirit of the men sent them forward too. The alarmed Pettigrew ordered an aide to see what was the matter, but the aide had scarcely started when Davis's brigade broke out of the woods with an "impetuous rush," and soon overtook the rest of the line.

But there was no Brockenbrough. The aide asked if he should ride to see what was the matter with that brigade. No, said Pettigrew, it might come along. Then he made the remarkable statement that if the brigade failed to advance, it was a small matter — thus referring, in the aide's opinion, both to the lack of numbers in Brockenbrough's command and to its "state of demoralization." Yet, in a few moments, that brigade also emerged from the woods, though there is lacking, again, any record of what had happened.

A hundred yards or something more behind, Pettigrew's first line followed the second, and behind the second line, at a similar interval, came Trimble's command.

So also, on the other flank, Armistead's brigade moved out behind Garnett's. And there, men have always delighted to tell, the grizzle-haired brigadier walked to the front of his line, and drew his sword, and on its tip placed his old black hat, holding it high as a rallying point, like the white plume of Navarre at Ivry. Yet, with the perversity that dogs romance, after a while the point pierced the felt, so that the hat kept slipping down to the hilt, and the general would have to hoist it up again.

2

Webb, on Cemetery Ridge, still with no battery to replace Brown's, had grown desperate. He rushed an aide to Cowan, ordering or requesting him to move to the clump of trees. Cowan hesitated, being under Doubleday's command. But, looking toward the trees, he saw an officer waving his hat frantically. (It was Webb, who by now doubtless saw the advance.) The hat-waving, for some reason, convinced Cowan, and he gave the order, "*Limber to the right, forward!*" The distance was only three hundred yards, and Cowan recognized a crisis. He had the drivers flog up the horses, and took the guns over at furious gallop, as light artillery often appeared in pictures of battles, but seldom on a battlefield.

The guns, in fact, were moving so fast that the first of them could not be stopped in time and went on to the north side of the trees, where it was pulled up and unlimbered. The other five guns went into position a little to the rear of where Brown's battery had been.

Even while the guns were being unlimbered, Cowan caught sight of the Confederates. He shouted the distance and the time-setting for the fuzes, and then galloped over to give instructions to the sergeant of the other gun.

He found the sergeant preparing the guns for action, though the field of fire was much limited by troops in front.

3

Now, in less than five minutes from starting, Pickett came to the top of the low rise, and the whole attacking force was in view. Most of the Union infantrymen had nothing to do but to watch. First they saw a line of skirmishers, the men seeming to be about six feet apart. A hundred yards behind this line was a similar one, and another hundred yards back came the

column of assault — to the north, under the red flags, six brigades in three lines; to the south, under the blue flags, three
brigades in two lines. All who saw admired the well-dressed
ranks, under the spaced colors, the regiments and brigades separated by proper intervals, all moving as on parade, even with
some mounted officers. At the northern end there may have
been a little raggedness, because Brockenbrough's men still
lagged.

The lines moved deliberately and quietly, at route step — 110
to a minute. At a thirty-inch stride they therefore came on, every
minute, a little less than a hundred yards. Lee, that psychologist
of battle, had perhaps calculated upon this very deliberation, this
sense of an overwhelming power, to help demoralize his opponents. Certain it is that more than one Union soldier, looking
out at those flag-dotted lines, remembered his Bible and thought,
"Terrible as an army with banners." A brigade-commander
wrote that the perfect order and steady advance gave the column "an appearance of being fearfully irresistible."

By and large, however, the veterans of the Second Corps were
not to be frightened by shows. In fact, as they looked out at the
lines advancing across the open fields, a horrible and yet inspir-
iting analogy popped into their minds. They remembered how
they themselves had thus charged at Fredericksburg against an
enemy that waited behind a stone wall, and how they had futilely met the fire and taken sickening losses, only to drag back
in defeat. Now, the other way round! The hill was not so steep
or the wall so high — but they would serve.

Addressing the 69th Pennsylvania, Colonel O'Kane, using the
old Bunker Hill battle-cry, told his men to hold their fire till
they saw the whites of the eyes. Then — though, indeed, most
of them had been born in Ireland — he reminded them that this
was the soil of their own state; he concluded: "Let your work
this day be for victory or to the death!" (It was.)

In the 80th New York, Gates's little regiment, a color-bearer jumped up on some stones, and waved his flag at the advancing lines, shouting for them to come on. All the men then stood up, and some of them started shooting, and had to be told to hold their fire until the Johnnies got within decent range.

Most of the men were relieved to be rid of the strain of the cannonade and the waiting, and one of them was heard to cry out, "Thank God! There comes the infantry!"

Even an esthetic feeling came to some of them, and an officer of the 126th New York wrote in a letter just after the battle, "Beautiful, gloriously beautiful, did that vast array appear in the lovely little valley." (His own regiment was to accomplish something toward making those lines far from beautiful in a few minutes.)

By now the Union lines were again receiving some artillery fire, but the Confederates were always chary of shooting over their own men, and probably limited themselves to solid shot.

No one on Cemetery Ridge paid much attention to this scattered cannonade. Hays even had his men stand up in line behind the wall, and there, obviously wishing to keep them from being idle and growing apprehensive, he shouted orders in his stentorian voice, and drilled his regiments in the manual of arms.

The artillerymen needed no artificial activity — except for the four Second-Corps batteries that were out of long-range ammunition. Osborn's guns were thundering from the hill; Cowan's, from the clump of trees. Daniels joined in, and the right-wing batteries of McGilvery's line. From Little Round Top the gunners of Rittenhouse's battery brought their six Parrotts to bear at the range of a mile and a quarter.

Watching from Cemetery Hill, the obviously excited correspondent of the Philadelphia *Morning Post* jotted down some staccato sentences, the only description of the charge that can be called strictly contemporaneous. Noting the time as 3.15, he wrote:

A great attack is now being made on our left center by a powerful column of rebels. We can see them advancing in hosts. Their lines are half a mile in length. [Doubtless as yet he saw only Pettigrew's brigades.] They have a mile to march before they strike our line. All our artillery has opened upon them and we can see them falling in hundreds. [Some exaggeration.] In a few minutes they will strike our line and the fight will be at close quarters.

4

Shortly after coming into view, Pickett's leading brigades arrived at the line of Dearing's guns, and passed through the intervals. The gunners raised their hats, and cheered the infantrymen on, shouting encouragement.

Alexander, noticing his good friend Garnett, whom he had not seen for some time, pulled his horse over and rode forward with him a little way; then they parted, wishing each other good luck and saying good-bye. A gentlemanly gesture, in fine disregard of the Yankee artillery fire? Perhaps it inspired the infantry, but still one wonders why Alexander was not already organizing his artillery to advance in support. In fact, the moment he left Garnett, that was what he set about doing.

Pickett himself, with his four aides, was riding about twenty yards in the rear — a good position from which to keep his eye on things and to issue orders. Once the lines had passed the crest, with the clump of trees now plain in view, the time came for initiation of the maneuver which was necessary to unite his division with Pettigrew's command. The order given was "Left oblique!" This meant that each soldier turned forty-five degrees to the left, so that the whole line sidled toward Pettigrew's, without altering its general north-south alignment. The watching Yankees, though puzzled as to the necessity of the maneuver, were deeply impressed by the parade-ground precision with which it was executed under artillery fire.

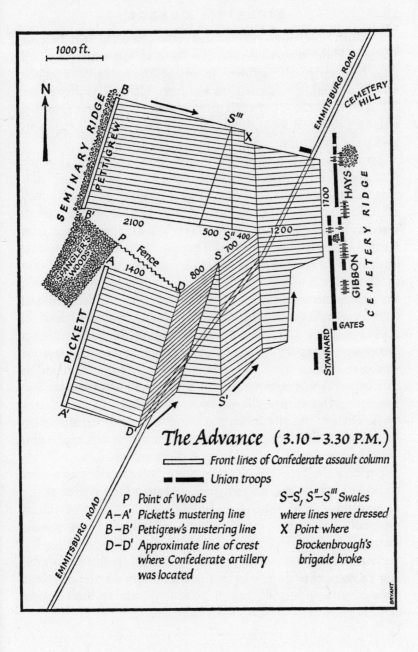

The Advance (3.10 - 3.30 P.M.)

▭ Front lines of Confederate assault column
▬ Union troops

P   Point of Woods
A–A'   Pickett's mustering line
B–B'   Pettigrew's mustering line
D–D'   Approximate line of crest where Confederate artillery was located

S–S', S"–S'" Swales where lines were dressed
X   Point where Brockenbrough's brigade broke

BRYANT

By this time, indeed, that fire was definitely troublesome. Colonel Hunton was hit, and his horse at the same time; still able to keep to the saddle, he swung the mortally wounded mount around, and started for the rear. Colonel Williams was knocked from the saddle, fell upon his own sword, and thus died like an antique Roman; his little mare kept with the regiment, and went on in the charge.

Though both Hunton and Williams were of Garnett's brigade, that command should have been having the easier time of it, since Cowan's five guns, firing at long range with no advantage of enfilade, could not cause heavy casualities. Kemper's brigade was receiving head-on fire from Rorty's guns, full enfilade from Rittenhouse's on Little Round Top, and a raking fire at various angles from Daniels's battery and several of McGilvery's. The most troublesome guns were Rittenhouse's rifles, firing at very long range but with the advantage of height, enfilade, good visibility, and reliable percussion shell. Under such conditions the skilled gunners could fire almost as at practice. Their natural target was Kemper's brigade, but any slight excess of elevation would land their shells in Garnett's line. The official report of this latter brigade commented upon the small loss from artillery fire during this part of the advance, except for that caused by a single battery "on the mountain"; this one enfiladed the entire line "with fearful effect, sometimes as many as ten men being killed and wounded by the bursting of a single shell."

Fortunately for the Confederates, Rittenhouse's six guns could be fired for only a short time, and then the advance passed beyond the line of sight of all but two guns. These, served by unusually skillful gunners, continued to deal out heavy punishment.

Also from the same flank, probably not always distinguishable from Rittenhouse's fire, was that of McGilvery's batteries. Kemper's advancing brigade passed obliquely through their line of sight. "The mark was a fair one," wrote a watching Third Corps man, and added, "He was a poor artillerist who could not hit it." As one of McGilvery's captains declared, "We had a splendid chance at them, and we made the most of it. . . . We could not help hitting them at every shot." Yet Union artillerymen, like their Confederate counterparts, were often over-optimistic. Lack of Confederate comment on the effects of this fire is strik- ing. Certainly Kemper's brigade was not seriously shattered.

Yet the fire was already so severe that a stream of slightly wounded was making for the rear, and with them were joined some men, as always, who were merely pretending to be wounded. The "play-out" whom Sergeant Easley was watching suddenly dropped, saying that he was hit. When Easley de- manded to see the wound, the man got up and ran, the sergeant in hot pursuit with leveled rifle. To Easley's chagrin, the fugitive dodged between two regiments and got away.

But many wounds were genuine. So it was with Private Byrd of the 9th, who was hit in the arm, slightly, but enough to dis- able him from using a rifle. He asked to be allowed to go to the rear, but the officer was doubtful. The sergeant — a man to be remembered among Americans who have joked when the going was hard — intervened with the words, "Lieutenant, they have winged our Byrd."

Not susceptible to humor was the case of Captain Spessard, of the 28th. His son, serving in the same regiment, was struck down. Men saw the major kiss the body tenderly, and lay it out gently on the ground; then raising his sword, he continued with the charge.

Having advanced slightly over half the distance in about eight minutes, under artillery fire for half of that time, Pickett's first line came to a point of shelter. A swale in the gently rolling terrain hid them from observation, and sheltered them from most of the fire. Because of the movement on the oblique, the left first came to this low place and was halted there. The rest of the division had to come up and re-dress on a new line.

The utility of this maneuver, which must have been planned in advance, was twofold. The halt in the swale permitted the regiments to be re-formed and re-dressed in comparative security. The swinging forward of the right flank meant that the line, when it again advanced, would be parallel with the general trend of the Union line, an important consideration. By fortunate accident, the direction of the swale was the same as that of the Union line.

Up to this time the losses, while far from insignificant, had failed to be crippling or demoralizing. Once the lines had been re-dressed, the division would be ready to resume the advance, scarcely weakened as a military force.

5

While Pickett had been moving forward, Pettigrew was advancing at equal pace. No complicated maneuvering was required. The right guide of Archer's brigade had merely to keep his eyes on the clump of trees and advance directly toward it. Pettigrew and Trimble, along with their aides, were on horseback, making a good show. The red flags at proper intervals moved forward steadily. There was the advantage of a downhill slope.

At first, the column was well behind Pickett's. Once his division had begun its oblique, this interval steadily lessened, since Pickett's men, thus sidling, were moving forward only about two thirds as fast as Pettigrew's. This, again, had doubtless been considered beforehand, and calculated with some degree of accuracy.

As far as artillery fire was concerned, Archer's and Pettigrew's brigades suffered scarcely at all. They may have received an occasional wild shot from Cemetery Hill, but probably no gun was firing directly at them except Cowan's single piece which had been carried north of the clump of trees. As far as this part of the advance was concerned, the men of these two brigades could have remembered only a downhill march under a blazing sun. Even Davis's brigade suffered very little during the first part of the advance — "not a gun was fired at us," that brigadier reported.

The reason was obvious. The gunners on Cemetery Hill naturally sighted at the most inviting target, and this was the left of the Confederate line, Brockenbrough's unlucky brigade. Captain Edgell of the 1st New Hampshire Battery reported: "I fired obliquely from my position upon the left of the attacking column with destructive effect."

The casualties in that brigade were probably troublesome almost from the beginning. Once the range had closed a little so that the Napoleons became more effective, the losses grew more serious. The brigade was small; its morale was low, and even at the beginning there were probably many "play-outs." Soon this small body was receiving the concentrated fire of sixteen Napoleons, three 20-pound rifles, ten smaller rifles. A well-aimed round shot could take out both front- and rear-rank man, and an occasional well-placed and properly exploding shell could open up a gap of several files. The brigade was not in good condition to take this pounding.

No official report of Brockenbrough's is extant, and in other reports and in reminiscences there is what we can call a conspiracy of silence, to cover up the details. Only here and there, in a few words, did someone put into writing some milder version of those "shafts of detraction" that were certainly the common talk, in the next few weeks, around the campfires of the Mississippi and North Carolina regiments. Seeking a scapegoat, some even went too far, maintaining that Brockenbrough's Virginians never really got into the charge at all, or else gave way "before they were fairly under fire." Actually the brigade did better than the statements of its worst detractors suggest. The four flags, with the line beneath them growing steadily shorter, as the men closed up to fill the gaps, advanced past the right flank of the troops on the sunken road, and down the slope past the hot ashes of the Bliss barn.

Just beyond the barn was a low place, and there Pettigrew probably halted the division to dress the line. Brockenbrough's regiments, doubtless coming up a little after the others, halted there too. As with Pickett, who by now was again advancing, the pause cannot have been for long, perhaps not for more than a minute or two.

6

Longstreet, able in spite of some smoke from bursting shells to scan the field, must have been moderately well pleased, though there is nothing to indicate that he ever lost his pessimism. Still, the head of the column had advanced more than half way, with no crippling loss. A considerable number of men, individually or in little groups, were coming back from both Pickett's and Pettigrew's fronts, slightly wounded and doubtless some skulkers, as was to be expected. But the flags were all held high, and were going forward; formation was well maintained; Pickett had executed the tricky left-oblique and was converging upon Pettigrew's left. Pettigrew, having re-dressed, was resuming the advance.

So far, not bad! But, with his keen general's eye, Longstreet was already beginning to sense that the brigade on the far left was getting shaky. Besides, the real test was just about to begin, when the front brigades would meet the shock of canister.

As for the Union lines, some wishfully thinking Confederates saw signs of demoralization there. Probably Longstreet did not so deceive himself. As a realistic thinker, he could only suppose that fresh batteries and infantry reserves were already converging toward Cemetery Ridge.

7

In reality, though batteries and brigades had started moving, they were not yet close. Neither Meade nor Hunt had acted quickly, in spite of appeals from the commanders on Cemetery Ridge. The less than six thousand infantrymen and the few hundred artillerymen with their broken batteries that already held the line were listening in vain for the cheers that might herald the approaching brigades or the ringing bugle notes that meant batteries moving up.

Undoubtedly many an individual soldier would have been ready to run if he saw the chance. But as for anything to be called demoralization in a military sense, there was none. On the contrary, various incidents show the Union soldiers in a high state of aggressive pugnacity. For instance, well to the left was the position of McCandless's brigade of the Fifth Corps, the Pennsylvania Reserves. Half a mile to the north the men could see Kemper's flank moving, and they had only to rest quiet to avoid trouble. But, against orders, they broke away, by twos and threes, ran to the north, and formed a line of scattered sharp-shooters, firing at long range into Kemper's flank. Several of them were shot down by the skirmish-line of Barksdale's Mississippians.

8

Again, as the second stage of the advance began, Brocken-brough's brigade remained the critical one. Still, the four flags went forward, but a Mississippian, who was close to the left of Davis's brigade, later declared that many of the Virginians remained in the shelter of the swale. So, now, beneath the flags, scarcely more than a skirmish-line was advancing. Moreover, watching from his vantage point, Longstreet saw blue uniforms mustering for a flank attack. Hastily he sent off an aide to warn Pettigrew.

Now was the time for the troops along the sunken road to advance for the protection of the left flank. Close to the outskirts of the town some of their skirmishers moved forward, firing, against the skirmishers of the Eleventh Corps. But elsewhere no troops supported them, and their advance died out in this futile popping of skirmishers' rifles, having no effect upon the troops that Longstreet had sighted preparing for a flank attack.

What he had seen can only have been the 8th Ohio, a remarkable regiment under a remarkable commander. At this time, its action was so audacious that even the watching Union soldiers scarcely believed what they saw, and the report began to circulate that the commanding officer must be drunk.

But Lieutenant Colonel Franklin Sawyer was sober. He had been ordered to hold his position, and rather than retreat he was ready to fight the whole Confederate army. He was far enough to the north so that if he had merely stayed there, the attack might have missed his regiment entirely. But Sawyer was one who believed that a bold attack is the best defense. He mustered his men, who seem to have equaled him in audacity, to the grand total of about 160. He drew the regiment up in a single rank to make it look bigger. Then he ordered an attack upon six brigades of Confederates. Moreover, his orders were, not to stop and fire, but to charge.

At the same time, tearing down the Emmitsburg road on the double came all of seventy-five New Yorkers of the skirmish-line reserve. They had been well off to the north, and could have lain low, but Captain Samuel Chapman Armstrong of the 125th saw the opportunity. Whether they joined the Ohioans in the charge or fired from behind a fence is uncertain. At least they added a few dozen rifles at a critical moment.

Surely there can have been few more audacious attacks in the

history of warfare, but also we are given to understand that
fortune — in some cases, at least — favors the bold. So it was.

What Sawyer struck was Brockenbrough's already faltering
line which was now, so to speak, tottering forward, awaiting the
push that would overthrow it. Even still it must have outnumbered the Ohioans. But, as Sawyer and his men charged, the
Virginians did not stop to make any count. They dissolved as a
fighting unit, and went to the rear, the flags and the colonel with
them. Lieutenant Dunaway, Brockenbrough's aide, as he later
wrote, stayed long enough to fire his pistol at the advancing
Yankees, but this is the only claim to heroism at close quarters
that the brigade registered for the day. The Ohioans took some
prisoners, but did not capture any of the colors.

After this success, Sawyer changed front, putting his men
behind a fence, and the regiment began firing into the Confederate flank.

9

The loss of Brockenbrough's little brigade might be considered
of no great significance. But when a flank began to crumble,
there was always the question of where it would stop. Pickett,
alarmed, sent two aides galloping across, to try to rally the men,
though Brockenbrough's were past rallying and the others did
not need it. From the third line Lane swung his brigade to a
left-oblique to bolster up that flank, but one regiment and part
of another failed to get the order and kept ahead, thus further
increasing confusion.

Immediately, Osborn's gunners swung their muzzles toward
Davis's line. A shell struck the ranks of the 11th Mississippi,
killing five men.

The most serious general effect, however, was one of morale.
The Army of Northern Virginia was not used to seeing a brigade,
even a small one, go streaming off to the rear, with all its flags.

Everyone who saw it must have suffered a real shock. Even Pickett's men sensed that something disastrous had happened on the left; since they could not see very well because of the smoke and confusion, they tended to exaggerate.

10

Pickett sent Captain Bright back to Longstreet, to report that the Union position could now, it appeared, be carried, but could not be held without reinforcements. Riding back, Bright was appalled at the number of obviously unwounded men who were making for the rear. Ungenerously, he later stated that these were "parties of Pettigrew's command," though one can hardly see how such parties would have got to the rear of Pickett's line. With poor judgment, as he later confessed, Bright wasted precious time trying to halt some of the stragglers and turn them about.

"What are you running for?" he asked.

One man looked up in surprise at the mounted officer also heading rearward, and called back, "Why, good gracious, captain, ain't you running yourself?" As Bright had enough humor to admit, appearances were against him.

He found Longstreet, characteristically, sitting on his fence, alone and imperturbable. The aide gave his message. Just then a gentleman in civilian clothes came cantering up on horseback, and even at this crisis there was a pause for amenities.

The gentleman was no less than Lieutenant Colonel James Arthur Lyon Fremantle, of Her Majesty's Coldstream Guards, a visitor with Lee's army. In spite of his high rank with a famous regiment, Fremantle had never seen a battle until he arrived at Gettysburg. On this afternoon he had been riding about from place to place, trying to get the best view, and managing to see very little. Just now, however, he had passed through the woods, and must have crossed the path of the fugitives of Brockenbrough's brigade. He assumed them all to be wounded, and the sight brought to his mind a highly British comparison — "a perfect stream of them flocking through the woods in numbers as great as the crowd in Oxford Street in the middle of the day."

Now he called out, as Bright remembered, "General Longstreet, General Lee sent me here, and said you would place me in a position to see this magnificent charge." Then, to shift to his own record, he added, "I wouldn't have missed this for anything."

At the moment, no words could have been more untactful or inappropriate. Longtsreet laughed, but the laugh must have been bitter. "The devil you wouldn't!" he said, "I would like to have missed it very much; we've attacked and been repulsed: look there!"

Then, to return to Bright's testimony, Longstreet added, "The charge is over." He turned to the aide, "Captain Bright, ride to General Pickett, and tell him what you have heard me say to Colonel Fremantle."

Bright started off, but the general called again, "Captain Bright! Tell General Pickett that Wilcox's brigade is in that peach orchard [he pointed], and he can order him to his assistance."

As with so much in connection with Longstreet on this day, this twice-reported incident has been variously interpreted. His statement that the charge had already failed may seem premature, and can even be called defeatist. But Longstreet was in a position to observe the whole engagement, and his conclusion may also be considered merely realistic. In any case, his attitude could not be carried to the troops in the front line, or have any influence upon their conduct.

There is also the question of why Longstreet did not, to save time, send direct orders to Wilcox. The reason probably is that Longstreet did not think at this point that there was any use of sacrificing this force in a hopeless attempt to retrieve the situation. But, though he was of the opinion that the charge had failed, he could not act wholly on that assumption, and if Pickett, who was closer to the front, felt that reinforcements were needed, the decision should be his. Moreover, Wilcox may already have been placed under Pickett's orders, and Longstreet's words have been intended to serve as a reminder.

11

During the time it took Bright to deliver his message, the advance was continuing. Pickett's lines still moving by the oblique. Finally, however, after more than half the distance had been traversed, this sidling march brought Pickett's left to touch Pettigrew's right. The command along Pickett's line must then have been "*Forward!*"

Tactically, the Confederates had triumphed. They had completed a necessary series of somewhat complicated maneuvers, involving careful timing and executed under fire. Even the great Frederick might well have been pleased. Now, all complications solved, the single column began to advance directly against the Union position.

12

The next problem for the two divisions was the Union skirmish line. Already the Confederate skirmishers, having made contact with the enemy's, had halted and were allowing themselves to be absorbed into their own regiments. Now, as the main Confederate line swept down, the opposing skirmishers were in the usual uncomfortable position. Honor required them to stay and fire a few shots, and so did tactics, since the advancing line would thus be thrown into some confusion and forced to empty its rifles. But if the skirmishers stayed a little too long, they would

be caught between the enemy's fire and that of their own
line.

At this moment, as might have been expected, there came
a clatter of hoofs, and along the skirmish line galloped a big
man on a very tall light bay horse, in major-general's uniform,
white shirt-front flashing in the sunlight. He was in easy range
of the Confederates. "Don't shoot him! Don't shoot him!"
called out Colonel Mayo of the 3rd Virginia, reacting to the
chivalrous code that urged the sparing of an officer being conspicuously valiant. Thus aided for the moment, Hancock passed
on, in safety.

Whether by his example or by natural courage and firm discipline, the Union skirmishers did as well as could be expected,
though most of them, in the face of two advancing divisions,
could merely fire a shot or two and then run for it, or be over-
taken by the Confederate line and surrender.

From the skirmishers and from the Confederates there was
firing, and on both sides a few men fell. In front of Garnett's
brigade the skirmishers of Gibbon's division, largely from the
Philadelphia Brigade and the 19th Maine, fought so stub-
bornly that Garnett's men had to fire and then halt to load
and come on again. Some of the Confederates later considered this the first Union line and took the credit for
having defeated it.

But in a minute it was all over, and the skirmishers were
running back, full tilt — all except the casualties and the prisoners and a few who had merely dropped into some little depression
to let the shots of both sides go over them, in the hope that no
Confederate would stop to bother with them.

The fifty skirmishers of the 106th Pennsylvania fell in with
the two companies of their regiment which was on the right of
the 72nd. As their captain put it, he had no orders, "but it was
one of those actions in which every soldier felt that his duty was
to be in the fight."

13

Just about then, all along the Confederate line, the canister struck — no long-range pummeling, but murderous shotgun blasts. On the north it was the worst, where Woodruff's six Napoleons roared against Davis's brigade. Arnold's five rifles were not so devastating against Pettigrew's, but they were bad enough. Pettigrew's horse was shot, and the general went ahead on foot.

Garnett's men took the fire from Cushing's and Cowan's rifles. Kemper's men had to face frontal canister from the two guns that Rorty's men (Rorty was dead) could keep in action. Also, from the flank, Daniels and McGilvery's right-wing batteries were throwing canister, though for some of them the range was excessive.

In any case, for both divisions, the time was past for that parade-ground march with dressed lines, and the mounted officers riding gayly back and forth, and the flags advancing steadily. Many of the mounted officers were down, and the flags were dropping and coming up again and the lines were ragged — but still they came on! Now many of the soldiers marched "in a half stoop" with their heads bowed, as if walking into a storm.

From this time on, naturally enough, the Confederate accounts of the charge cease to be orderly, and lapse into flashes of sharply remembered but uncorrelated incidents and words — as Colonel Mayo remembered, "everything was a wild kaleidoscopic whirl."

Sometimes they even remembered who was speaking, as when it was Garnett, still on horseback, calling out, "Steady, men! Close up! A little faster; not too fast! Save your strength." Or words of other officers: "Steady, boys!" "Don't fire!" "Not too fast on the left!" "Close up!" Yes, most of all, as gaps opened, "Close up!" "Close up!" and still, "Close up!"

And other words also: "Major, take command; Colonel is down."

So too one of them remembered a lieutenant waving his sword and crying out, in words that mingled hysteria with literal and figurative truth, "Home, home, boys! Remember, home is over beyond those hills!"

Pickett himself had come riding to the Codori house and the big barn. About there he halted. The general of nine brigades (or eight, it would be now) was not supposed to go up with the front rank, but to exercise command from where he could best observe the situation.

Ahead, the men of his first line pressed on, heads futilely down against the storm of canister. Still there was no rebel yell; that shrill cry would go up when the moment came for the final rush. Now men were calling out to be allowed to fire back. The ones who had thought it would be an easy victory had lost that hope now. Ahead they saw, through the smoke of the cannon-fire, the low stone wall with the pairs of flags rising from behind it, and the gleaming rifle-barrels thick beneath the flags. The black gun-muzzles were spurting canister, and there was no look of anyone running away. So Garnett's and Kemper's men pressed ahead, waiting for the rifle fire.

14

Farthest advanced of the Union troops were Stannard's Vermonters. At the south of the line they held a little entrenchment of dirt and rails about a hundred yards in front of the other regiments. The 14th was on the left, the 13th next to it, a little to the rear, with Lieutenant Brown still carrying his hatchet instead of a sword. The 16th, having just been driven in from the skir-

mish line, was being re-organized behind the others. The men of
these regiments had done their first fighting on the preceding
day, but they had been well drilled and they were good natural
material for soldiers. Vermont was almost a frontier state, and
many of the men were life-long experts with rifles.

Now they lay and looked out over the little earthwork, and
heard their officers calling, nervously perhaps, since they too
were inexperienced, "Steady, boys! Hold your position; don't
fire till the word is given; keep cool; lie low until the order is
given to fire!" The brigade had nothing on its left, but anyone
could see that that did not matter, because the advancing Confederate line did not extend as far south as that of the Vermonters.

The tone of the officers' voices changed. They were calling,
"Make ready, take good aim, fire low!" The lines rose up and the
command came, "Fire!" — and then the crash of the first volley.

15

Kemper's brigade had been having the bad end all day, merely
because of the chance that it had happened to lead the column
of march that morning. Having been heavily pounded by the
artillery during the cannonade and during the advance, now it
took the first rifle fire, a devastating outburst, from in front and
from the oblique.

Again, with the musketry, smoke began to cover the field, and
add to the confusion. Also, troops that were subjected to the
punishing fire from one flank inevitably began to edge away to
the other — "to drift," as it was called. Still Kemper's men did
not break, and the flags, though they might go down for a
moment, came up again, and the line moved forward, now firing
back, even though it sidled off. Thus moving, and growing
shorter all the time, it would now not hit the Vermonters' line
at all.

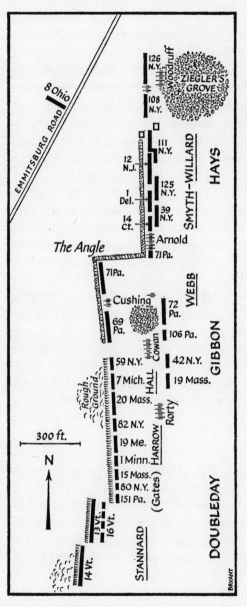

8 Ohio

EMMITSBURG ROAD

126 N.Y.
Woodruff
ZIEGLER'S GROVE

108 N.Y.

111 N.Y.

12 N.J.

1 Del.

125 N.Y.

39 N.Y.

14 Ct.

SMYTH-WILLARD

HAYS

The Angle

Arnold

71 Pa.

71 Pa.

Cushing

WEBB

72 Pa.

69 Pa.

106 Pa.

Cowan

GIBBON

59 N.Y.

42 N.Y.

HALL

7 Mich.

19 Mass.

20 Mass.

Rough Ground

82 N.Y.

Rorty

19 Me.

HARROW

1 Minn.

15 Mass.

(Gates)

80 N.Y.

151 Pa.

DOUBLEDAY

300 ft.

N

13 Vt.

16 Vt.

STANNARD

14 Vt.

BRYANT

Union Position
During the Advance

Divisions, e.g. GIBBON
Brigades, e.g. <u>HALL</u>
Batteries, e.g. Rorty

 One gun

〜〜〜〜 Stone wall

ıııııııııı Entrenchment

▬▬▬▬ Union troops

Woods

16

By this time Garnett's brigade and most of Archer's had come up to about 250 yards. At the word of command, the veterans of Gibbon's division sprang up — men who had known every battlefield from Balls Bluff onwards, Pennsylvanians and New Yorkers, men of Massachusetts and Michigan, frontiersmen of Minnesota, tall lumbermen of Maine. By regiment and brigade their line blazed with fire, and the smoke rolled out.

The shock of the lead slugs struck the Confederates. Half the flags went down. Along the line everywhere men dropped. Then the flags came up again, as others rushed to pick them up. The formation vanished, as the officers went forward waving their swords and the men followed them in fragments of lines, and clumps and bunches.

As they came up, with rifle fire added to canister, the slaughter was crippling. The color-guard of the 1st was shot down to a man. The flag of the 8th fell four times. Ahead, the men no longer saw the pairs of flags and the glitter of sun on rifle-barrels, but only eddying smoke and the red flashes behind it.

And through it all, canister and musketry, Garnett still rode on his black horse, untouched; Kemper, on his sorrel.

17

To the north of Garnett's line, Archer's brigade was involved with the two strong and high post-and-plank fences that edged the road. Farther to the south the fences had mostly been knocked down, and did not cause much trouble. Coming up to the first fence the Tennesseans and Alabamians beat at it with their musket-butts, but some unknown and unknowing Pennsylvania farmer had built it too stoutly to be thus knocked down. There was nothing to do but to go over the top; as they did, they offered a fine mark to the Pennsylvanians firing from just south of the Angle. Men toppled from the planks.

Where they went over, the road was a little below the surface of the ground, and a Tennessean remembered that many of them lay down in blissful quiet and safety for a moment, before going over the second barrier.

The worst of it was that the fences were on a diagonal. The line of the regiments went over like a wave that breaks on a slanting beach. This wrecked the formations, so that in spite of the fire each company had to halt for a moment to dress.

Even so, the little regiments went on and up the slope with such a rush that Colonel Fry thought victory was sure. And when he fell, shot through the thigh, with his fifth wound, he cried out, "Go on; it will not last five minutes longer!"

Farther to the north, Pettigrew's and Davis's brigades had not yet quite come within musketry range, the line of Hays's division being some eighty yards behind that of Gibbon's because of the jog in the stone wall. But these two big brigades were in no happy state of mind. They were coming close to the fences now, and just about as their left began to go over, they could expect to take the musketry fire. Already the canister was blasting them.

18

Amazingly, in all the brigades, when one would expect only excitement and hurry, sometimes there appeared a curious calm and almost a sense of leisure — though, of course, both of these are probably nothing but over-compensations for excitement and hurry. But men even paused and passed polite words, and later remembered the words.

Thus, as the lines were approaching the wall, a lieutenant of Armistead's brigade rushed to the left, grasped one of Archer's captains by the hand, and exclaimed, "Virginia and Tennessee will stand together on these works today!" (He thus supplied a key line for one of the best of the scores of poems later to be written about the charge.)

So also Private William Monte of the 9th Virginia, coming up the slope, was heard to exclaim, "What a sublime sight!" Then drawing his watch from his pocket, he remarked, "We have been just nineteen minutes coming." He thus supplied some valuable testimony as to the time consumed in the advance, and also his own last words, since immediately afterwards he was killed by a shell.

19

If we then take the moment of Monte's death as twenty minutes after the start of the advance, we find the situation approaching a major crisis. Against Hays's front Davis's and Pettigrew's brigades and Archer's left-flank regiments were still advancing steadily, not yet fully under rifle fire. Most of Archer's and all of Garnett's brigade, going up against the Angle, had been slowed by canister and by the rifle fire of three regiments; the Confederates were now firing back and inflicting punishment and they were inching ahead. But Kemper's brigade had been stopped by the frontal fire of Harrow's and Hall's brigades, and the enfilading fire from Stannard's and Gates's regiments. Kemper's men were firing back; he himself, still on horseback, was keeping them up; here and there some push went forward, only to be blasted by the rifle fire.

At this juncture occurred one of the strangest episodes of the fight, and the one which contained the possibilities of either success or failure, as accident or quick thinking might determine.

Kemper's brigade, already "drifting" to the left, began to move by the left flank — not toward the Union lines, but northward, to mingle with Garnett's brigade. It was not a planned movement, but can be plausibly explained. The guide for Kemper's brigade must now have been left. At the same time, there was much confusion, and men were falling rapidly. Suppose then that the left guide and some officers near-by were shot down, and a gap opened. Conscientious men and officers next in line moved toward the left to close the gap, and finding no guide, pressed on farther to find him, thus mingling with troops of Garnett's brigade, though in the confusion no one realized the error. Almost in a moment, a movement to the left could thus be established; once established, it could not be easily stopped. Company officers, even regimental officers, supposed that some order had been issued and they had failed to get it; they could not take the responsibility of stopping the movement. Besides, to officers and men alike it seemed sensible. Now, instead of pressing closer into the heat of the Union fire, they were moving parallel to it, and were also getting farther away from the deadly flanking fire from the right.

An error or momentary confusion on Kemper's part confirmed the movement, or may even have helped initiate it. Impetuously, the orator overcoming the general, he rose in his stirrups, pointed to the left with his sword, and shouted, "There are the guns, boys, go for them!" As one of his officers commented later, "It was an injudicious order." It sounds, however, more like an orator's exhortation than a general's command.

But, for better or for worse, Kemper was to shout no more commands. A bullet struck him, inflicting a seemingly mortal wound. "Old Buck" Terry, colonel of the 24th, took the brigade then, but there must have been some moments of uncertainty of command. Both Terry and some officers of Garnett's brigade tried to stop the rush to the left, but unsuccessfully.

So nearly all the brigade streamed off to the left, the blue flags one behind the other, the men being fired at, and themselves loading and firing as they went. On the right much of the 11th had already become separated, and did not move to the left. Here and there along the line individual men or little

groups stayed where they were, finding some spot of shelter.
The terrain also had its influence. Gibbon's front could be
readily attacked at either end, but in front of Hall's brigade was
some rough, bushy land, studded with good-sized rocks. It was
not a place where anyone would want to take a brigade, but it
was ideal for skirmishers and sharpshooters. So, once started to
the left, the flags naturally went on beyond this rough ground,
but just as naturally, allowing for the Confederate soldier's
individuality, many men peeled off and advanced here, singly or
in little groups, taking shelter behind the rocks and firing at the
infantry or at Cowan's gunners. Cowan had to shift some of his
guns from their main business and hold these sharpshooters
under control with some blasts of canister to keep his gunners
from being picked off. Some of these Confederates boldly
worked up close to the line of the 7th Michigan.

The flags, however, went on beyond the rocky ground, and
just to the north of it most of the brigade came pouring in behind
Garnett's and right into the flank of Armistead's, which was just
coming up. So far that brigade of the second line had not
suffered as heavily as the others, though it had absorbed enough
artillery fire to fall into some confusion. Now, with the sudden
inrush of Kemper's men, confusion became universal in Armistead's brigade too. The whole front, from the Angle to the
rough ground, measured a little less than two hundred yards, and
into it had crowded nearly all of Pickett's men, and at least half
of Archer's.

20

At this time the men of the nine Union regiments on Gibbon's
front line were in various states of activity and of mind.

On the south, Harrow's men smelled victory. The Confederate line had advanced against them, had apparently been unable to stand the fire, and had gone hastily off to the north, leav-

ing many dead. Harrow's men now had no one to fire at.

In the center Hall's two regiments toward the south were in much the same state, except that they could keep up a fire against the Confederates who were sheltering themselves among the rocks and bushes. The men of the 20th Massachusetts were shouting: "Fredericksburg!"

But the 59th New York, Hall's right-flank regiment, and the two Pennsylvania regiments near the Angle had no such sense of victory — at the most, they could only be glad that they seemed to have brought the enemy to a halt, or almost. The Confederates were blazing back at them, and men were dropping everywhere. Besides, even through the smoke the Pennsylvanians and New Yorkers could see the flags. No one on that firing line would have stopped to count, but probably fifteen blue flags and three red ones, each indicating a regiment, were massed on this narrow's front.

Once those flags started moving forward, the men with them might well overwhelm, by sheer weight of numbers, the regiments defending the Angle.

And, for some reason, the Angle was not strongly held, even though it was especially exposed to attack. With the aid of eight guns, now close to exhausting their canister, only 375 infantrymen were spread along 500 feet of front. Their only protection was a low stone wall with some rails on top; it might protect a man's lower legs, and that was about all; a charging Confederate could go across it anywhere.

Most badly placed of the three regiments was the 71st Pennsylvania, just rushed forward to the Angle, with nothing on its immediate right at all and its left resting uncertainly on Cushing's two guns. The men of the 69th Pennsylvania were well accustomed to their position, but their left flank had no infantry support. It merely stopped at the gap in the wall where a space had been left for Cowan's guns to fire through. South of that gap the 59th New York held the line, its right in the air, like the left of the 69th. This vital stretch of almost two hundred yards was thus held by what we may consider three isolated regiments, each with at least one flank exposed.

This, however, was the only part of the line that had some defense in depth. Behind the clump of trees was the 72nd Pennsylvania, a large regiment, for Gettysburg, numbering about 350, reinforced by a hundred men of the 106th. Somewhat farther to the south were two fragmentary but veteran regiments, the 42nd New York and 19th Massachusetts.

21

To the north Hays's men, crouched behind the wall, watched the Butternuts come on. They were ordered to keep low, and to hold their fire until the advancing troops got entangled with the fences — a little over two hundred yards in front of their own left. Then, as the line began to come over the first fence, Hays's great voice shouted *"Fire!"* In excitement the men forgot the orders, and stood up, and a sheet of flame burst from their line.

Theirs was a different situation from that of the badly outnumbered Union troops at the Angle. Hays could bring 1700 muskets to bear, and eleven guns. His men extended farther north than did the advancing Confederates, so that the 108th and 126th New York, and Woodruff's battery, could deliver a converging fire.

On the other side — with Brockenbrough gone and most of Archer's men in front of the Angle, with losses already heavy in the other two brigades and Trimble still too far back to be of use — Pettigrew probably had not more than 2500 men. His front line, which alone could do any firing, would be less than half of that, since it had taken heavier losses. If the second line had come up and begun mingling with the first, the resulting confusion would have off-set the accession of numbers.

Almost immediately the slaughter in Pettigrew's and Davis's brigades was crippling. The men fired back; many of them, though the line had largely gone to pieces, moved up the slope in spearheads under the flags. But the flags kept going down, and anyone could see that the Confederates could hope for little on that front, unless Trimble's two brigades pressed forward and drove the attack home.

22

At the moment, the situation was more hopeful on Pickett's front. In spite of losses the men massed below the Angle can scarcely have numbered fewer than three thousand. At odds, thus, of something like eight to one, they had a chance to overwhelm the three little regiments opposing them on the narrow front.

But this concentration of numbers had only been attained by a sacrifice. The brigades had fallen into some disorder because of losses during the advance, and now the piling in of Kemper's men from the right and of Armistead's from the rear was resulting in utter confusion. Theoretically, the Confederates should now have been six ranks deep; actually, the ranks had almost vanished. One of their officers described them as a "mingled mass, from fifteen to thirty deep" — a great swarm of men. The color-guards were keeping the colors up, but many men had lost the colors. Colonels were looking for their regiments. Majors had succeeded to the command of regiments, and did not know it. Captains looked around to see only a faithful sergeant and half a dozen men. Such a good soldier as Sergeant Easley had lost his men entirely.

Besides, of all this force only the men in the front could do any firing, and they had to face canister as well as musketry. With men thus placed the natural prejudice in favor of living tended to take over. Physically, there was no barrier to prevent any front-rank man from rushing ahead. But, as Civil War soldiers noted, there seemed to be in such a situation an imaginary line beyond which no man could advance and live. Psychologically, by mass reaction, the soldiers seemed caught between discipline and courage on the one hand, and prudence on the other. They would stand their ground and fire, but they would be hard to get moving forward again.

Having reached a point about twenty yards from the wall, the front then even sagged back — "recoiled," as one of their officers reported. Nevertheless, that mass of men was an asset likely to be decisive. Once started moving, it could sweep along, and might go on to victory.

So, partly by design and partly by accident, the situation had become that classic one in military history — column against line. Column can generally break line, and so it has been in the record of battles since Epaminondas sent his massed Thebans against the Spartan line at Leuctra. But column must sacrifice front to attain depth, and thus its flanks may become vulnerable. An alert line can lap around the flanks of the column and tear it to pieces.

Already three Union generals had grasped the situation, and were rushing to organize a counterstroke. From the rear of Hays's division Hancock saw the opportunity; he struck spurs, and galloped southward. Gibbon, on foot, was hurrying toward Harrow's brigade. Off to the south Stannard suddenly realized that his Vermonters might become agents of the destiny of a nation. It was a time to be measured in seconds.

23

Still the musketry crackled from both sides at the Angle, and now at last came release for a hero. As the desperately wounded Cushing directed the fire of his guns, he shouted an order. A bullet entered through his open mouth, killing him instantly, leaving no external mark. Sergeant Fuger took over, but they were close now to the last of the canister.

24

Thus, at the moment, the battle hung in balance, and the decision might well go to the side that could first make a new push. The immediate advantage lay with the Confederates — their men thick on the slope below the weakly held Angle. There, too, the generals were close at hand — Garnett still at the front on his black horse; Armistead coming up from the rear on foot. On the other side, Hancock had half a mile to ride, and Gibbon was unhorsed, and Stannard would need time to bring his regiments up.

PART VIII

High-water Mark

Everything is confused the worst kind.
— PRIVATE FREDERICK MANNES

So IT HUNG for a few seconds, while Hancock's horse took a leap or two, and the rifle fire was a dense crackle, and men dropped on both sides.

In those seconds, Webb ordered up his only supports — the 72nd with a hundred men of the 106th — forward on the right-oblique from behind the clump of trees, to fill the gap between the Inner Angle and the trees, as a second line behind the 71st.

Almost as the 72nd began to move, something broke the deadlock for the Confederates. Perhaps it was the mere pressure of men behind, perhaps something Garnett did; perhaps the rush forward of some unremembered captain or sergeant. All at once they came on at the Angle — Tennesseans, Alabamians, Virginians, all together! On a narrow front, a blunted wedge, they surged up the slope, on the run, raising — now for the first time — the high-pitched Rebel yell.

Looking from behind the wall, the men of the 71st saw themselves far outnumbered. They were holding a new and exposed position, and were a little shaky in discipline and morale. Against them, under the blue and red flags, came a wild swarm of yelling men.

From the flank Cushing's gunners fired canister. Some artillerymen ran, and some stayed to fight. Then, as the Rebels rushed the wall, the 71st — color-bearers and officers too — broke in wild flight, all but a few of them.

Those few stayed, firing to the last, and then were killed or surrendered. Among these was Sergeant Major Stockton, with a few men around him. They stuck it out, until the Confederates lapped around them, and then they threw up their hands.

There was a great surge of triumph in Confederate hearts. If one Yankee regiment broke and ran, why not others, why not all of them? But, the trouble was, they did not. A little way south the Confederates could see another regiment, beyond two guns, still holding to the wall. And, looking ahead past the backs of the panic-stricken, running fugitives, they now saw a solid line move in, nearly filling the gap between the wall and the trees. They fired at that line, and then the men in the line fired back, a solid opening volley.

Among the Confederates who had come over the wall, men went down, and suddenly those who were left realized that things were not as wonderful as they had looked for a moment. At the same time they realized that there was no pressure of men coming on behind them, and that they themselves had no particular formation and no special officer in command. They ebbed back over the wall. From its western side, where they had additional protection because of the slope, they began firing at the regiment ahead.

2

There was one good reason why the men at the wall had no leader. In the fire of that newly appeared regiment, Garnett had gone down. Hastily looking at the body, his aide saw that the general was dead. He took the watch from the pocket, a valuable instrument of war and a memento; he left the sword. (Rest, perturbed spirit!)

3

On the other side, those who had seen the rout of the 71st were almost as shaken as the Confederates had been by the rout of

Brockenbrough's men. The worst effect was on the 72nd, which was coming up, Webb leading the advance, just in time to have the rabble of fugitives go tearing around its right flank. Webb halted a fleeing artilleryman at sword's point, jabbing at him. Hysterically the fugitive screamed, "There's no use my going back, all the men are gone, killed!" But discipline was stiff in the artillery; once halted, he returned.

Behind the line of the 72nd, Lieutenant Haskell, riding back from delivering a message, found himself in the right place at the critical time; he spurred his horse into the path of the fugitives, drew his sword, and struck with the flat at the running men. "Halt!" he shouted. "Face about! Fire!" Some of the men halted. Then Webb, on foot, joined in the work of rallying them, and part of the 71st re-formed behind the line of the 72nd.

But almost immediately Webb was back with the 72nd. He saw the need for a quick counterstroke, to drive the Confederates from their suddenly acquired stronghold on the other side of the wall. The 72nd stood and fired, its own men dropping by twos and threes from the heavy fire against them. Webb ordered the regiment to charge, but it would not budge. Partly Webb was at fault; he did not give the order through the colonel, and he himself was so new to the brigade that the men hardly knew him. He shouted with all his might, but the musketry drowned him out. He gestured with his sword. Finally he seized the staff of the colors in the hands of the color-bearer, and strove to take the colors himself and rush forward. The color-bearer stuck to his staff, and wrestled with the general. At the same time Haskell was riding up and down behind the line of the regiment, also trying to get the men to advance, even crowding them with his horse.

But the men of the 72nd and those of the 106th on their left were much as the Confederates had been a few minutes before. They stood their ground and fired, but would not advance.

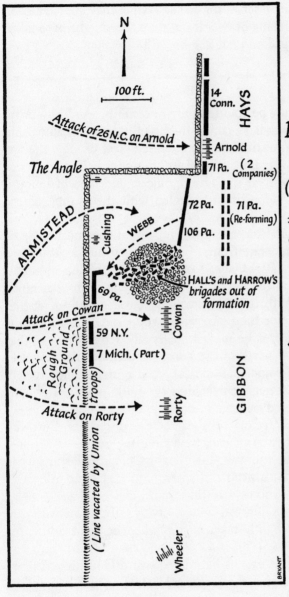

N

100 ft.

Attack of 26 N.C. on Arnold ➔

The Angle

ARMISTEAD

Cushing   WEBB

69 Pa.

Attack on Cowan

59 N.Y.

7 Mich. (Part)

Rough Ground

Attack on Rorty ➔

(Line vacated by Union troops)

14 Conn.

HAYS

Arnold

71 Pa.   (2 Companies)

72 Pa.   71 Pa. (Re-forming)

106 Pa.

HALL'S and HARROW'S brigades out of formation

Cowan

Rorty

GIBBON

Wheeler

BRYANT

High-Water Mark

(Ca. 3.30 P.M.)

⌇⌇⌇⌇ Stone wall

⟅⟅⟅⟅⟅ Entrenchment

Woods

━━━ Union troops in formation

⩘⩗⩘ Union troops out of forma- tion.

The Confederate troops were in dis- order, and their po- sitions cannot be accurately shown.

They held the wall south from the Angle, and were also among the trees. (See text.)

Logically it made no sense, for on the skyline they offered a good mark, and were taking heavier losses than they might have taken if they had charged and got it over with.

4

Still the time must be counted only in seconds. And now Armistead, the old black hat again at the tip of his sword, came pushing toward the front through the confused press of men, the flag of the 14th following him, other flags. In no formation whatever, just as they made their way ahead, officers and men of his regiments came on behind him; mingled with them, men of the other brigades.

As he came out from the press, he was at the south edge of the narrow Confederate front; at once he saw the situation and the opportunity. Right ahead of him was a Union regiment firing from behind the low stone wall, with two guns just north of it. Farther north the Confederates held the wall. What to do was to make for the place where the Confederates already were. At a little trot he moved diagonally across the front toward the spot just north of the guns, and behind him followed several flags and some hundreds of yelling men. They took a flank fire from the regiment behind the wall, and the stubborn Union gunners fired canister at such close range that a Confederate remembered feeling the heat of the discharge. But still, behind the gray-haired general, the rush came on.

Then he was at the wall, Lieutenant Colonel Martin of the 53rd with him. Armistead turned to him: "Martin? We can't stay here, we must go over to that wall."

In reply, Martin jumped across, crying, "Forward with the colors!" He had hardly taken a step when he went down, his thigh shattered.

Armistead leaped up, his hat-tipped sword held high, calling, "Come on, boys, give them the cold steel! Who will follow me?" The wall was so low here that he only had to make a high step to get over it. He went up the slope toward the slashing, where some abandoned guns were standing — and beyond the guns, the solid line of a regiment firing.

Behind him came a rush of colors and men, but not so many men as there might have been — a hundred, some said later; others, three hundred or more. No one knew.

They were mostly Virginians and seemingly of Armistead's own brigade, but some of Archer's men were with them.

Colonel Magruder of the 57th Virginia, going over the wall, was hit by one bullet from the 72nd and by another from the 69th simultaneously. The two crossed in his chest, and he went down mortally wounded.

Though those who went over were not many, they came on a broad enough front to sweep over the two guns by the wall and drive back the right wing of the regiment there.

5

That regiment was the 69th. Its right company along the wall was I; then, A, F, and D. As the Confederate rush came, orders were shouted for the three right companies to fall back and change front. I and A did so, but the captain of F was shot down at the moment, and that company failed to get the order. The attackers poured in upon F. Its men, overwhelmed, had to surrender. The edge of the Confederates came at Company D, but those men stood their ground; there was a wild flailing of musket-butts. A few of Cushing's artillerymen were with them — "fighting with handspikes and rocks and anything we could get our hands on." Then the Confederates brushed by, and went on.

In a moment the regiment was thus left with one company captured, two thrown back at right angles, and seven still in line at the wall, firing at the swarm of men in front. At the same moment, the left flank was probably turned too, although nobody may have noticed it in the confusion. Cowan's guns, firing canister from the left-rear of the regiment, were spraying the men from behind with stinging gravel and an occasional de-flected canister ball. The 69th was in about as bad a situation as a regiment ever was, but it stayed — with the Stars-and-Stripes and the green flag of Ireland both flying.

The only immediate reinforcement was General Webb him-self. Having given up the 72nd as a bad job, he set out to join the 69th. His reason was probably more personal than military. He felt disgraced by the behavior of most of his brigade, and merely wished to maintain his honor by joining his one front-line regiment. He walked, because running — even toward the front — was not considered quite fitting for a general. (Let us hope that he walked rapidly.) A bullet grazed his thigh, but he kept on.

He had started along the edge of the trees, and just about then the Confederates had come over the wall. Thus, as it happened — perhaps a unique occurrence — Webb and Armistead, two generals, both on foot and advancing, passed each other within about ten paces. Webb joined the right-wing companies of the 69th, and did what he could to encourage their stand.

One of those men later declared with fine understatement, "It was, you might say, a fight at close quarters. . . . Everybody was loading and firing as fast as they could." And he added, matter-of-factly, "We thought we were all gone." As a man of I Company put it, "We followed and fired and loaded as we fell back, looking and praying for help." But they stayed.

6

The 72nd still held the crest. Against them now, from the Angle, through the slashing, came the wild rush of Confederates. The 72nd stood and fired. Probably the men could see that the attackers were only a desperate few — a spearhead with no spear behind it. Ahead of the flags, leading the rush, was a gray-haired officer, waving a sword with a black hat on top of it. Dozens of men of the 72nd and of the two thrown-back companies of the 69th were firing at the tip of the spearpoint. Just before reaching one of the abandoned guns, the gray-haired officer toppled, his sword and hat almost striking the gun.

Their leader gone, too few to press ahead into the frontal fire of better than four hundred rifles, most of the Confederates dropped and took shelter, firing back. But some of them began to work into the clump of trees and around the thrown-back flank of the 69th. No Union infantry was in the trees to stop them. A few advanced forward, beyond where the general fell. One of these was Sergeant Easley, who had been at Armistead's side. Easley went a step or two farther, dropped behind the abandoned gun, and kept firing until a shot smashed his ramrod. Also, the men who advanced into the trees went farther than Armistead.

This, then, was High-water Mark.

7

Across the field those near Longstreet congratulated him that his column had stormed the Union position. The general was not inclined to accept the congratulations, seeing too many signs of confusion in the troops.

He himself had not been able to do much to aid in the attack, but he had done what he could — sending two messages to Pickett and one to Lane.

8

Now let the galloping horse move forward a little, to have brought Hancock to where Colonel Devereux, standing by the

line of his 19th Massachusetts, with Colonel Mallon's 42nd
New York on its right, looked anxiously toward the clump of
trees, which largely hid the area around the Angle. Without
seeing for certain, Devereux knew that the Angle must have
been overrun. He had seen the fugitives of the 71st; he had seen
that Webb was in trouble with the 72nd. He heard the shots,
just at the other side of the trees. He wished to get into the
fight, but hesitated to leave his post without orders. "We must
move," he was saying impatiently to Mallon. Just then he saw
Hancock come galloping from the north. He halted the general.
"See, general," he cried. "They have broken through; the colors
are coming over the stone wall; let me go in there!"

Hancock, his horse reined back on its haunches, spoke sharply
to the point, "Go in there pretty God-damned quick!"

The general spurred on to the south, and Devereux shouted
to his men and to Mallon.

9

The seconds ticked away. When Armistead had gone over the
wall, there was a hundred-yard gap between the men of the 106th
and the thrown-back companies of the 69th, fighting without
supports. What the Confederates might have done is obvious.
Pouring into that gap, one or two brigades should have overwhelmed the 69th, and rolled up Hall's and Harrow's line from
the flank. The other brigades, pushing on through the trees
between the 106th and 42nd, should have outflanked them both,
and then taken Hays's line with an enfilade fire, so that Pettigrew and Trimble could have advanced with the frontal attack.

But can we even, any longer, think in terms of brigades? The
brigadiers were down, and many of the field officers. The regiments were in confusion, and the men themselves uncertain
even as to whom to obey or to follow. Between the time when
Armistead went over the wall and the time when the chance had

been lost, probably less than two minutes ticked away. Historians
write of the Hundred Days of Napoleon; so we might write of
these Hundred Seconds of the Confederacy. Then — almost
literally — the road lay open to Washington.

10

But before the second-hand could swing into its third circuit,
Devereux had shouted orders to the two regiments — rallying,
as he wrote, "New England's sturdy courage and Ireland's fiery
valor." On the right-oblique, at the double, the two little regiments, about two hundred men, moved sidling, neither quite a
line nor quite a column; the Tammany boys were leading, the
Bay Staters trailed. There was little keeping of formation, but
the veterans knew what was expected. As one of them put it,
"The order was to go in; but we did not pay much attention to
any order, but went in."

Ahead they could see more Confederates, coming over the
wall — not in regiments or companies, but men alone and in
little bunches, hurrying up to the farthest front, the final chance
for victory.

In the middle of the tree-clump and between it and the wall,
the two regiments met the Confederates — those that had come
across with Armistead and the others. At deadly close range the
rifles blazed, and the men dropped. The color-bearer of the 19th
went down mortally wounded, but rose with a convulsive effort
and waved his flag in the face of the enemy, not ten yards distant.
The color-bearer of the 42nd also went down.

The Confederates probably had more men, but Devereux and
Mallon had their regiments under better control, and their men
were equally determined. No Confederate would go through
there unless a lot of killing should be done!

They settled to that bloody work on both sides. But the gap
was plugged — after a fashion and for a time at least, since two

hundred men hardly cover a front of a hundred yards. And even with this help for its left, how long could the over-pressed 69th hang on?

11

So, from close to the Inner Angle across to the trees, the men of the 72nd and the 106th, unwilling to charge, stood their ground, and took their losses, and fired back. In the trees was the 42nd; partly in the trees and extending out into the open stretched the thin line of the 19th. Then came the hard-hit men of the 69th, fighting in two directions, taking heavy losses but holding to their little front of stone wall as if it were Gibraltar itself. Webb was with their right-wing companies, but the situation offered no chance for generalship.

Many of the 69th were lying prone behind the wall, since the fire on their front was too much to take, but they were still staying there, loading as best they could. Captain Hill of the 19th Massachusetts, which itself was doing no bad job, took occasion to notice the 69th. He later complimented its men in terms which were all the more telling for their fine Yankee understatement, "They were doing some pretty good fighting." He also expanded a little: "The 69th appeared to be fighting on their own hook. They did not yield one inch, and the enemy swarmed right over them, but whenever they got a chance to get in a shot here and there they let the enemy have it."

Still the second-hand had not completed another circuit. Time might seem to have run out for the Confederacy, but many of the Confederates did not know it. When such men still press forward on a battlefield, who can say that they may not succeed?

12

To the left of the 69th was that gap in the wall, held by no infantry, covered by Cowan's fire. There some wildly adventuring Confederates charged for the guns. (Yet it was a shrewdly planned attack; they waited to catch the gunners loading, and they had the support of the skirmishers in the rough ground.) A young major, waving his sword, led the charging men, and they were only a few. They flung back the right wing of the 59th New York, and dashed for the battery, two hundred feet away. "Take the guns! Take the guns!" they were yelling.

To load at all under the murderous rifle-fire was close to impossible, but Cowan called for double canister. As he spoke, his lieutenant dropped at his side. Private McElroy shouted, "Captain, this is our last round!" and Cowan shouted back, "I know it, Jake." Then Jake went down with three bullets in his face. Private Gates rammed the charge home, and fell with a shot through both legs.

The Confederates, the major still leading, were well up the slope.

Suddenly, Hunt himself was with the battery, on horseback; forgetting to be a general, carried away by excitement, he was firing his revolver, as he yelled, hysterically and irrelevantly, "See 'em! See 'em!"

Then Gunner Mackenzie threw up his hands as the signal, just as he fell across the trail of his gun, wounded. From each of the five guns spurted the blast of canister.

As the smoke cleared, there were no Confederates in front. The body of the young major lay closest. (On the monument of Cowan's battery, you will read, "Double canister, at ten paces.")

Also, as they looked around, they found Hunt pinned beneath the dead body of his horse. They hurriedly pulled him loose, and mounted him on a sergeant's horse, and he spurred off, shouting back over his shoulder to Cowan, "Look out or you will kill our men!" The captain was a little miffed that instead of being congratulated on his determined stand he had been warned against such an elementary mistake as shooting into the men along the wall.

Then, canister exhausted, the men dragged the guns back behind the crest.

13

At the moment Gibbon was trying to get the 19th Maine to swing out and take Pickett's men on the flank. But the men were too excited to listen to orders — "All yelling, hallooing, shooting." Then Gibbon felt a stinging blow in the left shoulder, and the blood from the wound began trickling down from his hand. He grew faint, and was helped from the field.

14

And still Pettigrew's North Carolinians and Mississippians, with a few Tennesseans and Alabamians, advanced up across that gently sloping field, which one soldier incongruously noted was "covered with clover as soft as a Turkish carpet." Against them from behind the wall there was the unbroken smoke and flame of the musketry, and from the flanks the batteries were firing canister. Well could a post-war poet lament:

> Ah, how the withering tempest blew
> Against the front of Pettigrew!

Here, more than elsewhere, men noted that through the noise of the firing they heard a kind of great moaning and the cries of the wounded. One described it as strange and terrible, not any recognizable shouts or yells, but the unleashed primitive cries of men wounded and men fighting, a vast mournful roar.

Pettigrew's men now showed scarcely anything that could be called a line, but had disintegrated into clumps of men around the flags, advancing as they might, halting to fire back, moving ahead once more if anyone would lead.

Company A of the 11th Mississippi, the University Grays, had lost touch with the field officers. "For God's sake, John," shouted Lieutenant Baker to Captain Moore, "give the command to charge!"

"No, I cannot take the responsibility."

So Baker himself shouted the command, and the remnant of the company dashed forward, each man pretty much for himself, but with Baker leading.

In the same regiment, Private O'Brien, the color-bearer, fell dead. Privates Griffin and Smith stooped together to pick up the flag, but Smith got it. After a few steps both Smith and Griffin went down wounded. Private Marion picked up the flag, went a step or two, and fell dead. Then Private Marable raised it, and went on.

On the right, some North Carolinians of the 26th charged desperately at Arnold's guns, only to be blown to pieces by double canister, that battery's last shots.

Behind the stone wall, the five New York regiments and the men of Connecticut, Delaware, and New Jersey — four deep in places — kept up their devastating fire in spite of their own losses. Colonel Sherrill, commanding the New York brigade, was shot through the abdomen and carried off dying. Colonel MacDougall of the 111th took command until he was wounded, and then the brigade went to Lieutenant Colonel Bull of the 126th. Colonel Smyth, commanding the other brigade, was wounded in the face, but maintained his command.

Hays, watching the situation, saw an opportunity. The attack on his right, which he had feared, had not materialized, and so he could use the 126th. No troops were in its front, and he ordered it to swing forward, to a line with the skirmish-reserve under Captain Armstrong and with the 8th Ohio, thus to pour a flank fire into every Confederate attempt to advance. In addition, two of Woodruff's Napoleons — those murderous four-and-a-half-inchers — were rolled down by hand to join this flanking line.

Somewhere into the front of Davis's brigade, now that the

range had shortened, the Jerseymen were firing their blasts of buckshot. According to one account much of that brigade disintegrated suddenly — perhaps when it met this fire.

In the ranks of the 14th Connecticut the few men who had breech-loaders fired so rapidly that the barrels grew too hot to use. The loaders poured precious water from their canteens down the barrels to cool them.

Yet still the Confederates came on. Since later their own compatriots slandered them, let the enemy testify. Colonel Smyth reported that all along his brigade-front they advanced to within thirty or forty feet, and "fought with a fiery determination that he had never seen equalled" — and he had seen much valor. Colonel MacDougall was willing to shorten the distance to "within a few feet."

Pettigrew, unhorsed, climbed the fences along the road, and advanced half way up to the wall. Then he was wounded in the left hand, painfully. He sent an aide, also on foot, to Trimble, to hurry the third line forward.

Still the men struggled on. Nearly every regiment preserved the pitiful tale of its farthest advance. Lieutenant Colonel Graves of the 47th North Carolina seems to have taken the largest body of men forward. He kept 150 under his command, telling them that supports would come. None came, and finally the men that were left had to surrender.

Mostly it was a few men here or there beneath a flag or behind some officer or sergeant. But if such a group pushed ahead and neared the wall, these remaining were never more than a dozen, and could do nothing, at the last, but surrender. Thus a sergeant of the 26th North Carolina and one man carrying the flag came up to the wall. The Union men pitifully held their fire, and one of them cried out, "Come over on this side of the Lord!" So the two surrendered. Thus also it went with some men of Company C of the 2nd Mississippi. The University Grays reported that Lieutenant Baker fell within ten feet of the Union line, and the

11th Mississippi claimed that Private Marable planted the colors on the wall, before he went down wounded, to be captured along with the flag.

As the Union men remembered, no armed Confederates ever got so close. But in the smoke and excitement, who could be sure?

The Jerseymen recalled particularly one "smooth-cheeked lad," who ran ahead of the others, only to fall dead within twenty feet. There was another Confederate who reached the little barn at the north end of the wall, and from behind it, refusing to surrender, fired one shot before he fell.

But what gain was all this slaughter but a tale to be told and a few Union casualties? From the military point of view all it was accomplishing was to keep Hays from sending reinforcements to drive the Confederates back from the trees.

15

What was happening elsewhere at the moment was to a remarkable extent tied up with the actions of that unusual lieutenant, Frank Haskell.

Last seen, he was trying to urge the 72nd to charge. Like Webb, he gave this up as useless. Looking around, he saw himself the only mounted man in sight, and he did not know where to find General Gibbon. As a staff-officer, Haskell was allowed much latitude of action, and as a natural-born soldier, he was quick to act. Instantly, he sized the situation up. The critical spot was the Angle. Troops were needed, not only to plug the gap, but also to drive the Confederates back and regain the wall. Where could troops be found? He looked to the north, but the roar of musketry along Hays's front told him that no troops could be spared. He thought of Doubleday, but he had no great regard for Doubleday, and did not think that that general would send help. Then he realized that there was little or no firing along the lines of Hall's and Harrow's brigades. He struck his spurs in, galloped down past the clump of trees, and came to Colonel Hall, calmly standing in the rear of his line.

"How is it going?" Hall asked.

"Well, but Webb is hotly pressed, and must have support or he will be overpowered. Can you assist him?"

"Yes."

"You cannot be too quick."

"I will move my brigade at once."

"Good."

The lieutenant galloped on to take the same word to Harrow. Hall turned to shout his orders. Actually, two of his regiments had already gone to the clump of trees, and the 59th New York had plenty to do on its own front. Hall tried to shift the 7th Michigan and 20th Massachusetts, but the excitement and the sound of the firing were such that orders could scarcely be heard. At the attempt to withdraw them from the line and face them to the right, both regiments, though veteran, fell into confusion. Finally, about half the 7th remained where it was, firing to the front. The rest of it and the 20th went rushing off to the clump of trees, in almost complete disorder, the men unable to hear any orders, and simply following after their sword-waving officers and the colors.

Riding on, Haskell could not find General Harrow, or at least could not, later, remember having done so. In some way, however, the idea of going to the rescue of Webb's shattered brigade was transmitted. Harrow's five veteran regiments, released by the shift of Kemper's brigade to the left, went rushing to the critical point.

All this action must have consumed several minutes at least. During this time the Confederates, thickly massed below the Angle, still remained in disorder, and had not managed to do anything of military significance. What they apparently needed was a Lieutenant Haskell.

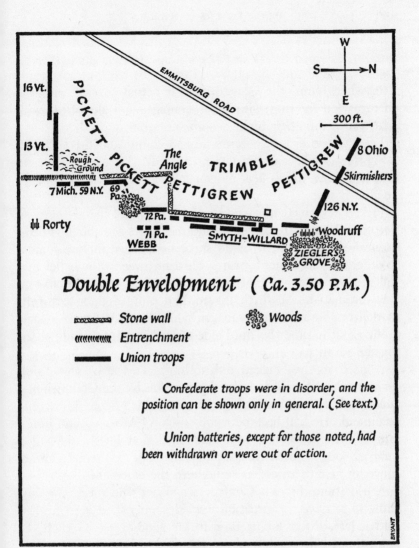

Double Envelopment (Ca. 3.50 P.M.)

~~~~~~~~~~ Stone wall   🌳 Woods

ᴍᴍᴍᴍᴍ Entrenchment

████ Union troops

Confederate troops were in disorder, and the position can be shown only in general. (See text.)

Union batteries, except for those noted, had been withdrawn or were out of action.

16

Everywhere, thus, the Confederates in actual contact with the enemy were fighting with great courage, and doubtless with great skill. But their higher command seemed paralyzed.

Lee gave no orders, because he had committed the battle to Longstreet, or because he saw no remedy. Longstreet gave no orders, because in his best judgment he believed the combat to be already lost.

Pickett remained near the Codori house, and made one positive contribution. Receiving Longstreet's message about Wilcox, he immediately sent, in rapid succession, three mounted aides to order those brigades forward. He sent three in the belief that the fire was so heavy that only one of them might be able to ride through it. All three arrived, and proceeded, successively, to deliver the same message, considerably to Wilcox's amazement. By the time the third aide arrived, he was already ordering the advance.

Aside from this, Pickett did nothing. To the present point, he had behaved well, but now his position by the Codori house could no longer be justified as one from which he could exercise command. He had become wholly useless. At this point, honor and military procedure both demanded that he should gallop forward, join his own troops, and either inspire them to an advance, or give them orders suitable to the emergency.

At this time the only Confederate officer who was doing anything to retrieve the situation was Alexander, and even he had started late. After taking time to say good-bye to Garnett, he had galloped desperately about the field, appalled to find that most of his batteries had got so low in ammunition that there was no use in advancing them. In the end he was able to send eighteen guns forward, but these moved largely as individual pieces or by sections, lacking any coherence into batteries.

This plan to advance the artillery and thus support the infantry on its right flank was a favorite one with both Alexander and Longstreet. Its possibility of success, however, rested upon the crippling of the Union artillery in the great cannonade. But most of these batteries were not seriously damaged; moreover, they could no longer fire at the Confederate infantry, now that it was so closely engaged with the Union infantry. Accordingly, all the gunners along McGilvery's long line opened enthusiastically on the advancing guns, and with every advantage. Not only were they already in established positions, but also they could concentrate at about three to one. As a result, most of the Confederate guns were smothered. Some of them were not even withdrawn, but were left beside their slaughtered teams, as the artillerymen took shelter.

Only a few of the guns managed to fire effectively. At the moment, most of Hall's and Harrow's brigades were jammed at the edge of the trees, six or more deep. Some Confederate gunners, recklessly taking the chance of firing into their own troops, sent several shells into this mass. These plowed through the crowded men and exploded with frightful results, the loss falling most heavily upon the 20th Massachusetts. But either these were lucky shots, or else the fire from McGilvery's line became too heavy for the gunners. By the time, almost immediately, when a decisive movement of infantry began, the Confederate guns were unable to do anything to prevent it, although the maneuvering regiments exposed a most vulnerable flank.

17

By this time, Hancock had scarcely completed his ride, since all these events are to be telescoped within a few minutes. In fact, thus riding to put Stannard's brigade into action, the general must have arrived there while Devereux's two regiments were still rushing toward the clump of trees. From his moment of first seeing the move of Kemper's brigade to the left, Hancock had decided to throw the Vermonters upon Pickett's flank. Stannard, himself, had had the same idea, and by the time that Hancock spurred up, shouting orders, Stannard already had his men in motion.

Now the long months of tedious close-order drill suddenly paid off for the Vermonters. From double-ranked line the 13th swung into column of fours, and marched north toward the enemy, in front of Harrow's now vacated line. Then came the command, *"Change front forward on first company!"* The men broke from column, and moved out, along the edge of the rough ground, going into line of battle within easy range of the flank of that disorganized mass of men just below the Angle. As it moved, the regiment turned upon Orderly Sergeant James B. Scully, twenty-year-old ex-dry-goods-store clerk of Burlington, who thus became, as a Vermont historian has put it, "the pivot of the pivotal movement of the pivotal battle of the war."

Before the regiment could complete its maneuver, the alarmed Confederates opened fire. Some of the left-wing companies of the 13th, thus caught while in motion and unable to reply, wavered for a moment, but one of Stannard's aides rallied them, and they went on into line.

The 13th was a big regiment, still mustering probably more than four hundred rifles. Company by company, as they came into line, the Vermonters opened fire. As the roar of musketry intensified and the smoke rose up, the Union soldiers fighting desperately to hold the wall, or struggling in the clump of trees, or firing from the skyline beyond the trees, all sensed that the battle had turned. Some of their own troops, they would not care which ones, had come in upon the enemy's flank and were tearing at it.

Still that musketry intensified, as the 16th Vermont, with farther to go than the 13th, moved out from behind its sister regiment and opened fire. The 13th was pushing forward, shortening the range, until the officers fired their revolvers.

The Confederates reacted, trying desperately to shift men to form a front against this new attack. An alert and active officer was trying to rally the men and face them around. A Vermont marksman picked him off. No troops ever mustered would be likely to withstand, for long, such a surprise attack driven home upon their flank.

Looking from higher up on the slope, Doubleday was waving his hat and shouting, "Glory to God, glory to God! See the Vermonters go it!"

At this moment the Union troops, in the classical tradition of Marathon and Cannae, had accomplished that quintessence of military consummations — a double envelopment. On the south the line of the Vermont regiments extended out well toward the road, with close to 900 rifles in action. On the north the 126th New York, Armstrong's skirmishers, and the 8th Ohio stretched beyond the road in a more thinly held line, totaling about 450 rifles, strengthened by the two Napoleons. Each flanking line concerned itself with the Confederates in its immediate front, but the distance between the two lines was only about 1200 feet, easy range for the rifles. Anything fired a little high had a possibility of hitting some farther-off Confederate, and the report for Garnett's brigade states that it was "receiving a fire in front, on the right, and on the left." Almost certainly, even, stray bullets from the Ohioans and New Yorkers hit some of the Vermonters, and vice versa.

At this moment of possibly imminent victory, Hancock was observing the battle from the left of his line, near the position of the 14th Vermont. As he was just addressing Stannard, a Minié ball passed through the pummel of his saddle, and pierced deep into his groin, driving along with it a bent tenpenny nail from the saddle along with some splinters of wood. Stannard's aides caught him as he slumped, and eased him to the ground. They staunched the blood that gushed from the ugly wound, and called for stretcher-bearers. But the general refused to leave the field, and continued to observe the action.

18

Though generals went down, there was no ceasing in that savage struggle around the Angle. Well might a private of the 72nd, testifying under oath in later years, protest that he could not be expected to be clear and exact, because at such a moment, "Everything is confused the worse kind!"

On the flank the Vermonters had fired eight or ten rounds by this time, and Pickett's badly punished men had been able to form scarcely anything that could be called a front against this new and unforeseen attack.

The 69th still held. Now, indeed, the Vermonters on one side and on the other the troops fighting in the grove had taken some of the pressure off.

Beyond the 69th and in the clump of trees, as confusedly as the Confederates below the Angle, Hall's and Harrow's men, eight regiments mingled, held back the spearpoint. Some of them had fired upwards of fifteen rounds by now, and received as many, all at close range.

North of the trees the 72nd and 106th stood doggedly and fired, their own dead marking in a straight line the position from which the men would neither advance nor retreat. At the same time, the two companies of the 71st that had not been involved in the rout held their little stretch of wall between Arnold's guns and the Inner Angle; they did good service by enfilading the line of the east-west wall, and so preventing the Confederates from establishing themselves there.

On the other side, Confederate riflemen, three and four deep, lined the wall south from the Angle, beneath a row of red and blue flags. Mostly they fired straight ahead at the regiment on the skyline, but the right of their line could fire, on the oblique, at the Yankees between the trees and the wall. To fire meant being fired back at, but the Confederates had the advantage of being behind the wall. At their right two abandoned guns stood in a no man's land. (Just at the Angle the wall and bank were highest, and in that protection — right on the bare rock that you can still see — Sergeant Major Stockton and his comrade prisoners of the 71st lay and considered their case. Close on both sides of them were Butternuts, loading, popping up to fire over the wall, ducking down to load again. One of them had water sloshing about in his canteen, and Stockton asked for some, but the Reb refused.)

The most advanced Confederates were still fighting at close quarters among the trees — those who had followed Armistead in the first rush, and the others that had gone forward later.

But time had been for any chance of victory for the Confederates, and most of them must now have known it. Not more than fifteen minutes had probably elapsed since that great moment when they had seen the Blue-bellies run from the Angle and the flags go backward. But so much had the situation altered, so many things had shifted, that the memory of that event was as of something that had happened to them at Chancellorsville or Sharpsburg. They had even lost their advantage in numbers, and were now fighting, over all, about man for man. Indeed, since many of the Confederates were not on the firing line, they found themself outnumbered at the critical points. So, in the clump of trees, the Union troops must have totaled well over a thousand, and the Confederates had only the remnants of the few hundred who had crossed with Armistead and never been heavily reinforced. But the Confederates, taking advantage of all the cover, fought back, not even giving ground when the Yankees pushed up to within a few yards.

Major Rice of the 19th Massachusetts remembered no lack of Confederates, there in the thick underbrush, "The grove was fairly jammed with Pickett's men, in all positions, lying and kneeling. Back from the edge were many standing and firing over these in front. . . . Every foot of ground was occupied by men engaged in mortal combat, who were in every possible position which can be taken while under arms, or lying wounded or dead." But — significantly, perhaps — there was no Rebel yell, though the air was full of Union hurrahs.

On both sides organization was lost. By this time few Confederate officers were left. The Union officers, however, could do little except wave their swords excitedly and join in the shouting. As a soldier put it, "Every man fought on his own hook." The confusion gave some advantage to the Confederates, since unorganized men could do well enough at holding a line, but could not so readily advance to thrust others from a position. The Union lines even showed a tendency to retire, by a kind of automatic action, since a man fell back from the front to load and was not likely to advance quite so far again when it was his time to fire. Once, to stop such backward creep, the file-closers of the 19th Massachusetts joined hands and kept the line steady by main force.

The men were jammed in to an average of six deep. When a man had loaded, he pushed his way to the front to fire. Sometimes he had to dodge around to get a place through which to point his musket, and in the confusion men might be shot from the rear. With men firing from everywhere the noise of the discharges was deafening.

Sometimes the lines even surged together, and there was a sudden swinging of clubbed muskets. In one of these encounters, Private De Castro of the 19th knocked down the color-bearer of the 14th Virginia, he himself using the staff of the Massachusetts state colors as a club. He seized the Virginia flag, brought it back, and thrust it into the hands of his colonel.

A soldier of the 19th Maine remembered the men fighting "in some places within rifle-length of each other and other places hopelessly mingled." Men in the rear picked up some of the

plentiful stones, and hurled them over the heads of their comrades.

Everything, Colonel Devereux remembered, seemed trembling
in the balance — "Whichever side could get a motion forward
must surely win."

19

Far off to the south, approaching the Emmitsburg road almost
half a mile beyond the Codori house, Wilcox was bringing two
brigades forward — his own Alabamians, about 1050; Perry's
Floridians, a mere remnant, of less than four hundred. By far
too few, and by ten minutes too late!

Also about this time, Hill ordered Wright's brigade forward.
The Georgians came out on the open slope below the crest of
Seminary Ridge, but it would take them twenty minutes to
march across and bring support to Pickett. Longstreet ordered
them back. By now there was no question; the men at the Angle
could not maintain themselves much longer. No call to expose
another brigade to the devastating artillery fire! It might be desperately needed later to repel a counterattack.

What, indeed, if he had summoned all his reserves — Posey
as well as Wright, and Mahone behind them? When it came
to reserves, were not the Confederates fighting in Union terri-
tory, and would not Union troops be able to get there faster?
Better, thought Longstreet, to husband all these brigades. In all
probability, Lee agreed. At least, though present, he did not
countermand the order sending Wright back.

Indeed, the game of mustering reserves was one that two
could play. Meade and Hunt had been slow, but now the batteries and brigades were coming fast. Wheeler's, the 13th
New York, three 3-inch guns, got there first, and swung into
line near Thomas's old position. Not far behind and driving
hard were Weir's C of the 5th U. S., Fitzhugh's K of the 1st

New York, Parson's A of the 1st New Jersey. The infantry too was moving. Robinson's hard-fought division of the First Corps was marching to fill that gap on Hays's right. Off to the south the men of the Third Corps, knowing from the firing that the Second was hard-pressed and remembering that it had come to help them on the day before, had been clamoring to go to the fight; now two brigades were marching, and close at hand. Also, a brigade from the Twelfth and two from the Sixth were moving. Still others were available. If the contest was to be decided by the throwing in of reserves, the Confederates, with only three brigades uncommitted, were badly outweighed.

20

On Hays's front, the fight continued desperately. A Union officer, writing a letter on the next day, remembered that the Confederates seemed to come on in three waves. If so, this might mean that Pettigrew's two lines and Trimble's one maintained some kind of integrity to the very end. But, in general, lines had ceased to mean much.

Old Isaac Trimble, on his mare Jinny, had come riding up to the road with his two brigades of North Carolinians, weakened by casualties and stragglers. At the road, looking ahead into the smoke where Pettigrew's men were still advancing gallantly, he felt a sudden hope, and called out to his aide, "Charley, I believe those fine fellows are going into the enemy's line."

As he was trying to get his own men over the fence and forward, a bullet smashed his left leg and wounded the mare. He could still keep to the saddle, but he advanced no farther.

Instead, he sent a message to Lane, couched in the best military third person, "General Trimble sends his compliments to General Lane, and wishes him to take charge of the division, as he has been wounded." Then he told the aide to add, by way of compliment, "He also directs me to say that if the troops he had the honor to command today for the first time couldn't take that position, all hell can't take it."

Though Trimble had stopped, his regiments went ahead, in the good Rebel fashion of taking the flags forward and having the men follow. Some of Scales's men on the right, following behind Archer's regiments, even went to the Angle. On the left, some of Lane's men advanced to "within a few yards of the stone wall."

All would not serve! Soon in little groups and singly, the wounded hobbling along, the men came streaming back. Trimble with his shattered leg, still sitting the wounded mare, looked right and left and everywhere saw men making for the rear. With the shock of his wound the fighting spirit and the hope had gone out of him.

An aide, willing to attempt the impossible, was asking whether he should rally the men and renew the charge.

"No," said the general, "the best thing the men can do is to get out of this; let them go."

"Little Jim" Lane, unhorsed, short on inches but all fighting-man, still pushed the attack, and ordered what was left of the 18th and the 33rd to move against the flanking force. But the colonel of the 33rd lacked Lane's fury for the battle. "My God, general!" he exclaimed, "Do you intend rushing your men into such a place unsupported, and when the troops on the right are falling back?" Persuaded that the action would only result in a sacrifice of men, Lane revoked the order.

Even where they were, the men were swept by musketry from in front and by musketry and canister from the left. Soon the few left in those regiments also went back. They were the last Confederates to leave that part of the field.

21

But still they fought at the Angle, men on both sides tense with the feeling that something soon must break. And still, though almost forgotten in the crowded story, some Confederates hung on at the right of the line, and a few of them even made a try for victory.

When, long ago, Kemper's brigade had moved to the left, many of the men, singly and in small groups, had remained in the rough ground. A few of these, it must have been — now that everything was almost over — finally made a dash at what was left of Rorty's battery. Rorty's guns fired, and Wheeler's newly arrived battery hit the charging men with canister from the flank. They must have been few even to begin with, and only a baker's dozen can have come up to the guns. For a few wild moments, the artillerymen fought them off with swabs and rammers, and wildly swinging handspikes. Then the guns were saved. As for the few Confederates who made that wild charge, no one can say whether they were all killed, or whether some surrendered, or whether a few made their way back. Indeed, except that they must have been Kemper's men, no one can say even who they were; only in Union records do we read of the attack, and not much, even there.

Less heroic, but even more surprising, is that story of some men of the 11th Virginia. As it had happened, when Kemper's brigade moved to the left, a large part of the 11th with some men of other regiments became separated, and stayed where they were, facing the Vermonters. Soon they saw these troops move off, as if retreating. In turn, the Virginians moved forward, and occupied part of "a hasty trench and embankment," which had just been abandoned. Here the story is circumstantial, specifying that the position occupied was not a stone wall, and that they could not see very well from it — true enough, since the position of the Vermonters was not at a stone wall and was on low ground. The Virginians were in a high state of elation, believing that they had broken the enemy's line and that the rest of their own army would soon come marching up to complete the victory. But almost immediately they became mystified, and soon horrified with disappointment; for, looking back, they could see no troops advancing, but only a field strewn with dead and wounded. Several captains were present, and they decided to send back for reinforcements. They picked a certain "Big foot Walker," who was a "long-legged, big-footed fellow," accustomed to serve as a courier, a fast runner.

Fearing that he might be shot down, they soon sent another man, and they anxiously watched the two of them, one behind the other, cross the field and go over the rise. Then, unmolested, they remained in possession.

Finally, the captains decided that everything must have gone wrong. Concluding that there was nothing to do but retreat, they ordered the men to go back in small groups, so as not to attract fire from the artillery to the south — another confirmatory detail, since these would have been McGilvery's guns.

Soon, only Captains Smith and Douthat remained. Smith stayed to tie up a wound in his leg which he had got during the advance, and which had started to bleed. Douthat stayed so as not to desert a comrade.

Suddenly Douthat picked up a musket and fired. Looking over the little entrenchment, Smith was horrified to see a column of Union troops close at hand and seeming to advance obliquely in their direction.

He jumped up, exclaiming, "What are you doing!"

Douthat dropped his gun, and replied, "It's time to get away from here!"

The two of them ran for it, Smith forgetting his wounded leg. They managed to get a good start before being noticed; though they drew fire, they were not hit.

The mention of this column is also a realistic detail, since it might well have been a brigade in its march between the Third Corps position and the Angle.

22

At this same time, four miles to the east, an engagement was occurring between Union cavalry under Gregg and Confederate cavalry under Stuart. The correspondence of time has led to the belief that Stuart attacked in co-ordination with Pickett, and that, if both had been successful, the two attacks would have met, thus cutting the Union army in two. Lee's only reference to this engagement, however, is in terms of defense, that it "effectually protected our left." Certainly, in the event of a Confederate victory Stuart would have been happy, as he himself declared, to harry the Union rear. But there seems to be no good evidence that his movement was in any proper sense of the word co-ordinated with that of Pickett.

At this very time, also — as closely as can be determined with allowance for fourteen degrees of longitude — there was being enacted, more than nine hundred miles away, a scene which would have been of the utmost interest to all of those fighting at Gettysburg. A lieutenant general of the Confederate army was walking to meet a major general of the Union army who was similarly advancing. The two met beneath a small oak. Pemberton was arranging with Grant the terms for the surrender of Vicksburg.

23

Even yet, in the Homeric phrase, "they fought like raging fire," so that the musketry seemed to be a steady roar. Still the Confederates held their strong position behind the wall, and still some of them fought among the trees. Still, all along that concave line from the Vermonters on the left to the Pennsylvanians on the right, the others fought back, and now with growing confidence.

A small reinforcement came up. Gates was bringing his two

little regiments along, firing at the enemy on the oblique as they came. They pushed in with the other troops among the trees.

Still, among the Confederates behind the wall, Sergeant Major Stockton and his men of the 71st lay waiting their moment. They had been told to go to the rear, but had stayed where they were, sheltering themselves, looking for a chance to escape. They agreed that when Stockton gave the word, they would all jump over the wall and run for it. Then they suddenly realized that they were no longer in complete shelter, but that there was firing from the left. They looked around, and saw Blue-coats, off in that direction, outflanking the Angle.

What had happened was that the Confederates attacking Hays's front had finally been driven back, and some of the Union troops had jumped the wall, and were swinging around to the left to fire at the Confederates who still held the wall.

At the same time, the Union troops along the crest and among the trees felt the tension rising. Some of them probably saw Hays's men moving out, and certainly all of them heard the Vermonters' musketry.

The ever-active Haskell had ridden back. He was still the only mounted man, but his horse was mortally wounded. He himself had been hit on the leg by a spent ball, which had failed to pierce his uniform and the two layers of underwear, but had bruised him badly. Now he began to work with the fragments of the 71st which had rallied, doubtfully, behind the line of the 72nd. He addressed an officer, "Major ——, lead your men over the crest, they will follow."

The major was having none of heroism, and replied, "By the tactics I understand my place is in the rear of the men."

"Your pardon, sir," said Haskell in heavy irony, "I see your place is in the rear of the men. I thought you were fit to lead." He turned to another officer, "Captain Sapler, come on with your men."

The captain was no more heroic, "Let me first stop this fire in the rear, or we shall be hit by our own men."

"Never mind the fire in the rear; let us take care of this in the front first."

Then Haskell rode toward the sergeant who held the colors of the 72nd — the national flag, since that regiment carried no other. Six men had already gone down as they held those colors; Wills, O'Donnell, and Finnessey are remembered by name, and the others not; now it was Sergeant Murphy. A bullet had hit the staff, smashing it, and he merely held the stump.

Anything to get the line started! By now the tension was so high that there began to be little surges ahead.

"Sergeant," cried Haskell, "forward with your color!" Then he spoke with the words of melodrama that came naturally to the men of that war, "Let the Rebels see it close to their eyes once before they die."

At last there was movement. Grasping the stump of the staff in both hands, Murphy waved the flag above his head, and rushed forward.

Haskell was shouting, "Will you see your color storm the wall alone?" But only one man followed.

Toward the wall ran the sergeant, and then went down, the flag with him.

As he toppled, something happened among the men of the 72nd, and some of the 71st along with them. There came a great roar, and without orders the men dashed forward.

Thus it happened also among the trees, at the same time, so that it was all one impulse rather than two. No command was shouted. There came a sudden spontaneous yell, and the line surged ahead, flags to the front. "A strange resistless impulse!"

During a few seconds there was a wild melee, while the last desperate Confederates tried hopelessly to stop the rush — as Haskell remembered, "thrusts, yells, blows, shots, and undistinguishable conflict." Rifles were fired at such close range that men's clothes were scorched by the flashes. Musket-butts swung; bayonets jabbed! Stones flew through the air. Men dropped their weapons, and took to slugging and wrestling.

Only for seconds! The charging men were not to be stopped; those others had neither the numbers nor, any more, the spirit to stand against them. Along all the stretch south of the Angle, the blue wave swept down, then over the wall. Everywhere behind the wall and out in the field, handkerchiefs and bits of white cloth were fluttering and Confederates were throwing up their hands, and shouting, "Don't shoot!"

PART IX

Repulse

> We gained nothing but glory; and lost our bravest men.
> — CAPT. J. T. JAMES, 11th Virginia

IT WAS FINISHED! All that was to happen afterwards may be quickly passed over. In fact, may it not be so with everything that happened between this moment and Appomattox? All men, we might think, should agree that it would have been better if Lee had surrendered his army, cornered somewhere in Maryland or Pennsylvania, and that all should thus have been spared the horrors of Chickamauga and the Wilderness, the long agony of Petersburg, and the march through Georgia, and Andersonville — since in the end it was to happen.

2

During the last stages of the fight at the Angle, Pickett had remained near the Codori house, perhaps on the slight rise to its north. His aide, Captain Bright, one of his strong defenders, placed him "some two hundred yards behind the command," and this point would be approximately that distance.

He was only an agonized spectator of the disaster. At times he was apparently alone, having sent all his four aides on missions. About the time of the Union counterattack, he had come to a decision. He turned his horse's head, and rode to the rear.

Though the action was not heroic, the motives may have been good. With no aide left to send, he could have had some vague idea of asking for supports to be advanced. At this time, however, the general seems to have been almost distraught. Thus, a lonely figure on horseback, he rode rearwards.

3

We may take the time of the Union countercharge as being just about four o'clock, perhaps a few minutes before that time. Only from Cemetery Hill could the Union troops get some general view. Captain James Stewart looked out, and exclaimed in proper language for a former private of the Regular Army, "By God, boys we've got 'em now. They've broke all to hell!" Major Osborn, from the same vantage point, saw that the Confederates were retreating, "no two men together, but each man was running by himself to gain the cover of the hills within his own lines."

The alert correspondent of the Philadelphia *Morning Post* wrote another staccato dispatch:

> We have won a great victory. The fight is over and the rebel lines hurried back in wild disorder. . . . The field is covered with rebel dead. Wild cheers ring out from every part of our lines. Thousands of rebel prisoners are being brought in. Sheaves of battle flags and thousands of small arms are being gathered in by our men. The rejoicing amongst our men is indescribable.

Closer at hand, a captain in the 80th New York recalled:

> As the ground over which they had come was swept by our fire, most of those near our line sank to the ground and gave up the attempt to get away.
>
> Our men shouted to them to come in and promised not to hurt them, and at the words hundreds rose up and came into our lines, dropping their arms and crouching to avoid the fire of their own artillery which was pouring upon our position.

4

The Confederates who did not surrender retreated without order. One of them claimed that he and some others fired back to cover the retreat, and doubtless a few of them did. But the Union accounts suggest very little such firing, and the Confederate reminiscences fail to indicate much of the heroic. June Kimble was frank: "For about a hundred yards I broke the lightning speed record." Then, having a horror of being shot in the back, he turned around and backed off for a while. If a sergeant could so confess, the retreat of the average soldier must have been almost panic-stricken. Pickett's men, naturally, did not follow the longer, oblique course of their advance, but went straight back, thus mingling with the men of the other divisions.

There was not much musketry fire against the retiring Confederates — partly from a spirit of chivalry and a feeling that there had been enough killing, partly because the Union troops were busy rounding up prisoners. At least one regiment, the 13th Vermont, had orders not to fire.

The Union artillery, especially the newly arrived batteries, opened with shell and shrapnel. As Osborn judged, the fugitives were so scattered that this fire did them little damage, though it may have further demoralized them. This latter judgment is confirmed by Confederate accounts, two of which mentioned the troublesome fire from the battery on Little Round Top. The Confederate gunners replied, but they were still shooting high. (This firing, however, should be noted as proof that shortage of ammunition was not a serious factor in the defeat. In reality, only some of Alexander's guns ran out, and even for them the shortage was probably temporary.)

5

About this time General Meade, accompanied by only one aide, his son, rode up from the rear. His timing had been bad; he had ordered reserves up, but so late that the troops already in position had had to do all the fighting. Meade, not even yet realizing that the crisis had passed, came to the 10th New York Battalion, a small body of men doing provost-guard duty. He hurriedly ordered them up to the line. The men started marching, though dubious that their hundred rifles could do much.

By this time unwounded Confederates had come over the wall as prisoners in such numbers as to be embarrassing. The ground was strewn with muskets, and one Union officer had the horrible thought that the Confederates might pick up these muskets and suddenly attack from the rear. But the prisoners had had enough fighting, and were content to go rapidly behind the line, even though almost no guards went with them. As they came over the low crest, they entered the zone of their own artillery fire, and began to hurry to get through it. Seeing this sudden rush of butternut, Union officers and men who were behind the crest jumped to the conclusion that the Confederates had broken the line.

"See them come pouring over!" cried a staff-officer, guiding a fresh battery up. "The old Second Corps is gone!" In a moment, however, everyone saw that the Confederates had no arms.

Meade was still riding up to the crest. Who should meet him but the ever-present Haskell?

"How is it going here?" asked the general sharply and eagerly.

"I believe, general, the enemy's attack is repulsed."

A look of surprise spread over Meade's face, and he inquired incredulously, "What! Is the assault already repulsed?"

"It is, sir."

By this time Meade had arrived where he could see the prisoners, captured flags, and fugitives. He spoke simply, "Thank God."

Then moving his right hand as if to take off his hat and wave it, he halted that motion, and instead merely waved his hand, and cried, "Hurrah!"

6

By this time most of the troops had jumped the wall, and were down toward the road, collecting prisoners and flags, and now and then, as soldiers are likely to do, a personal memento. One of the souvenir-hunters (a sharpshooter named Smith, after the war, declared that he was the man) cut the general's insignia from Garnett's uniform.

Since it was a custom for surrendering officers to give up their swords, some of the Union officers were burdened with more swords than they knew what to do with; even Stockton, a sergeant major, remembered having a dozen of them.

But only Lieutenant Brown gained any real profit. As the 13th Vermont had closed in, Brown had gone with them, flourishing his hatchet. When prisoners were being captured, Brown saw a lieutenant, still wearing his sword. Brown demanded it, but the other hesitated. Then the Vermonter swung the hatchet up above the Confederate's head, like an Indian warrior brandishing a tomahawk. The Confederate quickly unbuckled his belt and passed it over, along with sword, scabbard, and pistol. Brown buckled the belt on, and wore the captured sword from the field.

There was more than a little expression of chivalrous feeling. Union troops shared the contents of canteens and haversacks with the prisoners. One Confederate remembered, "Many of them taking off their hats as we went to the rear, and remarking that we had 'done well,' 'No troops could have done more,' and then offering us a part of their rations."

A few exchanges of words have been remembered. A proud Second Corps man reported, "One of them said to me distinct, 'If we'd known it was you'ns we'd never come across.'" Another remembered a discouraged Johnnie saying, "Doggoned if we've been any match for you Yanks today anyway. Every rooster fights best on his own dunghill!"

Many of the Confederates had the fixed idea that they could be defeated only by Yankees in tremendous numbers. They were surprised and genuinely puzzled to discover how few troops had been opposing them. As a wounded sergeant was lying near the trees, a Confederate lieutenant colonel came up. He looked around, and then asked where the reserves were. With impudence, the sergeant replied, "We can lick you with one line, these days, colonel."

Similarly a captured colonel inquired, "Where are the men who fought us?"

"Here," said a captain.

"My God!" the colonel exclaimed, "if we only had had another line, we could have whipped you." Then, gazing about with astonishment, he continued, with great emphasis, "*By God, we could have whipped you as it was!*"

7

Even at this time, in a last desperate throw for victory, Wilcox was still advancing.

As he came over the rise, he could see no troops left to support. Not knowing anything better to do, he advanced straight ahead against the whole Union army. Even the men in the ranks saw the absurdity of it.

Off to the north Colonel Veazey of the 16th Vermont noted the new advance, and gave orders to his regiment, which was still firing into Pickett's flank. The Vermonters reversed their line. Having first marched north to attack Pickett's flank, they now marched south against Wilcox's flank. Four companies of the 14th Vermont joined them.

Almost simultaneously, the Alabamians and Floridians were hit by this flank attack, by frontal fire from the rest of the 14th Vermont, and by the converging fire of McGilvery's batteries, many of them using canister. After a few minutes the lines went to the rear. On the left, the 2nd Florida had become too closely engaged to retreat, and most of the men surrendered to the 16th Vermont.

In a military sense, however, this seemingly futile and even pathetic attack was not within some results. By drawing the 16th away, Wilcox made it possible for a large number of Pickett's men to escape capture. Moreover, the attack alarmed some Union commanders out of all proportion to reality, because it suggested that Lee had more troops available than had seemed likely and that still another assault might be expected. Except for Wilcox's advance, Meade might have launched the great counterstroke which he had already planned.

Some Union officers saw this attack for what it really was. One of them described it as aimlessly "wandering across the field." Another called it "a ridiculous demonstration."

8

The confusion and excitement of those moments of victory were expressed in the words of a Pennsylvanian, "After the fight was over, these troops went in and a hurrah went up, and they were in front and we were hurrahing and some of them held up their hands and we were hollering to them." So also a Vermonter recalled, "I forgot all about the danger." Then he added, rather unnecessarily, "Must have been excited."

Even a division-commander was overcome. The impetuous Hays had had two horses shot under him, and out of twenty orderlies he had but six left. In the intense emotionalism of the moment, he expressed himself by kissing his young aide, David Shields. Then he exclaimed, "Boys, give me a flag!" He called out to two of his aides, "Get a flag, Corts; get a flag, Dave, and come on!"

Then, each of them trailing a captured flag behind his horse's tail, they rode along the divisional line, while the men were alternately firing at the retreating enemy and cheering and throwing their caps in the air, as their beloved general rode by. Such was the excitement that Shields could write later, "My horse seemed to be off the ground traveling through the air. I felt though a shot as large as a barrel should hit me in the back, it would be with no more effect than shooting into a fog bank."

9

This demonstration was seen from the Confederate lines, and thus offers one of the few points of co-ordination of time between the two armies. The observer was Major W. T. Poague, commanding the guns close to the Point of Woods. His orders were that as soon as the infantry should reach the crest by the clump of trees, he should move there with all speed, and then be governed by circumstances. Having seen Pickett's men apparently reach the objective, Poague had ordered his guns to be limbered up, ready to advance. But then he saw more and more Confederates retreating, and he hesitated. It was a hard decision for a young major, and no chief of artillery, either for corps or army, was present to give him the command.

As he waited in doubt, he saw General Pickett appear close at hand, on horseback, alone, looking intently to the front. Poague rode over, saluted, and asked for advice. Pickett did not reply, and did not even seem to know that he had been addressed, but he continued to gaze toward the smoke "with an expression on his face of sadness and pain."

Just then Poague saw a horseman, who can only have been

Hays, bearing a flag rapidly along the line of the stone wall. He addressed Pickett again, "General, is that Virginia flag carried by one of our men or by the enemy?" Again there was no reply.

Insistently, Poague then asked, "What do you think I ought to do under the circumstances? Our men are leaving the hill."

At last, Pickett replied, "I think you had better save your guns."

He then rode off. Poague decided that he should prepare for defensive action.

Just then Lee, who had spent most of the afternoon in that vicinity, came up, asking, "How are you off for ammunition, major?" Poague replied that he had some, and that he had ordered up his six howitzers with full chests.

"Ah! that's well," said Lee, "we may need them."

10

At the moment of victory and defeat, the two friends, Armistead and Hancock, were lying wounded.

Armistead had been heard, in some lull of the musketry, calling for help, "as the son of a widow." This we must take to be the code of some secret society; at least, the words gained immediate response. Some men of the 72nd Pennsylvania requested permission of their officer to go to his aid, and then carried him behind the Union lines.

As a wounded general, even though of the wrong side, he was granted much attention and every courtesy. A surgeon, Henry H. Bingham, soon arrived, but could only inform Armistead that he was dying. Bingham promised to deliver any personal effects that the general might desire forwarded to his family.

Armistead was, according to Bingham, a man "seriously wounded, completely exhausted, and seemingly broken spirited." The words that he then spoke were destined to become a small storm-center of controversy: "Say to General Hancock for me, that I have done him, and you all, a grievous injury, which I shall always regret." He was then carried to the hospital.

Hancock would not leave the field as long as the issue was doubtful. An ambulance then arrived, and the general permitted himself to be taken toward the rear. His fighting spirit was not quenched, and when the ambulance came to the Taneytown road, the general ordered it to halt while he dictated a message. Even at this time the Whitworth guns were firing from the north, and the nervous ambulance officer suggested to the general that it would be better to move on, since the Rebels were enfilading the road. Hancock snapped back, "We've enfiladed *them* — damn them!" He then dictated a two-hundred-word dispatch to Meade, rather lacking in continuity, but including the proud words, "I did not leave the field till the victory was entirely secured and the enemy no longer in sight." He even made use of the nature of his own wound to estimate the situation, "The enemy must be short of ammunition, as I was shot with a tenpenny nail." But his most interesting words were, "If the Sixth and Fifth corps have pressed up, the enemy will be destroyed." He was then taken to the hospital, and thus vanished any chance of a decisive victory.

11

By this time the Confederates in great numbers, still under long-range artillery fire, were coming up the slope toward Poague's guns. "The whole field," wrote a Confederate officer, "was dotted with our soldiers, singly and in small groups, coming back from the charge, many of them wounded, and the enemy were firing at them as you would at a herd of game."

Lee immediately rode among the men, attempting to steady them. Though one may feel a certain wonder that the commanding general should thus find nothing better to do than to attempt to rally broken troops, the duty of sergeants and captains, nevertheless the impression he made upon many beholders was magnificent. Some had noted, earlier in the day, his uncertainty and nervousness. But now Fremantle characterized his conduct as "perfectly sublime." The impression he made was such that many officers and men later remembered, or thought they remembered, his exact words.

Meeting Lieutenant Colonel Shepard, commanding the remnant of Archer's brigade, Lee took him by the hand, and said, "Colonel, rally your men and protect our artillery. The fault is mine, but it will all be right in the end."

To Pettigrew, he said much the same as to Shepard, but added, "General, I am sorry to see you wounded; go to the rear."

One man, so tired that he could hardly walk, remembered meeting the general and saluting. Lee asked, "Are you wounded?"

"No, general — only a little fatigued; but I am afraid there are but few so lucky as myself."

"Ah! Yes — I am very sorry — the task was too great for you — but we mustn't despond — another time we shall succeed. Are you one of Pickett's men?"

"Yes, sir."

"Well, you had better go back and rest yourself. Captain Linthicum will tell you the rendezvous for your brigade."

As the broken survivors passed, a wild mountaineer of the 24th Virginia, waving one of the few flags that had been saved, cried out, "General, let us go it again!" (Under the circumstances, the words seem almost a hysterical obscenity.)

Pickett rode up, and Lee spoke, "General Pickett, place your division in rear of this hill, and be ready to repel the advance of the enemy should they follow up their advantage."

Head bowed, Pickett replied, "General Lee, I have no division now. Armistead is down, Garnett is down, and Kemper is mortally wounded."

"Come, General Pickett, this has been my fight, and upon

my shoulders rests the blame. The men and officers of your command have written the name of Virginia as high today as it has ever been written before."

Some men came by, bearing the wounded Kemper. Lee turned to him, "General Kemper, I hope you are not very seriously wounded."

"I am struck in the groin and the ball has ranged upward; they tell me it is mortal."

"I hope it will not prove so bad as that. Is there anything I can do for you, General Kemper?"

"Yes, General Lee, do full justice to this division for its work today."

"I will."

Wilcox rode up, and spoke, "General, I have tried to rally my men, but as yet they will not stand."

"Never mind, general; the fault is all mine. All that you have to do is to help me to remedy it so far as you can."

An officer of the 18th Virginia heard him, once more, "It's all my fault! I thought my men were invincible."

"My fault! My fault!" he said again and again, as if by the confession the disaster itself might be lessened.

At one moment, with a calm that seems almost too much of an over-compensation, he found time to reason with an officer who was having trouble with a horse, "Don't whip him, captain; it does no good. I had a foolish horse, once, and kind treatment is the best."

Longstreet also maintained control of himself, well enough to earn from Fremantle the citation "admirable." He, too, rode among the men, and his words were, as Fremantle remembered, "All this will come out right in the end; we'll talk it over afterwards; but, in the meantime, all good men must rally. We want all good and true men just now."

But against one officer who came up to report that his troops would not rally, Longstreet lashed out in irony, "Very well; never mind, then, general; just let them remain where they are: the enemy's going to advance, and will spare you the trouble."

Thereupon he asked Fremantle if he had anything to drink, and with much satisfaction took a swig of rum from a flask, which the Englishman thereupon presented to him. But even the usually imperturbable Longstreet was somewhat shaken. Immediately after this he sent out conflicting orders to one of his commanders on the right, much to the chagrin of Sorrel who was forced to deliver them, even though he knew they were contradictory.

Other generals went to pieces badly. Pickett, Hill, and Wilcox were all reported in tears.

The worst of it was that all Lee's sublimity had little effect. Some officers, with bad judgment, attempted to form a line on the brow of the ridge. But this was still in full view from the Union batteries, and the line broke under their fire.

"Then commenced," wrote a Confederate officer, "a rout, that increased to a stampede." Officers were carried along with the mass. The demoralized men funneled into a little ravine on the back slope of the ridge and there, without distinction of commands, "pushed, poured, and rushed, in a continuous stream, throwing away guns, blankets, and haversacks."

Finally some officers picked a few resolute men out of the mass, flung a line across the ravine, and almost by physical force "dammed up" the last of the fugitives, several hundred strong.

12

As far as the Union troops on Cemetery Ridge were concerned, they were dog-tired and had taken heavy losses in repulsing a desperate attack made upon them by double their numbers; they were content to let things rest. They did little more than make faces, sending out skirmishers here and there to fire on a few of the advanced Confederate guns. Gradually the badly scattered regiments were got together again. There was much work to be done at collecting and escorting prisoners. The wounded of both sides had to be gathered in.

General Meade came along the lines. The men cheered him. A band that had turned up from somewhere played "Hail to the Chief," and a war-correspondent said, "Ah! General Meade, you're in very great danger of being President of the United States."

So, indeed, he was — if he had only pushed the fighting. And, as Hancock's note had indicated, he was not without a plan, to use the not badly damaged Fifth Corps and the almost intact Sixth against the Confederate right. This attack would actually have struck what was almost a vacuum, now that Pickett's and Wilcox's commands had been put out of action. With Hancock gone, Meade flinched, though the troops even of the badly shattered Third Corps sensed the chance for a decisive stroke, and were eager to be led again into action.

Lee, meanwhile, was doing what he could to prepare against an attack on Seminary Ridge. With three fresh brigades of infantry and a strong force of well-posted artillery, he could put up a strong defense. But Meade had never any intention of assaulting that position.

Another deterrent to the launching of a counterattack was the lateness of the hour. Quite possibly, the ever-shrewd Lee had had this contingency in mind, earlier in the day, when he had not seemed in a hurry to get his own attack started. "Saved by darkness," is a recurrent theme in military history.

13

Shortly before six o'clock the mop-up was completed, and the Union troops were ordered to resume their original positions in the line. The Confederate artillery was still firing, and as the 13th Vermont was marching back a shell exploded, killing one man and wounding several. Lieutenant Brown, always the humanitarian, stopped to see what he could do, and a second shell exploded over his head, stunning him. He revived, however, and was not forced to relinquish his command.

With the return of the Union troops to their positions, the mere action of Pickett's charge may be said to have ended. But, in a larger sense, much remains to be told.

14

Even after the wounded had been removed, the ground just inside of the Angle and the slope below the stone wall presented a scene of concentrated carnage. In a space not more than twenty feet in circumference a war-correspondent counted seven dead, three of which were piled on top of one another. Close by, in a spot not more than fifteen feet square lay fifteen bodies. An officer of the 126th New York, not given to exaggeration, wrote that the ground was "so thickly strewn with their dead that one could walk for rods on their dead bodies." Many corpses were horribly mangled by the canister.

There was other evidence of the intensity of the fire. From Confederate musketry the front of the stone wall was so spotted with black marks from where bullets had struck that it was compared to a target at which men had been shooting. Conversely, where Archer's men had crossed the fences along the road, one board, fourteen inches wide and sixteen feet long, showed 836 bullet holes. This would mean that, if they were spaced equally, one would not have been able to lay a hand on the board without covering several holes.

Forty-two Confederate dead were counted inside the Angle. The figure is of special interest as providing a datum from which to calculate the total number crossing the wall, since the wounded should equal about four times the dead. This would yield a figure of 210, but to it would have to be added some unwounded prisoners, and a number of men who went over the wall but escaped back over it at the end. Probably 300 is a minimal figure; considering the amount of commotion they caused, one can hardly see how they could have been fewer.

15

As soon as they had got back to their positions, the Union men doubtless started "rendering the butcher's bill," that is, figuring their losses on the basis of who was no longer with the company, and what had happened to him, if anybody knew. Many of the regiments had suffered more casualties earlier in the battle than in repulsing the charge. Reports on casualties were required, however, only for the battle as a whole. Still, several regiments reported losses for each day, and from regimental histories and other sources we can work out fairly reliable figures for all the units.

This presentation, however, is not concerned with losses during the cannonade or in the artillery. The former have already been considered, and to include them here would be to confuse two different kinds of fighting. (Merely for completeness, the loss in the Second Corps artillery, both during the cannonade and afterwards, totaled about 100; if Thomas's and Cowan's are to be included, another 25 should be added.)

We can start with the figure 3687, which represents the total loss July 1–4, as officially reported, of all the infantry units involved in the defense. A figure rather less than half of this would seem to be a reasonable one for the losses during the repulse of the charge. Approaching the problem from the other direction, by summation of the estimated losses of the individual regiments, we arrive at approximately 1500. The double method of approach seems to confirm this figure, and it probably cannot be far from correct.

Included in it would be a negligible number of prisoners, probably not more than thirty, from the skirmishers, the 71st Pennsylvania, and Company F of the 69th. Others were temporarily captured, but lay low — like Stockton and his men — and escaped during the Confederate retreat.

In the Civil War the usual proportion of killed to total casualties was about 17 per cent. In a close fight, such as that around the Angle, the proportion of dead would run higher, and we may use a figure of 20 per cent. In the conventional three-way classification the Union infantry losses may therefore be put at: killed, 290; wounded, 1180; missing, 30 — an over-all of about one in four of the men engaged.

One must remember, in considering such figures, that any man who was breathing when he reached the hospital was reported as wounded. About one wounded man in seven died later, and an even larger number were too badly injured ever to return to active service.

Losses varied according to the nature of the fighting to which the units had been subjected. Hays's division suffered about 18 per cent over-all, but losses in his regiments that fought from behind the stone wall were only around 16 per cent. The divisional average was raised by the 8th Ohio (35 per cent).

Gibbon's division suffered twice as heavily, its losses approaching 40 per cent, thus reflecting the heavy fighting at close range. The losses in Harrow's and Hall's brigades may be put at 32 and 37 per cent respectively; in Webb's, at 47 per cent. Among Webb's regiments the losses ranged: 71st, 34 per cent; 72nd and 106th, 47 per cent; 69th, 50 per cent.

Stannard's brigade, though engaged largely in the open, had taken the Confederates at a disadvantage; its losses were about 17 per cent. Gates's two small regiments suffered almost all of their huge casualties on July 1, and during the charge did not lose more than about 15 per cent.

16

Confederate losses are difficult to determine. Wholly trust-worthy reports exist only for Garnett's and Lane's brigades. With this beginning, however, and from the numerous more uncertain and less detailed reports for other units the losses can be calculated with some degree of reliability (see Appendix A), allowance being made for casualties during the cannonade.

For the three principal commands the losses may be tabulated:

	KILLED	WOUNDED	UNWOUNDED PRISONERS	TOTAL	PER CENT
Pickett	500	2007	375	2882	67
Pettigrew	470	1893	337	2700	60
Trimble	155	650	80	885	52
Total	1125	4550	792	6467	62

Actual casualties, that is, killed and wounded, total 5675, or 54 per cent of the 10,500 men making the advance.

Trimble's losses were naturally lower, since his troops formed the third line. The difference between Pickett's and Pettigrew's proportional losses is not great; if the summation is limited to Archer's, Pettigrew's, and Davis's brigades, the percentage works out at 70, a little higher than for Pickett's division. One must remember, however, that the factual basis is too doubtful to allow anyone to put much faith in exact percentages. In particular, the losses for Kemper's and for Brockenbrough's brigades are highly uncertain. The general conclusion, however, would seem to be that Archer's, Pettigrew's, and Davis's brigades fought equally as well as Pickett's.

According to Union sources, the number of unwounded prisoners was large. A detailed post-war study of the 11th Mississippi gives such loss as 13 per cent of the total, and I have used this figure for the six front-line brigades, for want of anything better. I have used a smaller figure for Lane's and Scales's brigades, which were not so closely engaged, and have assumed no unwounded prisoners at all for Brockenbrough's brigade.

By the standards of nineteenth-century European warfare the losses are extremely high. Gudin's division at Auerstädt lost 41 per cent; the Light Brigade in its famous charge, 37; the Third Westphalian regiment at Mars La Tour, 49. In the Civil War no comparably large body of troops seems to have suffered such heavy casualties in a single engagement. Hancock's division at Fredericksburg lost 42 per cent, probably all killed and wounded.

The losses of the different brigades show wide variation. Those officially reported for Garnett's brigade work out at 65 per cent. Those for Armistead's brigade are less certain, but yield a figure of 73. Data on Kemper's brigade are highly dubious, and I have finally taken its losses as being 60 per cent, chiefly on the assumption that it must have suffered about equally with Garnett's.

The losses of Archer's brigade for the whole battle totaled 65 per cent, and so those for the charge have been put at 56. For Brockenbrough's brigade we shall probably do justice if we assign a loss of a hundred men, or 17 per cent. The remainder of the divisional loss, which can be rather accurately determined, has been divided equally between Pettigrew's and Davis's brigades, and works out at 74 per cent for each of them.

Lane reported his losses officially in terms that yield the figure of 52 per cent. The same may reasonably be assigned to Scales.

Except for Garnett's and Lane's brigades all these figures are submitted with considerable diffidence. One has difficulty in seeing, for instance, why Archer's brigade should have lost so much less, proportionately, than Pettigrew's. Its men seem to have fought with great gallantry, and they advanced into the Angle. One should remember, however, that casualties are seldom an exact index of gallantry, and may reflect nothing more than luck. For instance, Archer's brigade advanced in a sector where it may have escaped canister entirely.

The losses of many individual regiments and companies were much higher than the average. We may, of course, expect some exaggeration, and also a tendency for only the hardest-hit units to make such reports. Among these claims are: 1st Virginia, 80 per cent; 9th Virginia, 81; 18th Virginia, 88; 11th Mississippi, 89; 8th Virginia, 92 per cent. The figure for the 11th Mississippi is based on a careful post-war study; that for the 8th Virginia has three different sets of figures behind it, all differing slightly, but working out at about the same percentage. According to Colonel Hunton, himself wounded, only ten men answered the first roll call after the charge; a lieutenant was in command. Such a figure, however, is of no great value, since it ignores the fact that stragglers would rejoin later.

A number of companies claimed over 90 per cent losses, and three reached the ultimate of 100 per cent. These last were the University Grays of the 11th Mississippi, the Color Company of the 38th North Carolina, and Company F of the 26th North Carolina. This last, which went into the charge with only some half-dozen men, also claimed that no prisoners were lost, and a list was prepared specifying the nature of the hurt that each man received.

The proportion of Confederate to Union losses is the measure primarily of the difference, under Civil War conditions, between an unsuccessful attack and a successful defense. Some credit should also be given to the quick-thinking Union leadership. Confederate courage, reckless and stubborn, increased the losses by carrying the fight to close quarters and maintaining it after all reasonable hope of victory had vanished.

In actuality the disproportion was probably greater than appears at first sight, because of the different methods of counting in the two armies. Lee's General Order No. 63 of May 14, 1863,

forbad the recording as wounded of those who were still able to
keep with their regiments, though in previous reports such men
had been so listed. As far as is known, Union reports still included such men. To attain a true comparison we should therefore either add a certain figure — say, 10 per cent — to the
Confederate reports or subtract it from the Union reports. Moreover, the 350 casualties and prisoners of Wilcox's two brigades
should be added, since the losses of the Vermont regiments
occurring in that engagement have been here included. Final
figures might then be: Union losses, 1500; Confederate losses,
7500, or five to one.

A Virginia captain, writing home to his father only six days
after the charge, summarized the result accurately enough: "We
gained nothing but glory; and lost our bravest men."

17

The proportion of losses resulting from various causes cannot
be very accurately established. In the Civil War a rule-of-thumb
credited one casualty in twelve to artillery-fire. The conditions
of the charge were such that the guns undoubtedly accounted for
a much larger than usual number of dead and wounded. Still,
most of the casualties were probably from musketry. (See
Appendix C.)

As for *armes blanches*, some eye-witness accounts of the final
melee contain generalizations, such as, "The bayonet was freely
used." In opposition may be cited the more circumstantial
observation of an officer of the 80th New York:

> A curious thing about this fighting was that, although
> all the men were armed with bayonets, no one seemed to be
> using them. Those nearest clubbed their muskets and beat
> each other over the head, while those not so close kept load-
> ing and firing as fast as they could.

The research for this work has not brought to light a single instance of a man killed or wounded by a bayonet, but this cannot be taken as conclusive evidence that not one was.

The only stab-wound credibly reported was in the shoulder of a Union soldier, apparently received from the color-bearer of the 13th Alabama, who that morning had attached a lance-point to the end of the color-staff. Corporal Bradley of Company D, 69th Pennsylvania, had his skull crushed by a clubbed musket. Since he is noted by name, and as something of a curiosity, serious casualties from that cause must have been extremely rare. A reliable witness also reported that he heard of another man so struck.

The throwing of stones in the fighting at the clump of trees is attested. The local trap rock weathers into conveniently shaped and sized chunks. Since it took you half a minute to load your rifle, throwing stones was a lot faster, and must have seemed highly satisfactory, particularly since you could hurl them over the heads of the men in front of you. Probably no one was killed by such a missile, and wounds inflicted might not have demanded hospitalization.

That some men dropped their weapons and fought barehanded seems certain. Most interesting is the testimony, under oath, of a member of the Philadelphia Brigade.

Q. There were personal conflicts?
A. Yes, sir; squabbles.
Q. What do you call a "squabble"?
A. When there is no organized fighting being done.
Q. You are not speaking of a fight in the sense that the men were shooting or stabbing each other.
A. No, sir; I call that a melee.

The chief actual evidence of close fighting which was observed afterwards was the considerable number of men with clothing burned from the discharge of muskets.

18

The total number of prisoners, wounded and unwounded, cannot be accurately determined. The captured men were herded to the rear or taken to hospitals, and were mingled with others taken earlier in the battle. Union estimates of prisoners therefore vary considerably, from 3000 to 5000. The Confederates could only lump together under *Missing* their unwounded and wounded prisoners and also the dead who had been left close to the Union lines. From reports of captures by different units we may roughly estimate the prisoners as 3750.

19

Casualties have not only numerical but also qualitative significance. Among the generals the losses of the two sides had fallen somewhat more heavily upon the Confederates. Of their eight generals, Garnett was dead; Armistead, mortally wounded; Kemper and Trimble, so severely wounded that they would never again be fit for active service; Pettigrew, slightly wounded; Pickett, Davis, and Lane, unhurt. Of seven Union generals, Hancock was so severely hurt that he probably never entirely recovered, though he was able to take the field; Gibbon and Stannard were wounded severely; Webb, slightly; Doubleday, Hays, and Harrow were unhurt.

In field officers, the Union regiments had lost heavily; six regiments came out commanded by captains, and the 1st Delaware was under a lieutenant. But the losses of the Confederates in field officers had been almost an annihilation. Pickett's division advanced with thirty-two, and only one returned unhurt. There is some argument as to who he was, but he was probably Major C. S. Peyton, who had, ironically, already lost an arm in an earlier battle. Of the thirteen colonels, seven were killed; one, mortally wounded; all the others, wounded. The three heavily engaged brigades of Heth's division suffered almost as severely. To quote from the official report, "in Archer's brigade but two field officers escaped, in Pettigrew's but one, and in Davis's all were killed or wounded." The loss in company officers, though not so carefully recorded, seems to have been proportionally almost as great.

This slaughter among the officers was never made good. For instance, the historian of the 11th North Carolina recorded his opinion that because of those losses "defective organization continued to mar the efficiency of the regiment to the end of the war." The historian of Pickett's division commented "a loss never to be fully repaired."

20

Symbols of victory in nineteenth-century warfare were guns and colors. Although the Confederates overran some guns at the Angle, none were captured permanently. On the other hand, the capture of Confederate colors was amazing and appalling. Not counting Brockenbrough's brigade, the Confederates had advanced with thirty-eight regiments, each under its own flag. Of these, twenty-eight were captured by the Second Corps and officially recorded. But Hancock reported, "There were undoubtedly thirty-three colors captured, the balance having been secreted as individual trophies."

In addition to the colors captured by the Second Corps, the 16th Vermont of the First Corps captured the flag of the 8th Virginia. Still another would have to be added to the total, since the 16th Vermont also captured the flag of the 2nd Florida of Perry's brigade. The grand total would thus have to be put at a minimum of thirty and maximum of thirty-five. Among the officially captured flags, nine were not identified; apparently, many of the colors of the North Carolina and Mississippi regiments bore no distinguishing mark.

Although the loss of the flag was usually considered a disgrace, its capture in the charge was rather the reverse, since those regiments which advanced farthest and fought most desperately were in the end most likely to leave their colors behind.

Pickett's division lost all but two of its colors, including all of those in Armistead's and probably all in Garnett's brigade. The flag of the 24th, of Kemper's brigade, was saved, doubtless since that regiment was well toward the right flank of the brigade, and after the movement to the left found itself at the rear.

Archer's brigade lost, by the report of its own commanding officer, four colors. He also stated that the one to be saved, that of the 7th Tennessee, was only brought back because a captain tore it from the staff, and concealed it under his coat when he retreated.

The men of the 126th New York had a special satisfaction in that one of their captured flags bore the name "Harpers Ferry" among its list of victories.

Congress granted fifteen medals of honor to individual soldiers for capturing flags. Like most grantings of medals, this one caused discontent. Men remembered that after the retreat the flags were lying around and were to be had for the picking up. There were also many stories that the man who turned the flag in had merely taken it from some comrade who already had it. Divisional rivalry was involved. Webb, as the story ran, was so disgruntled that Hays's men had taken away so many colors that he sent to ask for them back; Hays, contemptuously, told the messenger to help himself to half a dozen of those that were lying around.

This story can be accepted only with reservations, because the captured flags were, with two exceptions, assigned to the regiments which would naturally have captured them. Thus, all the identified flags of Pickett's division were credited to regiments of Gibbon's division, with one exception; also, with one exception, all the identified flags of Heth's and Pender's divisions were credited to Hays's regiments.

21

For "conspicuous gallantry" Cushing was given the posthumous
promotion to brevet lieutenant colonel. A medal of honor was
granted to Colonel W. G. Veazey for his spectacular handling
of the 16th Vermont. Also so honored was Major Edmund Rice
of the 19th Massachusetts, for "conspicuous bravery" in the
counterattack.

Under many military systems, after such a victory, citations
would have been granted to the units which had most distinguished themselves. If such a procedure had been followed, one
such would probably have gone to Cushing's battery. Among
the infantry regiments, the 8th Ohio was outstanding for its
audacious attack, and the 69th Pennsylvania for its equally
audacious defense. The 16th Vermont could scarcely have been
passed over. In addition, the 13th Vermont, 19th Massachusetts, and 42nd New York had shown remarkable valor at critical
moments.

22

The sun thus set — and for the first time — upon a triumphant
and jubilant Army of the Potomac and a shattered and despond-
ent Army of Northern Virginia. In later years there was a
tendency for Southerners to slur the battle over, and even to
say, "Both sides lost at Gettysburg." The incompleteness of the
Confederate casualty returns made this easier, since it was thus
possible to maintain that in the whole battle Meade had lost
more heavily than Lee. There was no such feeling on the evening of July 3.

To illustrate the Confederate state of mind, we may shift to
the interview, that night, between General John D. Imboden
and Lee. Summoned to receive orders, Imboden found his

commander so exhausted that he could scarcely dismount from his horse. Shocked by this weariness and by the sadness of the face, Imboden ventured to remark, when Lee stood silent, "General, this has been a hard day on you."

Lee looked up, and then spoke mournfully, "Yes, it has been a sad, sad day to us."

After another lingering silence, Lee commented on the gallantry of Pickett's men, and then after another pause, he cried out, in a loud voice, in a tone almost of agony, "Too bad! *Too bad!* OH! TOO BAD!"

Lee then gave the orders to begin the Confederate retreat, on a road which, as it happened, passed through Waterloo. Beyond, the road led to Hagerstown, and Appomattox.

PART X

Afterwards

Afterwards conducting a leading dry goods business.
— Tribute to Sgt. J. B. Scully

A DELIGHTFUL chapter of the Victorian novel was that last one in which the reader was told what happened to the characters later. Those of the charge, including some of the corps, divisions, brigades, and regiments, may similarly warrant a little more attention.

2

Lee's career may be considered well-enough known, and we may restrict ourselves to a few words about the apparent influence upon him of that afternoon at Gettysburg. In spite of the behavior that so impressed Fremantle, Lee was somewhat shaken. In his dispatches after the battle there is a noticeable occurrence of the words "Divine Power," "Providence," and "Supreme Ruler of the Universe." On August 8, in a very careful letter to President Davis, he offered his resignation. In the long run, however, he drew some profit from the disaster. He never again ordered a Napoleonic assault, and his army was thus spared another disaster. Lee continued to accept the responsibility for the attack and its failure; writing to Davis, he again absolved the army: "I am alone to blame, in perhaps expecting too much of its prowess and valor."

Longstreet continued as second-in-command, and was severely wounded in the Wilderness. Most of the troops remaining to surrender at Appomattox were of his corps, and he was with them. His post-war career can be better told in connection with the controversy about the charge.

Pickett, in spite of what seems almost a crack-up after the repulse, retained command of the remnants of his three brigades. His men were assigned the task of escorting the Union prisoners, and he had spirit left to protest at what seemed a second-class duty. Lee reassured him that the division had already won great glory.

Five days after the charge Pickett wrote to his fiancée. He mentioned, "My spirit-crushed, wearied, cut-up people." He deplored lack of supports. Of himself he wrote, "how I escaped it is a miracle." On July 23 he wrote a calmer letter, again blaming the failure on lack of supports. He was ready now to plan for a wedding, though a very quiet one — "with all the graves I have left behind me, and with all the wretchedness and misery this fated campaign has made."

Shortly afterwards, Pickett married the girl, but we can hardly say that he lived happily ever afterwards. He himself realized that his conduct during the afternoon had been such that he would be accused of cowardice. Lee and Longstreet, however, must have considered his behavior to be fitting; no general whose courage was in question could have kept his command in that army. Pickett retained the same division, but was never entrusted with a corps. In 1864 he was not brilliant. His career really ended at Five Forks, April 1, 1865, when he again lost most of his division. On this occasion, while his men were being crushed, Pickett was behind the lines and out of touch, enjoying a shad-bake. These were the last days of the war, and the scandal was somewhat hushed up. But Pickett thereafter had only some fragmentary regiments, and he was relieved of command the day before the surrender. Lee, seeing him at Appomattox, remarked, "I thought that man was no longer with the army." Coming from the ever-courteous Lee, the words "that man" have a ring of derogation. Pickett's post-war career was undistinguished; he died in 1875.

Garnett was dead. Since his uniform had been stripped of its insignia, his body was not identified, though special search was made. He was interred in some common grave, along with his own men. (Yet where may a general rest in more honor?)

Armistead died, but his dying words were soon being quoted as evidence that a Confederate general, in a final moment of insight, had denied the Confederate cause. As would be expected, his statement was embroidered and made stronger. After the war, Southern apologists denied that he could possibly have said anything of the sort. A careful and irrefutable statement by Bingham made such a defense impossible. Some Southerners then reinterpreted the words to mean, not a denial of the Confederacy, but a personal apology to his former comrades for hard feelings he had cherished against them.

Against all expectation, Kemper recovered, but was never able to resume command in the field. After the war he returned to politics, and served as governor of Virginia for a term, during which he notably supported civil rights for Negroes.

Pettigrew, having escaped Gettysburg with a slight injury, was mortally wounded in the skirmish at Falling Waters some days later. Trimble, his leg amputated, was left behind to be taken prisoner when the army retreated; though exchanged toward the end of the war, he was never fit for active duty.

Pendleton remained in his post as chief of artillery; and then returned to his beloved pastoral work at Lexington, in which he remained till his death.

Alexander won promotion to brigadier general before the end of the war, having rendered distinguished services and received many plaudits. After the war he lived a busy and successful life as an engineer and railroad executive. He was, like many veterans, stricken by the itch for writing. Counting his two official reports, he left six versions of his participation at Gettysburg.

Like Longstreet and others, he did not always bother to check what he wrote against what he had already written. Thus he quoted from one of his notes to Longstreet — once, that he would "direct" Pickett to advance; a second time, that he would "order"; a third time, that he would "advise." (But if generals were scholars, battles might never get themselves fought.)

Davis, the President's nephew, and "Little Jim" Lane continued to serve as brigadiers. In the post-war years Davis returned to his practice of law; Lane, to his career as a professor.

3

On the other side, Meade was hailed as a hero in many quarters, but Lincoln never forgave him his failure to follow up the victory. Though he remained in nominal command of the Army of the Potomac until the end of the war, he functioned under Grant's shadow. His short post-war career was undistinguished.

Hancock, though still suffering from his wound, commanded the Second Corps in the campaign of 1864, and won the highest praise from Grant. Assigned to command his own army in 1865, he was prevented from taking the field by the ending of the war. As a war-hero who could pull votes, he was nominated for the presidency by the Democrats in 1880, but lost to Garfield.

Gibbon quickly recovered from his wound. He retained his division in 1864, and was promoted to major general. In 1865, he took command of the Twenty-Fourth Corps, and led it to Appomattox. A thorough professional soldier, he remained in the army. In 1887, after a spectacular campaign, he defeated the Nez Percés under Chief Joseph, and then became that chieftain's fast friend.

The irrepressible Hays, still commanding his division, was killed in the Wilderness. Harrow, Stannard, and Webb continued to render good service throughout the war. From 1869 to 1902 Webb served as president of the College of the City of New York.

Hunt continued to serve as the principal Union artillery officer, but the latter part of the war offered fewer chances for spectacular employment of guns. As with artillery officers in general, he received little recognition of his services, reaching the rank of major general only by brevet, and reverting to lieutenant colonel after the war. In writing, he mentioned Malvern Hill and Fredericksburg, not Gettysburg, as the triumphs of the Union artillery.

4

A few characters, North and South, who are less notable in the strictly military sense, deserve a few words.

Of the three unusual lieutenants, Cushing was dead. Brown was soon mustered out with his regiment, and returned to civilian life in Vermont.

Haskell won golden opinions on all sides, being mentioned in the very highest terms in the official reports of Hancock, Gibbon, Harrow, and three regimental commanders. Gibbon later testified that Haskell "did more than any other one man to repulse that last assault at Gettysburg, and he did the part of a general there." As if he had not done enough already, he wrote a 40,000-word letter to his brother, describing the battle. Not only is this perhaps the longest letter ever written to a brother, but it may also be the most notable. It remains the most detailed and most vivid eye-witness account of the charge, and is considered a military classic. In recognition of his services Haskell was given command of the newly raised 36th Wisconsin, with the rank of colonel. He took his regiment through the Wilderness and Spotsylvania, and led it at Cold Harbor, on that black day for the Second Corps. Standing up to see that his men were taking cover properly, he was shot through the head.

Twice wounded on July 3, the indestructible Colonel Fry was

taken prisoner. He recovered, was exchanged, was promoted to the command of Archer's brigade, and survived Gettysburg by almost thirty years.

Captain Samuel Chapman Armstrong, who boldly led his skirmishers to harry the Confederate flank, became interested in the progress of the Negro, and was the founder of Hampton Institute.

Captain Cowan led his battery throughout the war. He had appeared so suddenly at the clump of trees and departed so soon after the crisis that no one was sure what battery his had been, and the reports credited Wheeler's, much to Cowan's chagrin. For a while he nursed a paranoia about the matter, but in the end justice was done. In later years Cowan became something of a professional veteran, never happier than when at a reunion by the clump of trees, especially when he could deliver an address.

Sergeant Major Stockton, and Sergeants Kimble and Easley survived the war. But Corporal Sturtevant, who had predicted his own death, was not mistaken. Also among the dead was Private George Stewart.

5

Pickett's division was reorganized and built up. In 1864 it served mostly to the south of the James but was sometimes a part of Lee's army. Its fate at Five Forks has already been mentioned.

Brockenbrough's brigade got into trouble again at Falling Waters on the retreat from Gettysburg. The colonel bumbled; as the result, the flags, which had escaped at Gettysburg, advanced without support, and were captured. The colonel's future service is obscure.

Heth's and Pender's divisions were also built up, and rendered excellent service. Heth remained in command. When Pender died of his Gettysburg wound, Wilcox was promoted, and the division took his name. Both the generals, with some remnants of their divisions, kept with the army until its final surrender.

6

The Union troops had suffered less heavily in casualties, and came out of the fight with a heightened morale. This was particularly true of Hays's old brigade. As he wrote jubilantly, "Harper's Ferry Boys have wiped out Harper's Ferry." From this time on, that brigade was a top-notch organization.

Among the Union regiments the 71st Pennsylvania, though with some excuse, had behaved badly, and the record of the 72nd was doubtful. Immediately after the battle Webb was described as "very angry." He ordered a court-martial, probably of some officers of the 71st, but the procedures were later dropped in the general good feeling of victory. Certainly there was much to be said for the 72nd. Its dead were thick along the crest; as one officer described it, "If they had been laid there by their comrades, they could not have been laid more in a line."

The Second Corps, built up during the winter by the accession of many regiments, fought well in the Wilderness, and at Spotsylvania it stormed the Bloody Angle, capturing most of a Virginia division. It was averaging, however, about four hundred casualties a day. To cap everything it was thrown against the entrenchments at Cold Harbor. If Pickett's Charge was Fredericksburg in reverse, the assault at Cold Harbor was Pickett's Charge in reverse. As its historian wrote, "the Second Corps here received a mortal blow, and never again was the same body of men." On June 22, 1864, in one of the battles around Petersburg, the "fought out" corps suffered a humiliating defeat.

The generally unlucky Philadelphia brigade was here much involved. These regiments, returned to the dubious leadership of General "Paddy" Owen, had — to say the least — failed to distinguish themselves at Cold Harbor; a few weeks later Owen was "mustered out, by order of the President," having barely escaped court-martial. By June 22 the 71st had already been mustered out, and the other three old regiments were down to mere fragments. On that day they were thought to have behaved badly; most of the 106th and its colors were captured. After this engagement the brigade was broken up, and the old regiments, what was left of them, were distributed to other brigades for the short time remaining of their terms of service. The men considered it mere vindictiveness.

Again built up during the winter, the Second Corps participated in the final campaign. It had by this time little in common with the corps that had fought at Gettysburg except its number, a few generals, and some of the old regiments, reduced to the size of companies.

The three nine-month regiments of Vermonters, their time having expired, were mustered out a few days after the battle. They went home, and were there received — not altogether incorrectly — as the heroes of Gettysburg. Some of the men re-enlisted, but Stannard's brigade, after two days of remarkable fighting, was a thing of the past.

James Scully, that pivotal sergeant, was among those who re-enlisted. After the war he returned to his home town — "afterwards conducting a leading dry goods business." By and large, the same or something similar, may be said for the vast majority of the citizen-soldiers, who made the charge and repulsed it — if they were fortunate enough to survive the war.

PART XI

The Story of the Story

It is so easy to fight battles on paper, so different from fighting them successfully on the ground.
— GENERAL JOHN GIBBON, *Recollections*

THAT AFTERNOON, no one knew that it was High-water Mark. During the night many Union troops labored at fortification, in the expectation that Lee might once more attack. Only with his retreat did men begin to realize that something symbolically decisive, even in the history of the world, might have happened there by the little clump of trees.

Officially and publicly the Confederates could never make such an admission while the war lasted. In their hearts many of them must have known — and more and more of them as the months passed — that the whole war after Gettysburg was merely, in the words of William Faulkner, a long "walking backward slowly." Longstreet was eager for one try more, but after the results of Chickamauga had been dissipated, he was ready to admit the inevitable. In January, 1864, he expressed doubt as to the future of the Confederacy and asked to be relieved of command. Nevertheless he continued to fight magnificently until Appomattox. Lee himself almost certainly realized that with the repulse had vanished all reasonable hope for a military victory.

Perhaps because of this deeper knowledge in their hearts, the Confederates labored the harder to minimize the defeat. Or, at least, they would explain it in some such way as almost to explain it away. One method was to account for the defeat by some one particular mistake, so that the bad result could seem to be almost accidental. Even in the midst of the firing this state of mind was apparent. As Brockenbrough's men were retreating, some of them were heard to say, "If old Jack had been here, it wouldn't have been like this." These may be taken as the first of the countless ifs and it-wouldn't-have-beens that were to be uttered in the years that followed.

These attempts at explanation did much to develop a legend of the charge, and this legend has had a great influence upon what has come to be considered fact. Implicit in these explanations was the idea that a different result would have been assured if the writer's ideas had been followed. From those who had been at Gettysburg this technique passed on to the historians. The present writer has attempted to keep the ifs and might-have-beens to a minimum, thinking that his work is to tell what happened, not what might have happened. He remembers Lee's words, shortly after the battle, "It is sufficient to show what was done and what was not done" — a rather cryptic comment, indeed, but one which may be taken to mean that there is no need to consider what "might have been done." We might also remember Gibbon's words of many years afterwards: "It is so easy to fight battles on paper, so different from fighting them successfully on the ground."

2

The first attempt to explain was merely to blame everything on the North Carolinians. Since the Virginians had pierced the Union line at one point, and the others had not done so, there arose among Pickett's men, almost immediately, a feeling that they had not been properly supported. To blame the North Carolinians was easy, for ever since colonial times Virginians had held a low opinion of their neighbors to the south. Possibly, also, this was a smoke screen among chauvinistic Virginians to cover up the indisputable fact that the first troops to give way were those of Brockenbrough's brigade.

Pickett himself adopted this attitude in his already-quoted letters and also, apparently, in his official report, throwing the blame upon the other brigades. One must write "apparently" because the report is not extant, having been destroyed at the specific request of Lee, who wrote — "we have the enemy to fight, and must carefully, at this critical moment, guard against dissensions which the reflections in your report would create."

Unfortunately, a Virginia war-correspondent, writing from Hagerstown on July 8, 1863, broke the story, producing what may be called the classical account of up-Pickett and down-Pettigrew. Seldom has there been a worse war-dispatch — based on ignorance and shaped by prejudice. It did not even mention Trimble's command, but with fine over-simplification made a straight contrast between Pickett's "brave Virginians" and "Pettigrew's division." Nothing is said about Brockenbrough's Virginians. Pettigrew's men were described as flying, panic-stricken, as retreating "pell-mell." Though there was no mention in this article of North Carolinians, popular feeling soon fixed the onus upon them.

Obviously, this article should not have been published, for two reasons. First, it was false; second, it was deleterious to the war-effort. It furnishes a good example of the kind of tensions which racked the Confederacy.

Naturally, the North Carolinians resented these slanders intensely. They made some efforts at counter-propaganda. But, having already been established as the villains, they could not readily argue their way out. One effect of this "explanation" has been the coloration of nearly all accounts of the charge which have been written since that time. From the newspapers and from common gossip this interpretation passed to such Southern historians as Pollard, thence to such Northern historians as Swinton, and thus was established in historical tradition.

Eventually the counterattack itself went to extremes, and thus arose the North Carolina slogan, "Farthest at Gettysburg." This claim rests upon geographical rather than military data — that some of the North Carolinians, advancing against the wall held by Hays's men, went farther east than Pickett's men did, even after these latter had broken the Union line. But a Virginian countercounterattack was quickly launched.

With the mass of *Official Reports* and reminiscences now available there is great difficulty in seeing how anyone can still maintain this derogatory attitude toward the North Carolinians or toward any of the other brigades except possibly Brockenbrough's. The only way to do so would be to believe that the writers of those reports and reminiscences, most of them officers of Lee's army, were all arrant liars. One would also have to conclude that the Union soldiers who testified to the valor of their opponents were linked with them in a conspiracy.

True, Lee himself is reported by Imboden as praising Pickett's division and questioning the conduct of the supporting troops. But is it not possible that Lee was referring to Brockenbrough's men? Also, we should perhaps remember, Imboden was a Virginian, and wrote his recollections long after the war, when the down-Pettigrew tradition was well established.

True, also, Pickett broke the Union line, and Pettigrew did not. But a consideration of Union records and of the whole situation, as here attempted, makes clear that this breaking of the line depended upon many factors besides mere valor.

3

Blaming it all on the North Carolinians could be satisfactory for Virginians and South Carolinians, but not for the Confederates generally, and particularly not for Mississippians, Tennesseans, and Alabamians, who had fought under Pettigrew's command. Some other explanation of the disaster must be sought, and the Confederates were caught in a dilemma. They had to maintain either that Lee had ordered an impossibility, or that the Confederate soldier could not accomplish what he was reasonably ordered to do. Perish the thought that either should be true! The explanation therefore had to be very vague. There could be mention of an "impregnable position," and the low Cemetery Ridge was magnified into "heights," and even "a mountain bristling with guns." Or the gallant little band of Confederates was overwhelmed by numbers. Thus the scant six thousand Union troops were multiplied into as many as forty thousand, and reserves were rushed in from all directions, until the odds were "sixty to one." But even these solutions were not satisfactory, for they naturally raised the questions why Lee thus recklessly assaulted a mountain and why he did not have better information about the number of Yankees holding it.

Then, not long after the war, the Confederates were supplied with a scapegoat. Though he had fought bravely, Longstreet had never been what may be called an extreme Southerner. After the war, he was among the first to accept the new situation and to begin labors toward a unified republic. By then accepting office under the Federal government, he outraged the South. In 1867 a newspaper noted him as one of those "who have dishonored the dignity of the white blood and are traitors alike to principle and race."

Immediately there was a new possibility to explain the defeat. If Longstreet was a traitor after the war, he might well have been a traitor during it, particularly at Gettysburg — he had disobeyed Lee's orders; he had obstructed and delayed; his defeatism had caused defeat. The public accusation began in 1872, and the chief accusers were Generals Jubal Early and "Parson" Pendleton. Longstreet, a good fighter, struck back. Like most controversies, this one generated more heat than light, and does not inform us greatly about the charge itself. It dragged on for years, but we may quickly pass it over. Longstreet, at times the most hated man in the South, was in a hopeless position. He might refute particular charges, but it did him little good. In a sense, we may say that the South could never forgive him for being right. He had said all along that the charge would fail, and he had been proved disastrously correct. But, having *said* that it would fail, had he not in some subtle and mysterious way, as if by sympathetic magic, *caused* it to fail? As late as 1904, a writer in the *Confederate Veteran* could publish the flat statement, "Longstreet, not Meade, defeated Lee at Gettysburg." No substantial charges were proved, and none possibly could be. Yet, again, a controversy had a profound effect upon the historical tradition, apparently because of the common belief that where there is so much smoke there must be some fire.

As far as these two controversies are concerned, the present writer can say only that he has read both sides of them both, but has thereby got little real information, and has therefore depended upon the *Official Reports* and other basic documents. He has read the evidence and tried to interpret it reasonably. He is not a North Carolinian, nor does he have any personal reason to defend Longstreet. The ideas that either the North Carolinians or Longstreet failed in their duty on July 3 seem to him, on the evidence, to be unfounded, and in fact utterly fantastic.

4

A third controversy involves Pickett's own conduct. Some went so far as to say that he was well to the rear, behind a large rock.

Among his bitter critics was Eppa Hunton, colonel of the 8th Virginia at Gettysburg, who afterwards was promoted to the command of the brigade that had been Garnett's. He wrote in his memoirs:

> It is very curious that Pickett should go down in history as the hero of Gettysburg, and finally lose his reputation to such an extent as to be dismissed from the army.

Hunton would not recognize the term "Pickett's charge," and on his tomb required the inscription, "Wounded in the charge of Pickett's Division."

Naturally most of these accusations circulated by word of mouth, and failed to get into print — at least, as with Hunton's memoirs, until long after the war. With this controversy as with the others, the present writer has tried to examine and appraise all the evidence.

Popular tradition, though it was harsh to Longstreet, was highly favorable to Pickett. The argument, in fact, was almost syllogistic. Pickett's charge was heroic; it was Pickett's; therefore, Pickett was heroic. The account in the Richmond newspaper that vilified Pettigrew's men reported that Pickett moved forward among his troops as if courting death by his own daring intrepidity!

The chief difficulty to be explained away, aside from the dissenting murmurs of a few veterans, was how Pickett survived without a scratch, when his three brigadiers and all his field officers except one went down. This could be done by the brief explanation that his escape was "miraculous."

Up to a certain point, in the present writer's opinion, Pickett's conduct was all that could be desired. He then suffered some failure of stamina, though probably nothing that should be called cowardice. More likely, not being a quick-thinking man, he merely became confused, and ended by doing what was not heroic. Thus, instead of going forward at the critical moment or instead of advancing to meet his men as they retired, he went to the rear, as Poague so clearly relates. The strong argument that he did nothing cowardly is that he was retained in command and that he kept the respect of his men and officers, with some exceptions.

5

Among the Union troops, since they had won the victory and could afford to be generous, the controversies were small. There was one involving Hancock and Hunt as to the proper handling of the artillery. There was another between Hancock and Stannard as to who ordered the flanking movement. The survivors of the Philadelphia brigade objected to Haskell's narrative, and published a pamphlet ridiculing and attacking it, but scarcely presenting any counter-evidence.

More than twenty-five years after the battle, the Gettysburg Battlefield Memorial Association and the Survivors' Association of the 72nd Pennsylvania became involved in a dispute which eventually went to the courts. The problem was where the regiment's battlefield monument should be located. The established policy was that such monuments should stand at some point where a regiment had been located in a regularly established line. This would have put the monument, along with those of the 42nd New York and the 19th Massachusetts, in the second line, where all three had lain in support during the cannonade. The two other regiments, secure in their own records, quietly accepted this position. The 72nd insisted upon thrusting itself forward.

The result was a lengthy trial, with the examination of witnesses ranging from former privates to General Webb. All this testimony, taken under oath and with cross-examination, was published verbatim; we have thus a unique historical document, although one which has not been used by historians, so far as I can discover, until the present work. From this document have been drawn many details, such as the story of Sergeant Major Stockton, and also much information as to timing and maneuvers.

Some of the testimony is of remarkable poignancy, even

though the heat of battle was so many years in the past. We have the boiling over of pride in the regiment:

Q. Did you see any Massachusetts or New York regiment come down and run over the Seventy-second?

A. I would like to see somebody say so! I would like to meet the man who said it!

We have the vivid personal memory:

Q. Where did you find the bodies in the angle; I mean of the Seventy-second people in the angle?

A. The most I can remember was one by the name of Metz belonging to my company — him and me were great chums — and he fell across the stone wall. He fell crossways across the stone wall.

Or we have the man lost from his regiment and looking desperately for his comrades, saying simply, "I thought that if I were to get wounded or killed, I wanted to be near somebody who knew me."

In the end the regiment won its suit, though on a technicality. The monument, a conspicuous one of a soldier in Zouave uniform swinging a clubbed musket, stands close up to the stone wall.

6

Two minor legends deserve brief mention. One is that one of the assailants was a woman — a young wife who disguised herself as a man to accompany her husband, went with him in the charge, and was killed at the Angle. The other is that of a Union soldier whose teeth fell out soon after the battle and who was always convinced that they had been shaken loose by the cannonade.

7

In 1957 President Eisenhower and Field Marshal Montgomery viewed the field, and allowed themselves some adverse comments on Confederate generalship that aroused a considerable to-do in the South. The suggestion that there should have been a movement around the Union left flank was an approval of Longstreet's idea, though probably neither of the modern soldiers knew what Longstreet had proposed. Also, we may doubt whether they knew that such a movement would have overstretched the Confederate line and would have run into the Sixth Corps.

8

In later years some veterans could never bring themselves to return to the field which could offer them only the memory of stricken comrades. Perhaps these were the ones of finer sensibilities. Many, however, returned on reunions, and fought their battle over. A bond of comradeship even developed between the survivors of the Philadelphia brigade and those of Pickett's division. The Virginians once entertained the Pennsylvanians in Richmond, and the latter reported that on that occasion they captured the city without losing a man. On another occasion, Pickett's men were guests at Gettysburg. In a simulated attack the Virginian oldsters marched up the slope toward the Pennsylvanians behind the wall, and then a photograph was taken as they shook hands across it. According to one story, on this or a similar occasion, the excitement rose to such a pitch that the Philadelphians refused to be driven from the wall even symbolically, and a conflict with walking sticks ensued.

At one joint reunion a keg of ice-cold beer was on tap at High-water Mark. The day was hot, like that one of July 3, 1863. Sampling the beer, the Confederate veterans declared that if it had been there on that long-ago afternoon, no one could possibly have driven them away from the clump of trees. Thus, sometimes, the hatreds and the horrors of the world, like its glories, pass away.

Appendices

Acknowledgments

Bibliography

Notes and References

Index

Appendix A

CONFEDERATE LOSSES

BASIC information as to Pickett's losses may be derived from the following. (1) *Return of killed and wounded* (OR, ii, 329). (Since this does not list missing, it is of limited value.) (2) *Return of casualties* (OR, ii, 339). (3) Peyton's report for Garnett's brigade, viz., total losses, 941 (OR, ii, 387). (The report is of July 9 when all the stragglers should have rejoined; it is presumably correct.) (4) Aylett's report for Armistead's brigade (OR, ii, 1000), viz., "more than two thirds." (This is dated July 12, and is presumably correct, though vague.) (5) The statement by Harrison in *Pickett's Men* (p. 102) that the losses for the division were 3393. (This was probably based on a roll call of July 4, before the stragglers had rejoined, and therefore may be high.)

W. W. Wood states that 300 men who had been under arrest in brigade guardhouses were returned to the ranks on the night of July 4; this seems an unduly large figure; not knowing what to do with this statement, I have neglected it.

For Heth's division the sources also are various. (1) The official returns of killed and wounded and of casualties, as cited above, are almost useless, since they give no missing, except for Archer's brigade; for this brigade the figures are confirmatory. (2) The letter of Capt. J. J. Young (OR, ii, 645) states that the division on July 4 numbered "only 1,500 or 1,600 effective men," but added that "a good many will still come in." (2) J. H. Moore states that the division numbered about 1800 when it recrossed the Potomac. (4) Shepard's report for Archer's brigade (OR, ii, 647) gives losses for the whole battle as 677. (5) Davis told his uncle the president that his brigade ended at less than 500 (OR, iii, 1000).

For Pender's division (the official returns again not giving the missing) we have Lane's report (OR, ii, p. 664) of 660 losses.

From these data a fairly satisfactory summation can be made. The chief point of doubt is the loss in Kemper's brigade. It seems too high if we assign to it the residuum of Harrison's figure, and too low if we take the *Return of Casualties*. In the latter case we have to believe that Kemper's brigade suffered only 40% in the charge, whereas Garnett's suffered 65% and Armistead's 73%. The return is dubious, as regards Kemper's brigade, for other reasons too, for instance, it lists only two killed for the 1st Virginia. I have therefore raised the casualties for Kemper's brigade approximately to equal those of Garnett's.

For Heth's division Young and Moore essentially agree, since a sufficient number of stragglers could have come in to raise Young's figure to Moore's. I have therefore taken the losses to be 4500 minus 1800, or 2700. The assignment of losses to the brigades is difficult. I have assumed that Brockenbrough lost about a hundred men. The 677 for Archer's brigade must be divided between July 1 and July 3. If we take its loss on July 1 as 177, the loss of July 3 was about 500 (57%); since Archer's men fought with great gallantry, it is hard to assign them losses much less, proportionally, than those of Garnett's brigade, with which they were mingled. Residual losses for the division (2100) would have to be equally divided between Pettigrew's and Davis's brigades.

We may assume that Scales's losses were proportionately the same as Lane's.

These figures have been corrected for estimated losses during the cannonade. They include, however, the unwounded prisoners, who were numerous, according to Union reports. The best source from which to estimate the proportion of unwounded prisoners is McFarland's careful post-war study of the 11th Mississippi, in which the unwounded prisoners are 13% of the total losses. I have used this figure for the five front-line brigades and a smaller one for Pender's brigades.

Civil War statistics (See Fox, p. 24) show 17% as the proportion

of killed to total casualties. In a close fight, such as that of Pickett's
charge, we may use the figure 20%.

From all these data we arrive at the table presented in Part IX,
#16.

Appendix B
THE PICKETT "LETTERS"

IN *Pickett and his Men* (1900) by LaSalle Corbell Pickett (the general's wife) appear the text of one letter by Pickett, the partial text
of another, and a brief quotation from a third (pp. 301, 316–8). I see
no reason to doubt that these are genuine though they may have
been edited. In 1913 appeared *The Heart of a Soldier*, presented as
Pickett's letters to his fiancée, some of them dated from the field of
Gettysburg, with an introduction which was substantially a reprinting of Mrs. Pickett's article in *McClure's Magazine* for March, 1908.
In 1928 appeared *Soldier of the South*, reprinting the letters from the
1913 volume and adding the two from *Pickett and his Men*, together
with a facsimile page of one of these latter, giving evidence of heavy
editing.

The letters of the 1913 volume, at least those dealing with Gettysburg, I have been forced to decide, cannot be considered original
historical sources. I have come to this conclusion regretfully, because
I would have been glad to use some of the vivid details there presented. From D. S. Freeman's note (*Lee*, ii, 563) I should conclude
that he did not accept these letters as authentic. In conversation I
have also found another Civil War expert to be so minded. Many
historians, however, have used them.

The letters fall under suspicion in many ways, a few of which may
be mentioned. (1) For the letters included in *Heart of a Soldier*, no
facsimiles are given, and I have come across no originals. (The fore-
words to both the volumes imply the existence of originals.) (2)

The omission from this volume of the genuine letters from *Pickett and his Men* is surprising. (3) In *Pickett and his Men* there are mentions of still other letters written by Pickett to his fiancée during the campaign, but they do not coincide in date with those of *Heart of a Soldier*. (4) The style of writing in *Heart of a Soldier* is lusciously sentimental, differing from that of the letters in *Pickett and his Men*. (5) The writer in *Heart of a Soldier* knows a great deal more than Pickett could possibly have known at the time when he was supposed to have been writing the letters. For instance, he mentions the battlefield place names, Little Round Top, Culp's Hill, Cemetery Ridge, Seminary Ridge. Most of these names were not known to the Confederates at the time of the battle, and do not occur in OR. Longstreet, for instance, once refers to Little Round Top as Rocky Hill. Again, on page 92 we have the sentence, "About half past three, Gary's pistol signaled the Yankees' attack upon Culp's Hill." How could Pickett, not yet even arrived on the battlefield, have known that Culp's Hill was attacked, much less that the Union troops were commanded by General Geary (not Gary), even much less still, that Geary had signaled the attack by shooting a pistol?

Possibly the letters may go back to some originals which have been very heavily edited. More likely, I believe, they are constructed, as data and occasional wordings would indicate, from Harrison's *Pickett's Men* or *Pickett and his Men*, which itself is largely based upon Harrison. In any case, I have not felt justified in making use of them.

Appendix C

FIRE-POWER AND LOSSES

ALTHOUGH it is stated in the text (Part IX, #17) that the losses resulting from different causes cannot be accurately determined, such matters — like the Sirens' song — are not beyond speculation.

Confederate losses may be broken down into those resulting from (1) long-range artillery fire during the advance, (2) canister, (3) musketry, (4) hand-to-hand weapons, (5) long-range artillery fire during the retreat. Of these (4) is negligible, and (5) is not important, and may be merged with (1).

Knowing the approximate number of guns firing during the advance, their possible rate of fire, and the approximate time during which the Confederates were exposed, we can calculate the number of long-range rounds fired. This would be around 1000.

Canister-fire can be similarly calculated, and works out at around 500 rounds. If each round contained 30 balls, the number of projectiles would be 15,000.

At the beginning of the advance about 5300 Union muskets were available; by the end of the engagement casualties had reduced these to about 4000. We may take an average of 5000. Some regiments, like the 8th Ohio, may have fired as many as 50 rounds per man; an average of 30 may be assumed. This would yield the total of 150,000 rounds, ten times the number of canister balls!

The "efficiency" of canister-fire was probably higher than that of musketry, since the firing was from a solid base and was performed by men who had more right to be called experts. On the other hand, the efficiency of long-range artillery fire was very low. One might suggest then that the approximately 6500 casualties should be split: Long-range fire, 500; canister, 1000; musketry, 5000.

Union casualties must have resulted almost entirely from musketry. The Confederates advanced with about 4800 men in the front (double-ranked) line. By their time of coming within musketry range this number had presumably shrunk to about 3000 because of casualties, stragglers, and the retreat of Brockenbrough's brigade. With this length of line they fired only a few rounds (say, 5), and then the move of Kemper's brigade to the left and the general massing in front of the Angle reduced this front to about 1800 men, that is, counting the men in two ranks, who would have been able to fire freely. Some others fired to the flanks, so that we may generally assume that about 2000 Confederates were able to fire. Obviously most of the men massed fifteen or twenty deep below the Angle could not fire. Moreover, the Confederates undoubtedly fired fewer rounds per man than the Union troops did, because they were trying to advance and were at the same time overwhelmed by a fire heavier than they were able to return. Probably 20 rounds per man firing would be adequate. This would yield a total of 40,000 rounds fired after the lines contracted, or perhaps 50,000 altogether.

Under the conditions, the efficiency of the Confederate fire was undoubtedly lower than that of the Union fire, especially since the Union troops were behind defenses which protected a quarter to a third of each man's body. We have assumed that about one Union rifle bullet in 30 produced a casualty. If we assume that one Confederate bullet in 35 was similarly successful, the result is just about 1500, or the number of Union casualties as determined from other data.

Appendix D

BATTLE-ORDERS IN CONFEDERATE BRIGADES

ALMOST nothing can be said to turn upon the arrangement of the Confederate regiments within their brigades. Nevertheless, it is a matter of some sentimental interest, and much data is available. The only order given in OR (ii, 647) is for Archer's brigade, viz., left to right, 5th Ala., 7th Tenn., 14th Tenn., 13th Ala., 1st Tenn. The chief sources for the orders are the Bachelder *Isometrical Drawing*, and the Warren-Bachelder map. But the order given by these for Archer's brigade does not coincide with OR, and therefore the authority of these maps cannot be altogether accepted. Still, Bachelder was interested in collecting this kind of information, and most of his data are probably correct. For instance, his order for Garnett's brigade is, left to right, 56–28–19–18–8. This is confirmed by Finley. His order for Kemper's brigade, left to right, is 3–7–1–11–

24. This is largely confirmed by Loehr's statement that the 1st held the center, and by various reminiscences indicating that the 11th and 24th were on the right of the line. Bachelder's order (all, left to right) for Armistead's brigade is 38–57–53–9–14; for Pettigrew's, 11–26–47–52; for Brockenbrough's, 55–47–40–22; for Lane's, 33–18–28–37–7; for Scales's, 38–13–34–22–16. In Davis's brigade the 11th Miss. was probably on the right and the 2nd Miss. on the left. Reminiscences in NCRegs suggest that the 55th N.C. was next to the 2nd Miss.; this would leave the 42nd Miss. next to the 11th.

Appendix E
WRIGHT'S REPORT

WRIGHT's report (OR, ii, 622) is the most inaccurate and exaggerated of any that it has been my need to study. It can be checked against the much more matter-of-fact Union reports and the highly circumstantial account in Ward. Wright claimed the overrunning of more than 20 guns; three was the probably correct figure. He mentions a rocky ravine, which does not exist on that part of the battlefield, and must be a confused memory of what I have termed the rough ground. No one would deny that the Georgians made a gallant advance; but the Union reports indicate that they never reached the stone wall, being repulsed by frontal fire from the 69th Pa. posted behind it and by a flank attack of the 106th Pa. Yet Wright could claim, "We were now complete masters of the field [!]."

One cannot help wondering to what extent this report influenced the decision to order Pickett's Charge — probably, not very much. Lee doubtless knew the kind of person that Wright was; besides, that Wright had advanced to a certain point on July 2 meant little as far as July 3 was concerned. Obviously the Union position could have been fortified and reinforced in the meantime. Yet Lee certainly took some comfort from Wright's exploit, and used it for propaganda purposes with the troops about to advance with Pickett.

Appendix F

THE BATTLEFIELD

THE battlefield itself is an important document, since it enables us to determine cover, distances, and therefore, on occasion, such other matters as time and numbers of troops. In general, the preservation of the battlefield has been excellent. (See the photographs in the text.)

1) *Terrain.* There is no evidence of erosion, and the contours are probably not changed significantly since 1863.

2) *Buildings.* The Bliss barn, burned before the charge, has not been rebuilt. The Codori barn is a post-battle construction, but on the site of the old barn and probably much resembling it. Aside from some unfortunate modern structures such as motels, the other buildings are about as they were. Except as they gave the Confederates a little shelter during the advance, the buildings were of no significance.

3) *Fences.* As can be determined by references to fences in the sources and from the Warren-Bachelder map, the fences remain about as they were, in location and construction, with one exception. This last is a more recent wire fence that runs north from the Angle, in front of Hays's position. As mentioned in the text, the Confederates had torn down most of the fences that would have impeded their march. Only the stone walls and the fences along the northern part of the Emmitsburg road are to be considered of military significance. Many of the fences must have had a growth of bushes and small trees along them; a possible significance of such growth is mentioned in Part III, #3.

4) *Fields and crops.* The field-pattern, being determined by the

fences, was about the same as now. Wheat was the principal crop; there are also mentions of fields of oats, rye, and corn. From the military point of view all of these, offering about the same degree of cover at that time of year, may be considered very much the same thing. The land between the Emmitsburg road and the Union position was apparently pasture; in front of Hays's position the field was in clover. The farmhouses had small orchards near-by.

5) *Tree-growth.* The area is an excellent tree-growing region, and trees have sprung up rapidly since 1863. In addition, through the years, the building of roads and the general maintenance as a park have tended to protect growth in certain places and to remove it in others. In considering the scene, one must make some allowances. a) Cemetery Hill had few trees, and so was a good artillery position, though now it would not be. b) Along Seminary Ridge at various places in front of the Confederate battery positions the tree-growth has been such as to obstruct the line of fire. c) The trees in the "clump of trees" are probably twice the size they were, and are more numerous. This is a matter of some military significance, since the clump in 1863 would have given less protection to troops behind it than it would now. d) Bushes and small trees had extended north and west from the clump toward the Angle. These had mostly been cut down, and thus formed the slashing. This was of some significance, since the Confederates advancing over the wall had much more shelter than they would have now, but also some impediment to their advance. e) What I have called the rough ground (see various maps in the text and photograph entitled "Hall-Harrow Line") may have looked just before the battle much as it appears now, i.e. a rather thick growth of bushes and small trees. On July 3, however, the trees had largely been cut down to open up a field of fire. Still, the rocks here offered a good deal of shelter. f) Post-battle growth of trees may have obstructed the field of fire which was available to McGilvery's guns (see photograph entitled "McGilvery's Line").

Appendix G

CONFEDERATE ARTILLERY

A WHOLE monograph would be required to discuss adequately the complicated evidence as to the location of the Confederate guns, especially those of Longstreet's corps. Historian Harry W. Pfanz of the Gettysburg National Military Park has collaborated with me on the problem, and our correspondence has been voluminous. I feel that we have been able to work out solutions to practically all the problems of location except as to that of certain of Cabell's and Poague's guns which were somewhere near the Point of Woods.

In the map of the cannonade (Part V, #2) the general results of these researches are embodied; but battalions and batteries are not specified. Some statement as to battalions appears in the text.

The difficulty arises chiefly from the fact that the reports in OR are few, brief, and remarkably vague as to location, though they cannot be neglected. "Troop Positions (Interviews)" must be our chief reliance for many details. But these reminiscences resulted from visits to the battlefield about thirty years later, and one sometimes doubts whether the officers' memories can always be trusted. Many reminiscences yield information on particular batteries. The Warren-Bachelder map is of little value, and the markers are along Confederate Avenue, far removed from the actual location of Longstreet's batteries.

The precise site of each battery is of natural interest to the descendants of artillerymen who fought there, but it is of no appreciable historical significance. As already stated, I believe that we can consider most of the problems soluble, but this is no place to present the voluminous data. The map may be considered, for practical purposes, sufficient.

Appendix H
THE UNION ARTILLERY

THE Union artillery offers comparatively few problems as compared with the Confederate artillery.

Osborn's batteries were in a V with the point turned approximately north, viz.:

Hill

Eakin

Bancroft

Dilger

Taft

Edgell

The batteries in the rear line fired through the gaps in the front line. The present markers are of little value in locating the battery positions, which can best be established from Osborn's article and from OR.

The Second Corps artillery is properly located by the battlefield markers.

Thomas's position was about at what might be called the south end of Cemetery Ridge, a long way from its monument. (See Benedict and Morgan.) As a battery of the Reserve, it was probably put into position by Hunt personally, but was doubtless under Doubleday's orders. There is no report for this battery.

Daniels's battery was a good way north of its battlefield marker, and may have been about where the Warren-Bachelder map locates it. Certainly it was well south of Cemetery Ridge, for the Confederates paid little attention to it.

Lt. Col. McGilvery was the second-ranking officer in the Artillery Reserve, and his assignment to this particular sector shows the importance that Hunt felt it to have. McGilvery's command was the First Volunteer Brigade, of which he had Phillips's, Hart's, and Thompson's batteries with him. He was also assigned Dow's, Sterling's and Ames's from other brigades of the Reserve and Rank's from the Horse Artillery. Cooper's, of the First Corps, later reinforced him. In his report (OR, i, 883) McGilvery mentions also "a New Jersey battery," but this must be an error since the two N.J. batteries can be located elsewhere. Hunt (OR, i, 238) lists the batteries. The markers for these batteries seem to be correct.

Appendix I

THE EVIDENCE

THE only contemporary evidence, strictly speaking, consists of the field itself, a few notes written during the battle, and the dispatches to the Philadelphia *Morning Post*. Everything else must be considered reminiscence, subject to conscious and unconscious editing. We have a few letters and newspaper dispatches written on July 4. Some of the Union reports are dated July 5, and most of them were written within a month. The Confederate reports were written mostly within two months. Reminiscences in the stricter sense began almost immediately (e.g., Jacobs, Palmer, both published in 1864), and continued to be written as long as veterans lived. In fact, the battle is probably the best attested of any in the war, and perhaps of any before the twentieth century.

The multiplicity of evidence greatly increases the historian's task, and I have sometimes paused over two conflicting and seemingly equally authoritative accounts to quote — "How happy could I be with either, were tother dear charmer away!" Even the reports, though on the whole the most reliable evidence, are not consistent. Not only are Union and Confederate reports contradictory, but also reports within the same army. Even the better reminiscences contradict one another wildly on particular points.

Yet one should not present too doleful a picture. By careful checking of one source against another, by application of the canons of historical criticism, by constant reference to the great yardsticks of time, space, and number — eventually the reality appears.

There is no single full and authoritative account from which to begin. Haskell's is the longest, and is deservedly famous. It is, however, primarily a personal-experience story, and it contains some errors, as would only be expected. What we have, then (as the long bibliography indicates), is a surprisingly large number of short accounts, representing different points of view, presenting different details, and supplementing one another. As a result, much of the story must be constructed by noting details from widely separated sources and fitting them together.

There should be a special word about the speeches, many of which have been quoted *verbatim*. I am not so trusting as to believe that these represent, in many cases, exactly what was said. Thus Fremantle, writing soon after the event, reported Lee's words to Colston as: "Don't whip him, Captain; don't whip him. I've got just such another foolish horse myself, and whipping does no good." Colston himself, writing years later, reported: "Don't whip him, captain; it does no good. I had a foolish horse, once, and kind treatment is the best." Yet, though the words vary, the idea is remarkably the same. I have used such quotations freely. While the words cannot be guaranteed, I see no reason to doubt that the sense has been preserved.

The reading and careful consideration of so many reminiscences has left me with a heightened regard for the reliability of the American soldier, as regards his own experiences. Deliberate attempts to deceive seem to be rare. Rare also are boastful accounts. Thus Sergeant Easley went over the wall with Armistead and advanced as far as any man, but in telling about it he is actually a little apologetic, because he had allowed himself to become separated from his company. Occasionally I read an account which seemed to me impossible, only to realize, as my own information increased, that it had something to it. A notable instance is Captain Smith's reminiscence upon which is based the story of the 11th Virginia (VIII, #21).

The trouble arises in the reminiscences when the attempt is made to describe, not the writer's own experience, but the situation as a whole. Even in such cases, however, we must remember that a reminiscence may be valuable in some parts and not in others. Thus Bright's narrative is excellent in its earlier parts, but like some other Confederate reminiscences it goes to pieces toward the end.

I estimate that for the preparation of this book I have had available, in longer or shorter form, the testimony of 450 participants, and of a few non-participating witnesses.

Appendix J
PROBLEMS OF THE ADVANCE

SOME problems of the advance seem rather too technical for inclusion in the text. The statement is sometimes made that Heth's division, being posted farther back, had farther to advance. Assuming that we know where each division was posted (and there seems to be no great controversy), the distance which Heth's right had to advance was actually about the same as that to be covered by Pickett's left. Reference to the map of the advance will show that Heth's left had to advance a slightly shorter distance; Pickett's right, a considerably greater distance. In my interpretation, I have decided that Pickett's right made up this distance (about 800 feet) at the time when the line was re-dressed. In any case, the time of Pickett's advance must have been determined rather by the right than by the left, and so his division would have needed more time than Heth's. Since the matter was successfully solved, I presume that it was foreseen and planned in advance. Such happy outcomes are rarely the result of accident. Did Heth's division start a little later, or was it held longer in the swale where it re-dressed?

If Heth's division was posted along the line of Seminary Ridge, as is usually supposed, it would have been off perpendicular. The tactical problem of "maintaining the perpendicular" during an assault was emphasized in the manuals, e.g., Casey. The division was about ten degrees off, with its left advanced. This would mean that the left of

Pettigrew's brigade would have been about 200 feet in advance of the right of Archer's. A variation of ten degrees would doubtless have been a matter of moment to the Prussian Guard, but we may question whether Heth's division even knew about it. The matter may have more or less automatically been adjusted by the lines dressing to the right. The fact that Davis's and Brockenbrough's brigades were delayed might have corrected, or even over-corrected, the difficulty.

Appendix K

FLAGS

UNION flags are not the subject of much controversy, and the statements in the text will probably occasion no argument. The second flag was regularly a state flag.

I have come to three conclusions as far as the Confederate troops in Pickett's Charge are concerned. (1) Each regiment bore one flag. The captures of flags, never more than one to a regiment and many mentions of "the flag" of a regiment would bear this out. See, e.g., the report for Archer's brigade, OR, ii, 647. (2) The Virginia regiments carried the blue Virginia flag. Poague mentions "a Virginia flag" (p. 75); Scheibert (*Drei Monate*) mentions blue flags. See also a passage on flags in J. E. Johnston Narrative, p. 602. (3) Most of the other regiments — perhaps all of them — carried flags in which red was the noticeable color, many of which were, as closely as words can indicate, the same as what is known now as the Confederate flag. Haskell (p. 105, 113) mentions red flags. The best description is Fremantle's (pp. 180f), who was writing his first impressions of Lee's army on June 22, and was referring to Pender's division:

> The colors of the regiments differ from the blue battle flags I saw with Bragg's army. They are generally red, with a blue St. Andrew's cross showing the stars. . . . The new Confederate flag has evidently been adopted from this battle flag.

Fremantle's use of the word "generally" should indicate that some of Pender's regiments carried another kind of flag, but I am not sure that we can trust him for such meticulous use of language. If so, these other regiments might have carried one of the other Confederate flags or a state flag. In view of the individuality of the Confederate service, some of the older regiments may well have carried a special flag.

Shields (p. 463) describes the captured flags as being "home-made affairs" of different kinds of cheap cloth. Since the once brightly colored sections had undoubtedly faded and the white sections had become dirty, many of these flags probably showed little color of any kind.

Acknowledgments

DURING the course of working upon this book, I have become in-
debted to a large number of people for criticism, advice, and other
favors. I wish particularly to thank the following: Bruce Catton,
Monroe F. Cockrell, Burke Davis, Clifford Dowdey, Fairfax Downey,
C. S. Forester, Richard B. Harwell, W. S. Howell, Col. H. C. Lauter,
Jr., Jay Monaghan, Joseph B. Newman, Ralph G. Newman, Louis D.
Rubin, Harold A. Small, Ray D. Smith, Kenneth M. Stampp, Glenn
Tucker, Jac Weller, Kenneth P. Williams, Don Worcester. The
members of the Kosmos Club (Berkeley) and of Symposion–Junto
have listened to my readings of sections of the book in preliminary
form, and have offered their suggestions.

I am under particular debt to the historians of Gettysburg National
Military Park, Dr. Frederick Tilberg, and Harry W. Pfanz. A special
acknowledgment to the latter is recorded in Appendix G. The Park
Library contains valuable materials.

I wish also to express my thanks, for courtesies rendered, to the
Historical Societies of Pennsylvania, Rhode Island, Vermont, Virginia, and Wisconsin, and to the Rhode Island Development Council.

The Huntington Library possesses, in the Nicholson Collection,
what is probably the outstanding assemblage of materials on Gettysburg. I worked there on two occasions, and wish to express my
appreciation for the cooperation extended to me, with particular
thanks to Dr. Lyle H. Wright and Mary Isabel Fry.

The Library of the University of California (Berkeley) has a good
basic collection on the Civil War, together with a surprising number

of less common items. I have used this collection to the full. Largely to aid my work, the Library also purchased the *Lost Cause* minicards, thus making available a number of items which would otherwise have been difficult to obtain. I wish to thank Dorothy Keller, Head of the Order Department, for her aid in this and other matters.

I also utilized to the utmost the miraculous Inter-library Borrowing Service, which brings the books to the scholar, instead of forcing him, as would have been necessary a generation ago, to go to the books. I therefore express a special endebtedness to Margaret D. Uridge, head of that department, and to her able and always-helpful assistants.

Through this service I obtained eighty-one titles from thirty-four different libraries. I list the latter, with my thanks: Library of Congress; State Libraries of California (Sacramento, and Sutro Branch), Louisiana, Massachusetts, New Hampshire, New York; Public Libraries of Boston, Los Angeles, Riverside, St. Louis; Hayes Memorial Library; Pennsylvania Historical Society Library; Libraries of the Universities of Alabama, California (Los Angeles and Santa Barbara), Chicago, Duke, Emory, Illinois, Iowa, Michigan, Minnesota, Ohio, Oregon, North Carolina, Princeton, Stanford, Texas, Virginia, Western Reserve, Yale; College Libraries of Oberlin and Swarthmore.

Bibliography

EXCEPT for the works listed under VIII and some of those under I and II, all the entries represent original sources, i.e., they offer original material or material which is not extant in original sources.

The bibliography is arranged:

    I. Bibliographies, Periodicals, Collections
    II. Military Background
    III. General Works
    IV. Works Chiefly on Gettysburg, with Material on Pickett's Charge
    V. Regimental Histories, etc.
    VI. Maps
    VII. Newspapers
    VIII. Secondary Works
    IX. The Battlefield and the Monuments

ABBREVIATIONS: — AW, *Annals of the War*; B & L, *Battles and Leaders*; CV, *Confederate Veteran*; DAB, *Dictionary of American Biography*; MOLLUS, Military Order of the Loyal Legion of the U.S.; NCRegs, *Histories of the Several Regiments . . . from N.C.*; NY at G, *New York at Gettysburg*; OLOD, *Our Living and Our Dead*; OR, U.S. War Dept., *War of the Rebellion, A Compilation of Official Records*; Pa. at G, *Pennsylvania at Gettysburg*; SHSP, Southern Historical Society Papers; Trial, see Supreme Court, Sect. IV of Bibliography.

I. BIBLIOGRAPHIES, PERIODICALS, COLLECTIONS

Annals of the War. Phila., 1879.
Bartlett, J. R., *Literature of the Rebellion*. Boston, Providence, 1866.
Battles and Leaders of the Civil War (R. U. Johnson and C. C. Buel, eds.) (4 vols.) N.Y., 1887–88.
Confederate Veteran (40 vols.). Nashville, 1893–1932.
Dictionary of American Biography (20 vols.). N.Y., 1928–37.

The Land We Love (6 vols.). Charlotte, 1866–69.

Military Service Institution of the U.S., Journal (61 vols.). N.Y., 1880–1917.

Nicholson, J. P., *Catalogue of the Military Library of* . . . Phila., 1914.

Our Living and Our Dead (3 vols. and one no. of vol. 4). Raleigh, 1874–76.

Southern Bivouac (5 vols.). Louisville, 1882–87.

Southern Historical Society Papers (49 vols.). Richmond, 1876–1930.

United States Service Magazine (5 vols.). N.Y., 1864–66.

U.S. War Dept., *Bibliography of State Participation in the Civil War.* Wash., 1913.

U.S. War Dept., *The War of the Rebellion, A Compilation of Official Records* (70 vols. in 128). Wash., 1880–1901. The material on Pickett's Charge is mostly in Series I, Volume xxvii, Parts I and II. (To save space, references to this volume are cited merely as i, ii, or iii.) Supplementary material is to be found in the same volume Part III, in Series I, Volume li, Parts I and II, and in the *Atlas*. About 70 Union reports and 50 Confederate reports bear directly upon the charge.

II. MILITARY BACKGROUND

[Anon.], *Instruction for Field Artillery.* Wash., 1863.

[Anon.], *Medals of Honor issued by the War Dept.* Wash., 1904, 1906.

Benton, J. G., *Course of Instruction in Ordnance and Gunnery.* N.Y., 1862.

Birkheimer, W. E., *Historical Sketch of the* . . . *Artillery, U.S. Army.* Wash., 1884.

Butterfield, Daniel, *Camp and Outpost Duty for Infantry.* N.Y., 1862.

Casey, Silas, *Infantry Tactics.* Columbia, 1864.

Gibbon, John, *Artillerist's Manual.* N.Y., 1860.

Gilham, William, *Manual of Instruction for Volunteers and Militia of the Confederate States.* Richmond, 1861.

Gorgas, Josiah, "Notes on the Ordnance Dept." SHSP, xii, 67.

Hardee, W. J., *Rifle and Light Infantry Tactics.* Memphis, 1861.

Henderson, G. F. R., *Science of War.* London, N.Y., 1912.

Hicks, J. E., *Notes on U.S. Ordnance* (2 vols.). Mount Vernon, N.Y., 1946.

Hill, D. H., *Address.* SHSP, xiii, 259.

Hunt, H. J., "Artillery Administration," *Military Service Institution of the U.S., Journal,* March 1891, 197.

Idem, "Artillery," *Mil. Hist. Soc. of Mass.,* Papers, xiii, 93.

Hunter, Alexander, *Johnny Reb and Billy Yank.* N.Y., Wash., 1905.

Jomini, Baron de, *Art of War.* Various editions, originally published 1836.

McCarthy, Carlton, *Detailed Minutiae of Soldier Life*. Richmond, 1882.
Mahan, D. H., *Advanced Guard and Outposts, with essential Principles of Strategy and Grand Tactics*. N.Y., 1864.
Roberts, Joseph, *Hand-book of Artillery*. N.Y., 1865.
Scheibert, Justus, *Der Bürgerkrieg in den Nordamerikanischen Staaten*. Berlin, 1874.
Scott, H. L., *Military Dictionary*. N.Y., London, 1864.
Wiley, B. I., *Life of Johnny Reb*. Indianapolis, 1943.
Idem, *Life of Billy Yank*. Indianapolis, 1952.
Wilhelm, Thomas, *Military Dictionary*. Phila., 1881.

III. GENERAL WORKS

These contain sections dealing with Pickett's Charge or with its background.

Alexander, E. P., "Confederate Artillery Service." SHSP, xi, 98.
Idem, *Military Memoirs of a Confederate*. N.Y., 1907.
Alexander Letters. Savannah, 1910.
Allen, William, "Reminiscences of the Field Ordnance Service." SHSP, xiv, 137.
[Anon.], *In Memoriam Alexander Stuart Webb*. Albany, 1916. (Includes address by Andrew Cowan.)
Bardeen, C. W., *A Little Fifer's War Diary*. Syracuse, 1910.
Birkheimer, W. E., *In Memoriam of Gen. John Gibbon*. N.p., 1896.
Blackford, Susan Leigh, ed., *Memories of Life in and out of the Army in Virginia* (2 vols.). Lynchburg, 1894–96.
Blake, H. N., *Three Years in the Army of the Potomac*. Boston, 1865.
Browne, Dunn (pseud. for S. W. Fiske), *Dunn Browne's Experiences in the Army*. Boston, 1866.
Buell, Augustus, *"The Cannoneer."* Washington, 1890. [The authenticity of this book has been impugned (see *Pa. Mag. of Hist. and Biog.*, Oct. 1956), but I believe it to contain authentic material on Gettysburg; it is, however, a minor source on Pickett's Charge.]
Carson, A. S., "Southern Soldiers in Northern Prisons." SHSP, xxiii, 158.
Chamberlaine, W. W., *Memoirs of the Civil War*. Wash., 1912.
Committee on the Conduct of the War, Report of, Pt. 1, 38 Cong., 2 Sess. Wash., 1863.
Crotty, D. G., *Four Years Campaigning in the Army of the Potomac*. Grand Rapids, 1874.
Dawson, F. W., *Reminiscences of Confederate Service*. Charleston, 1882.
Dooley, John (J. T. Durkin, ed.), *John Dooley, Confederate Soldier, His War Journal*. Georgetown, 1945.

Dunaway, W. F., *Reminiscences of a Rebel*. N.Y., 1913.

Early, J. A., Letter, March 12, 1877. SHSP, iv, 50.

Favill, J. M., *Diary of a Young Officer*. Chicago, 1909.

Fitzgerald, David, *In Memoriam Gen. Henry J. Hunt*. Wash., 1890.

Fremantle, A. J. L., *Three Months in the Southern States*. N.Y., 1864 (refs. are to 1954 edition).

Fuger, Frederick, *Family History*. Detroit, 1904. (More correctly Füger, but usually occurring as Fuger.)

Gibbon, John, *An Address on the Unveiling of the Statue of . . . Meade*. [Vancouver Barracks, 1887.]

Idem, "Gettysburg." *Phila. Press*, July 6–13, 1887.

Idem, *Personal Recollections of the Civil War*. N.Y., 1903.

Gordon, J. B., *Reminiscences of the Civil War*. N.Y., 1911.

Goss, Warren, *Recollections of a Private*. N.Y., 1890.

Haight, T. W., *Three Wisconsin Cushings*. [Madison], 1910.

Hancock, A. R., *Reminiscences of Winfield Scott Hancock*. N.Y., 1887.

Hays, Alexander, *Life and Letters of* . . . (G. T. Fleming, ed.). Pittsburgh, 1919.

Heth, Henry, Letter, June, 1887. SHSP, iv, 151.

Hoke, Jacob, *The Great Invasion of 1863*. Dayton, 1887.

Howard, O. O., *Autobiography* (2 vols.). N.Y., 1907.

Idem, "Campaign and Battle of Gettysburg." *Atlantic Monthly*, July, 1876, 48.

Hunton, Eppa, *Autobiography*. Richmond, 1933.

Jacobs, M., *Notes on the Rebel Invasion*. Phila., 1864.

Johnston, D. E., *Four Years a Soldier*. Princeton, W. Va., 1887.

Idem, *Story of a Confederate Boy*. Portland, 1914. [Later version of the above.]

Johnston, J. E., *Narrative of Military Operations*. N.Y., 1874.

Jones, E. R., *Four Years in the Army of the Potomac*. London, 1881.

LaBree, Benjamin, ed., *Camp Fires of the Confederacy*. Louisville, 1899.

Lane, J. H., Letter, Oct. 20, 1877. SHSP, v, 38.

Lee, Fitzhugh, *General Lee*. N.Y., 1894.

Lee, R. E., *Lee's Dispatches* (D. S. Freeman, ed.). N.Y., London, 1915.

Lee, R. E., Jr. *Recollections and Letters of General R. E. Lee*. N.Y., 1905.

Lee, Susan P., *Memoirs of William Nelson Pendleton*. Phila., 1893.

Lewis, J. H., *Recollections from 1860 to 1865*. Wash., 1895.

Livermore, T. L., *Days and Events, 1860–66*. Boston, 1920.

Long, A. L., *Memoirs of Robert E. Lee*. N.Y., Phila., Wash., 1886.

Longstreet, H. D., *Lee and Longstreet at High Tide*. Gainesville, 1904.

Longstreet, James, *From Manassas to Appomattox*. Phila., 1896.

Idem, "Lee in Pennsylvania." *Phila. Weekly Times*, Nov. 3, 1877 (also in AW, and SHSP, v, 54).

Idem, "Lee's Right Wing at Gettysburg." B & L, iii, 337.

Idem, Letter, Nov. 6, 1877. SHSP, v, 52.

Idem, "The Mistakes of Gettysburg." Phila. *Weekly Times*, Feb. 23, 1877 (also in AW, and SHSP, v, 257).

Lyman, Theodore, *Meade's Headquarters, 1863–65*. Boston, 1922.

Malone, B. Y., *Diary of . . .* [W. W. Pierson, Jr., ed.]. Chapel Hill, 1919.

Maull, D. W., *Life and Military Services of the late Brig. Gen. Thomas A. Smyth*. Wilmington, 1870.

Meade, George, *Life and Letters of George Gordon Meade* [George Gordon Meade, ed.]. (2 vols.) N.Y., 1913. (All refs. are to Vol. II.)

Morgan, W. H., *Personal Reminiscences of the War*. Lynchburg, 1911.

[Napier, Bartlett], *A Soldier's Story of the War*. New Orleans, 1874.

Oliphant [Col.?], "Brig. Gen. Alexander Hays." *U. S. Service Magazine*, ii, 262.

Paris, Comte de, Letter, Jan. 21, 1877. SHSP, v, 88.

Parks, Leighton, "What a Boy saw of the Civil War." *Century Magazine*, June 1905.

Pettigrew, J. J., *Notes on Spain and the Spaniards*. Charleston, 1861.

Pickett, George E., *The Heart of a Soldier*. N.Y., 1913. Reissued with changes as *Soldier of the South*, Boston, 1928. [I do not consider these letters authentic. See Appendix B.]

Pickett, LaSalle Corbell, "General George Pickett." SHSP, xxiv, 151. (From Richmond *Dispatch*, May 3, 1896.)

Idem, "My Soldier." *McClure's Magazine*, March 1908. (Reprinted with changes as introduction to *Heart of a Soldier*.)

Idem, *Pickett and his Men*. Atlanta, 1900.

Idem, "Wartime Story of General Pickett." *Cosmopolitan*. (Section on Gettysburg is in issue of April 1914.)

Poague, W. T., *Gunner with Stonewall* (M. F. Cockrell, ed.). Jackson, Tenn., 1957.

Poindexter, J. E., *Address on the Life and Services of Gen. Lewis A. Armistead*. Richmond, 1909. (See CV, Nov. 1914, 502.)

Ross, Fitzgerald, *A Visit to the Camps and Cities of the Confederacy*. Edinburgh, London, 1865.

Scheibert, Justus, Letter, Nov. 21, 1877. SHSP, v, 90.

Idem, *Sieben Monate in den Rebellen-Staaten während des Nordamerikanischen Krieges*, 1863. Stettin, 1868.

Shotwell, R. A., *Papers of . . .* (J. C. deR. Hamilton, ed.). (2 vols.) Raleigh, 1929. (All refs. are to vol. II; See also Shotwell, Sect. IV.)

Small, A. R., *Road to Richmond*. Berkeley, 1939.

Sorrel, G. M., *Recollections of a Confederate Staff Officer*. N.Y., 1917.

Stewart, W. H., *A Pair of Blankets*. N.Y., 1911.

Stiles, Robert, *Four Years under Marse Robert*. Wash., 1903.

Stine, J. H., *History of the Army of the Potomac*. Phila., 1892.

Swift, Eben. "The Military Education of Robert E. Lee." *Virginia Mag. of History and Biography*, xxxv, #2.

Talbot, E. A., *Samuel Chapman Armstrong*. N.Y., 1904.

Taylor, W. H., "The Campaign in Pennsylvania." Phila. *Weekly Times*, Aug. 25, 1877. (Reprinted in AW and SHSP, iv, 124.)

Idem, *Four Years with General Lee*. N.Y., 1877.

Idem, *General Lee: His Campaigns in Virginia, 1861–1865*. Norfolk, 1906.

Idem, Memorandum. SHSP, iv, 80.

Trimble, I. R., "Civil War Diary of . . ." *Maryland Hist. Mag.*, xvii, 1.

Tyler, M. W., *Recollections of the Civil War*. N.Y., London, 1912.

Walker, F. A., "General Gibbon in the Second Corps." MOLLUS, New York, *Personal Recollections*. 2 Ser., 320.

Idem, *General Hancock*. N.Y., 1895.

Walton, J. B., Letter, Oct. 15, 1877. SHSP, v, 47.

Wilcox, C. M., Letter, Mar. 26, 1877. SHSP, iv, 111.

Wise, J. S., *End of an Era*. Boston, 1899.

Woodruff, C. A., "In Memory of Maj. Gen. John Gibbon." MOLLUS, New York. *Personal Recollections*, 2 Ser., 290.

IV. WORKS CHIEFLY ON GETTYSBURG, WITH MATERIAL ON PICKETT'S CHARGE

Alderson, J. C., Statement, CV, Oct. 1904, 488.

Alexander, E. P., "The Great Charge and Artillery Fighting at Gettysburg." B & L, iii, 357.

Idem, Letter, Mar. 17, 1877. SHSP, iv, 97.

Idem, Letter, Feb. 23, 1878. SHSP, v, 201.

Idem, *Official Report*. SHSP, iv, 235. [This seems to be the genuine report, though it is not included in OR.]

Allen, W., "Lee's Invasion of Pennsylvania." *Century Magazine*, May 1887, 151. (Also in B & L, iii, 355.)

[Anon.], "Battle of Gettysburg." *Times* (London), Aug. 18, 1863, 1–7. By the Hon. Francis Lawley (?), cited as London *Times*.

[Anon.], *Dedication of the High-Water Mark Tablet*. [Collection of cards, circulars, etc., in Nicholson Collection, Huntington Library.]

[Anon.], "The Great Battlefield Forty-five Years Ago." Gettysburg Scrapbook. [Includes the dispatches to the Phila. *Morning Post*.]

Ashe, S. A., "The Charge at Gettysburg." NCRegs, v, 137.

Bachelder, John B., *Descriptive Key*. N.Y., 1870.

Idem, "Notes relating to the Services of the Troops at Gettysburg, 1863." MS in Nicholson Collection, Huntington Library.

Idem, "The Third Day's Battle." Phila. *Weekly Times*, Dec. 15, 1877.

Idem, *Gettysburg*. Boston, [1873].

Biddle, J. C., "General Meade at Gettysburg." AW, 205.

Bingham, H. H., Letter, July 19, 1882. SHSP, x, 428.

Bond, W. R., "Longstreet's Assault at Gettysburg." *Literary and Historical Activities in North Carolina, Publications of the Historical Comm.* Raleigh, 1907.

Idem, *"Pickett or Pettigrew?"* Weldon, N.C., 1888.

Idem, "Pickett's Men at Gettysburg." Phila. *Weekly Times* [Date?]. Gettysburg Scrapbook.

Bright, R. A., "Pickett's Charge." SHSP, xxxi, 228.

Brook-Rawle, William, *"The Right Flank at Gettysburg."* AW, 467.

Cabell, S. W., *The "Bulldog" Longstreet at Gettysburg and Chickamauga.* (Longstreet Memorial Assn.) N.p., 1938.

Carter, R. G., "Reminiscences of the Campaign and Battle of Gettysburg." MOLLUS, Maine Commandery, *War Papers*, ii, 150.

Christian, G. L., *Official Rep. of the History Comm. of the Grand Camp Confederate Vets., Dept. of Va.* (See CV, Apr. 1904, 161.)

Clark, George, "Wilcox's Alabama Brigade at Gettysburg." CV, May, 1909, 229.

Clark, Walter, *North Carolina at Gettysburg and Pickett's Charge a Misnomer.* N.p., 1921 (?).

Cockrell, M. F., *Where was Pickett at Gettysburg?* [Typescript].

Colston, F. M., "Gettysburg as I saw it." CV, Nov. 1897.

Cook, J. D. S., "Personal Reminiscences of Gettysburg." MOLLUS, *War Talks in Kansas*, Kansas City, 1906, 320.

Cowan, Andrew, Letters, July 2, Dec. 5 and 10, 1913. (In Library of Gettysburg Nat. Mil. Park.)

Idem, See also Sect. V and Sect. III Anon. *In Mem. Webb.*

Craighill, J. B., "Pickett's Charge at Gettysburg." Unidentified clipping. Gettysburg Scrapbook.

Crocker, J. F., "Gettysburg — Pickett's Charge." SHSP, xxxiii, 118.

Day, Walter E., *The Campaign of Gettysburg.* (By "Miles"). Boston, 1912.

Devereux, J. F., "Some Account of Pickett's Charge at Gettysburg." *Magazine of American History*, July 1887.

Doubleday, Abner. *Chancellorsville and Gettysburg.* N.Y., 1882.

Douthat, William, Statement. CV, xxxvi, 59.

Easley, D. B., "With Armistead when he was killed." CV, Aug. 1912, 379.

Finley, G. W., see Smith, Christopher.

Fry, B. D., "Pettigrew's Charge at Gettysburg." SHSP, vii, 91.

Galloway, F. R., Statement. CV, Aug. 1913, 388.

Harding, Milton, Statement. CV, Aug. 1911, 371.

"Harry," Statement. *Southern Bivouac*, ii, 522.

Haskell, Frank A., *The Battle of Gettysburg.* Various editions. My references are to Boston, 1958, Bruce Catton, ed.

Hazelwood, M. W., "The Gettysburg Charge." SHSP, xxiii, 229.

Houston, T. D., "Storming Cemetery Hill." Phila. *Times*, Oct. 21, 1881 [?]. Gettysburg Scrapbook. Includes letter of J. T. James. Cited as Houston-James.

Howell, F. A., Statement. CV, July 1911, 330.

Hunt, H. J., "Rejoinder." B & L, iii, 386.

Idem, "The Third Day at Gettysburg." B & L, iii, 369.

Hyde, T. W., "Recollections of the Battle of Gettysburg." MOLLUS, Maine Commandery, i, 191.

Imboden, J. D., "The Confederate Retreat from Gettysburg." B & L, iii, 420.

Irvine, R. H., "Brig. Gen. Richard H. Garnett." CV, Sept. 1915, 391.

Jackson, H. W., "The Battle of Gettysburg." MOLLUS, Illinois Commandery, *Military Essays and Recollections*, 1, 147.

James, see Houston.

James, R. T., Statement. CV, Sept. 1894.

Johnson, Gart, Statement. CV, Aug. 1893, 246.

Jones, J. T., "Pettigrew's Brigade at Gettysburg." NCRegs, v, 133.

Kimble, June, Statement. CV, Oct. 1910.

T. B. K[ingsbury], "Another Witness — Gettysburg." OLOD, iii, 457.

Idem, "North Carolina at Gettysburg." OLOD, i, 193.

Lane, J. H., Letter, Apr. 11, 1875. OLOD, iii, 460.

Lee, Fitz, Letter, Mar. 5, 1877. SHSP, iv, 69.

London *Times*, see Anon., "Battle of Gettysburg."

McConnell, C. H., "Pickett's Charge." *National Tribune*, Jan. 29, 1914. Gettysburg Scrapbook.

McCulloch, Robert, "High Tide at Gettysburg." CV, Oct. 1913, 474.

McKay, F. E., "A New View of Gettysburg." Phila. *Times*, Apr. 22, 1882 [?]. Gettysburg Scrapbook.

McLaws, Lafayette, "Gettysburg." SHSP, vii, 64.

McNeilly, J. H., Statement. CV, Feb. 1916, 92.

Martin, Rawley and Smith, J. H., "The Battle of Gettysburg." SHSP, xxiii, 183.

Martin, R. W., "Armistead at the Battle of Gettysburg." SHSP, xxxix, 186.

Mayo, J. C., "Pickett's Charge at Gettysburg." SHSP, xxxiv, 327.

Meade, George Gordon, *With Meade at Gettysburg*. Phila., 1930.

Miller, I. T., Statement, CV, Sept. 1895, 281.

Montgomery, W. A., "Farthest to the Front at Gettysburg." *North Carolina Pub. of the Historical Commission*, Raleigh, 1907, 433.

Morgan, C. H., "Narrative of the Operations of the Second Army Corps." In A. R. Hancock (q.v. in Sect. 3), 182.

Mulholland, St. Clair, "The Gettysburg Campaign." Phila. *Times*, Feb. 14, 1880.

Osborn, T. W., "The Artillery at Gettysburg." Phila. *Weekly Times,* May 31, 1879.

Owen, H. T., "Pickett at Gettysburg." Phila. *Weekly Times,* Mar. 26, 1881.

Pickett, G. E., "Address at Richmond." MS in Huntington Library.

Pleasonton, Alfred, "The Campaign of Gettysburg." Phila. *Times,* Jan. 19, 1878 (also AW, 447).

Plummer, J. W., Account. *Rebellion Record,* x, 178.

Porter, J. W. H., Statement. CV, Oct. 1916, 460.

Rafferty, Thomas. "Gettysburg." MOLLUS, New York. *First Series,* 1.

Reid, Whitelaw (Agate), "Thursday's Doubtful Issue — Friday's Victory." *Rebellion Record,* vii, Docs. 92 (from Cincinnati *Gazette*).

Reid, W. D., Statement. CV, Feb. 1911, 66.

Rhodes, J. H., "The Gettysburg Gun." *Rhode Island Soldiers and Sailors Historical Society,* #19.

Rice, Edmund, "Repelling Lee's Last Blow at Gettysburg." B & L, iii, 387.

Rittenhouse, B. F., "The Battle of Gettysburg as seen from Little Round Top." MOLLUS, Dist. of Columbia, *War Papers,* #3.

Robbins, W. M., "Longstreet's Assault at Gettysburg." NCRegs, iii, 101.

Rogers, Horatio, *Record of . . . Dedicatory Services . . . Batteries A and B, 1st R. I. Light Artillery.* Providence, 1887.

Rowan, Cleve, Statement. CV, June 1910, 286.

Scott, W., "Pickett's Charge as seen from the Front Line." MOLLUS, Calif., *War Papers,* #1.

Shields, David, "Capt. David Shields' Story," in *Alexander Hays, Life and Letters,* q.v., Sect. III.

Shotwell, R. A., "Virginia and North Carolina in the Battle of Gettysburg." OLOD, iv, 80. (See also Sect. III.)

Sigma Chi, "Northern Prison Life." *Land We Love,* ii, 39.

Smith, Christopher, "The Bloody Angle." Buffalo *Evening News,* May 29, 1894. Gettysburg Scrapbook. Contains letter of G. W. Finley.

Smith, J. B., "The Charge at Gettysburg." *Southern Bivouac,* Mar. 1887, 646. (Also in B & L, iii, 354.)

Smith, J. H., Statement. SHSP, xxxii, 189.

Smith, L. A., "Recollections of Gettysburg." MOLLUS, Michigan Commandery, *War Papers,* ii.

Straight, C. T., "The Gettysburg Gun." Typescript, Library of Gettysburg Nat. Mil. Park.

Stribling, R. M., *The Gettysburg Campaign.* Petersburg, 1905.

Supreme Court of Pennsylvania. May Term, 1891. #20, 30. Middle District. *Appeal of the Gettysburg Battlefield Memorial Association from the Decree of the Court of Common Pleas of Adams Co.* **Paper Book of Appellants.** [Cited as Trial.]

Swallow, W. H., "The Third Day at Gettysburg." *Southern Bivouac,* iv (n.s. i), 562.

Talcott, T. M. R., "The Third Day at Gettysburg." SHSP, xli, 37.

Thayer, G. A., "Gettysburg, as we Men on the Right saw it." MOLLUS, Ohio Commandery, ii, 24.

Thompson, R. S., "A Scrap of Gettysburg." MOLLUS, Illinois Commandery, *Essays and Recollections,* iii, 97.

Trimble, I. R., "The Battle and Campaign of Gettysburgh." SHSP, xxvi, 116.

Idem, "North Carolinians at Gettysburg." OLOD, iv, 53. (Also in SHSP, ix, 29–35.)

Troop Positions (Interviews). MS, Library of Gettysburg Nat. Mil. Park.

Walker, F. A., "Gettysburg." Boston *Herald,* Mar. 5, 1886.

Idem, "General Hancock and the Artillery at Gettysburg." B & L, iii, 385.

[Walker, J. H.], "The Charge of Pickett's Division." *Blue and Gray,* i, 221.

Idem, "A Survivor of Pickett's Division." *Blue and Gray,* ii, 27.

Watts, A. T., "Something more about Gettysburg." CV, Feb. 1898, 67.

White, H. A., "Gettysburg Battle." SHSP, xxvii, 52.

Wilkeson, S. [E.], "Details from our Special Correspondent." N.Y. *Times,* July 6, 1863, 1–4.

Wood, W. W., "Pickett's Charge at Gettysburg." Phila. *Times,* Aug. 11, 1877.

Young, L. G., "Pettigrew's Brigade at Gettysburg." NCRegs, v, 113.

Idem, same title (not same text). OLOD, i, 552.

V. REGIMENTAL HISTORIES, ETC.

Included here are works written from the organizational or local (state) point of view.

Adams, J. G. B., *Reminiscences of the 19th Mass. Reg.* Boston, 1899.

Adams, Silas, "The 19th Maine at Gettysburg." MOLLUS, Maine Commandery, iv, 250.

Aldrich, T. A., *History of Battery A, First Reg., R. I. Light Art.* Providence, 1904.

[Anon.], *Connecticut, 14th Reg.* Hartford, 1889.

[Anon.], *Dedication of the Monument,* [12th N.J.] N.p.; n.d.

[Anon.], *Hist. of the 5th Mass. Battery.* Boston, 1902.

[Anon.], *Hist. of the 121st Reg. Pa. Vols.* Phila., 1906.

[Anon.], *Maine at Gettysburg*. N.p., 1898.

[Anon.], *Michigan at Gettysburg*. Detroit, 1889.

[Anon.], "The 19th Mass. at Gettysburg." Typescript, Library of Gettysburg Nat. Mil. Park. (Much like the account in the Anon., *Rem. of the 19th Mass., v. i.*)

[Anon.], *Pennsylvania at Gettysburg* (4 vols.). Harrisburg, 1893.

[Anon.], *Reminiscences of the 19th Mass. Reg.* Salem, 1906.

[Anon.], *Reply of the Phila. Brigade Association to the Foolish . . . Narrative of Lt. Frank A. Haskell*. Phila. [?], 1910.

[Anon.], *72nd Reg. Pa. Vols. at Bloody Angle, Gettysburg*. Phila., n.d.

Bachelder, J. B., "The 72nd Pa. Monument Case." Gettysburg *Star and Sentinel*, Apr. 14, 1891. Gettysburg Scrapbook.

Banes, C. H., *History of the Phila. Brigade*. Phila., 1876.

Barbour, W. M., "A Brief Historical Sketch of the 37th N.C. Troops." OLOD, July 1873.

Benedict, G. G., *Vermont in the Civil War* (2 vols.). Burlington, 1886–88. (All refs. are to vol. II.)

Bicknell, L. E., Statement. B & L, iii, 391. (1st Mass. Sharpshooters.)

Bond, W. R., "Pickett's Men at Gettysburg." Unidentified clipping in Gettysburg Scrapbook.

Brown, J. W., *Signal Corps, U.S.A.* Boston, 1896.

Brown, M. M., *University Grays Company*. Richmond, [1940].

Bruce, G. A., *20th Reg. of Mass. Vol. Infantry*. Boston, 1906.

Chamberlayne, E. H., Jr., *War History and Roll of the Richmond Fayette Artillery*. Richmond, 1883.

Chamberlin, Thomas. *History of the 150th Reg. Pa. Volunteers*. Phila., 1905.

Clark, Walter, ed., *Histories of the Several Regiments . . . from N.C. . . .* (5 vols.). Raleigh, Goldsboro, 1901. See also Walter Clark in Sect. IV.

Clark, William, *History of the Hampton Battery F, Independent Pa. Light Artillery*. Akron, Pittsburgh, 1909.

Cowan, Andrew, *Reunion of Cowan's Battery*. N.p.; n.d. (Nicholson Collection).

Cowtan, C. W., *Services of the 10th N.Y. Volunteers*. N.Y., 1882.

Daves, Graham, "The 22nd N.C. Infantry." SHSP, xxiv, 256.

[Figg, R. W.], "*Where Men only dare to go*." Richmond, 1885.

[Fishburne, C. D.], *Historical Sketch of the Rockbridge Artillery*. SHSP, xxiii, 98.

Fleming, F. P., "The Florida Brigade at Gettysburg." SHSP, xxvii, 192. (From *Memoir of Capt. Charles Seton Fleming*.)

Flowers, G. W., "The 38th N.C. Regiment." SHSP, xxv, 245.

Ford, A. E., *Story of the 15th Reg. Mass. Volunteer Infantry*. Clinton, 1898.

Fuger, Frederick, "Cushing's Battery at Gettysburg." *Jour. Military Service Institution*, xli, 404.

Idem, "The Gettysburg Battle." Burlington *Daily Free Press*, June 2, 1911. Gettysburg Scrapbook.

Gates, T. B., *The "Ulster Guard."* N.Y., 1879. (80th N.Y.)

Goddard, H. P., *The 14th Conn. Vol. Regimental Reminiscences.* [Hartford, 1877.]

Goolsby, J. C., "The Crenshaw Battery." SHSP, xxviii, 337.

Griggs, G. K., "Memoranda of the 38th Va. Infantry." SHSP, xiv, 250.

Harrison, Walter, *Pickett's Men.* N.Y., 1870.

Hill, W. A., "The Seventy-Second's Position." [Phila.?] *Press*, July 9, 1891.

Hoke, W. J., "Sketch of the 38th Reg. N.C. Troops." OLOD, i, 545.

Holcombe, R. I., *Hist. of the 1st Reg. of Minn. Vol. Infantry.* Stillwater, 1916.

Irby, Richard, *Historical Sketch of the Nottaway Grays . . . 18th Va. Reg.* Richmond, 1878.

Johnston, W. F., "The Second Rockbridge Battery." SHSP, xxv, 281.

Jones, B. W., *Under the Stars and Bars, A History of the Surry Light Artillery.* Richmond, 1909.

Lane, J. H., "Twenty-Eighth N.C. Infantry." SHSP, xxiv, 324.

Idem, *History of Lane's N.C. Brigade.* SHSP, various issues, vii-x.

Lindsley, J. B., *Military Annals of Tennessee.* Nashville, 1886.

Lochren, William, "The First Minn. at Gettysburg." *Glimpses of the Nation's Struggle.* Papers read before Minn. Commandery. MOLLUS (Series 3), N.Y., St. Paul, Minneapolis, 1893, 42.

Idem, *Narrative of the First Reg. in Minn. in the Civil and Indian Wars.* N.p.; n.d.

Loehr, C. T., Statement. CV, Mar. 1898, 129.

Idem, "The 'Old First' Va. at Gettysburg." SHSP, xxxii, 33.

Idem, *War History of the Old First Va. Inf. Reg.* Richmond, 1884.

Love, W. A., "Mississippi at Gettysburg." *Pub. Miss. Hist. Soc.*, ix, 25.

McCarthy, Carlton, ed., *Contributions to a History of the Richmond Howitzer Battalion.* Richmond, 1883–86.

McDermott, A. W., *A brief History of the 69th Reg. Pa. Vet. Volunteers.* Phila., 1889.

McFarland, Baxter, "The 11th Miss. Reg. at Gettysburg." *Pub. Miss. Hist. Soc., Centenary Ser. II* (1918), 549.

Martin, W. J., "The 11th N.C. Reg." SHSP, xxiii, 42.

Moore, E. A., *The Story of a Cannoneer.* N.Y., Wash., 1907. (Rockbridge battery.)

Moore, J. H., "Heth's Division at . . . Gettysburg." *Southern Bivouac*, iii, 1885. (Also appeared as "Longstreet's Assault," Phila. *Times*, undated clipping in Gettysburg Scrapbook.)

Morgan, C. H., "Narrative of the Operations of the Second Army

Corps. . ." Appendix A in A. R. Hancock, q.v. Sect. III.

Murphy, T. G., *Four Years in the War*. Phila., 1866. (1st Del.)

NCRegs, v.s., Clark, Walter.

New York Monuments Commission, *New York at Gettysburg* (3 vols.). Albany, 1902.

Owen, H. T., "Pickett at Gettysburg." Phila. *Weekly Times*, Mar. 26, 1881. Gettysburg Scrapbook.

Owen, W. M., *In Camp and Battle with the Washington Artillery of New Orleans*. Boston, 1885.

Page, C. D., *History of the 14th Reg. Conn. Vol. Infantry*. Meriden, 1906.

[Palmer, E. E.], *The Second Brigade; or Camp Life. By a Volunteer*. Montpelier, 1864. (Stannard's brigade.)

Pennsylvania at Gettysburg, see Anon.

Reichardt, Theodore, *Diary of Battery A, 1st Reg., R.I. Light Artillery*. Providence, 1865.

Reilly, J. P., "An Incident of Gettysburg." Phila. *Inquirer*, Aug. 28, 1896. Gettysburg Scrapbook (69th Pa.)

Rhodes, J. H., *The History of Battery B, 1st Reg., R.I. Light Artillery*. Providence, 1894.

Robertson, John, *Michigan in the War*. Lansing, 1882.

Rogers, Horatio, *Record of Dedicatory Services . . . Batteries A and B, 1st R.I. Light Artillery*. Providence, 1887.

[Rowland, Dunbar], *Military History of Miss., 1803–1898*. (In *Miss. Official and Statistical Register*, 1908, 387.)

Sawyer, Franklin, *A Military History of the 8th Reg. Ohio Vol. Infantry*. Cleveland, 1881.

Searles, J. N., "The 1st Minn. Vol. Infantry." MOLLUS, Minn. *Glimpses of the Nation's Struggle*, Second ser., 80.

Seville, W. P., "History of the 1st Reg., Del. Volunteers." *Hist. Soc. of Del., Papers*, #5, 1884.

Simons, E. D., *Regimental History, The 125th N.Y. State Volunteers*. N.Y., 1888.

Smith, J. D., *History of the 19th Reg. of Maine Vol. Infantry*. Minneapolis, 1909.

Stevens, H. C., *History of the 14th Reg. Conn. Vol. Infantry*. Hartford, 1889.

Sturtevant, R. O., *Pictorial History, 13th Reg. Vermont Volunteers*. N.p.; n.d.

Tivy, J. A., *Souvenir of the Seventh*. Detroit, n.d. (7th Mich.)

Toombs, Samuel, *New Jersey Troops in the Gettysburg Campaign*. Orange, 1888.

Underwood, G. C., *History of the 26th Reg. of the N.C. Troops*. Goldsboro, 1901 [?].

Walker, F. A., *History of the Second Corps.* N.Y., 1886.

Walton, J. B., etc., "Sketches of the History of the Washington Artillery." SHSP, xi, 210, 247.

Ward, J. R. C., *History of the 106th Reg. Pa. Volunteers.* Phila., 1906.

Washburn, G. H., *A Complete Military History and Record of the 108th Reg. N.Y. Volunteers.* Rochester, 1894.

Webb, A. S., *An Address at Gettysburg . . . 72d Pa. Volunteers . . . Monument.* Phila., 1883.

White, W. S., "A Diary of the War," in McCarthy *Contributions,* v.s.

Whitman, W. E. S. and True, C. E., *Maine in the War for the Union.* Lewiston, 1865.

Williams, J. C., *Life in Camp.* Claremont, 1864. (14th Vermont.)

Willson, A. M., *Disaster, Struggle, Triumph.* Albany, 1870. (126th N.Y.)

Wood, W. N., *Reminiscences of Big I.* Jackson, Tenn., 1956. (19th Virginia.)

Young, C. P., "History of the Crenshaw Battery." SHSP, xxxi, 275.

VI. MAPS

The following maps may be considered original sources, although they all must be used with caution, particularly as regards locations of troops.

Bachelder, John B., *Gettysburg Battlefield (Isometrical Drawing).* Boston, 1863.

Brown, L. Howell, *Map of the Battle-field of Gettysburg* (accompanying Lee's report). OR, *Atlas,* Pl. XLIII, 1.

Cope, E. B., *Map of the Battle-field of Gettysburg, Pa.* OR, *Atlas,* Pl. XL, 2.

Hall, Norman J., Sketch-map accompanying his report. OR, I, 27, 1, 438.

Hazard, J. G., Sketch-map accompanying his report. OR, I, 27, 1, 479.

Howard, O. O., Sketch-maps accompanying his report. OR, I, 27, 1, 698–9.

Phillips, C. A., *Gettysburg. The Fight of July 3rd.* In Anon., *Fifth Mass. Battery.* Boston, 1902, 648.

[Warren, G. K.], *Map of the Battle Field of Gettysburg, Third Day's Battle.* (Cited as the Warren-Bachelder map.) Published by the Office of the Chief of Engineers, U.S. Army, 1876.

VII. NEWSPAPERS

In the originals or in reprints I have checked accounts in the following newspapers. (All dates are shortly after July 3, 1863.) The accounts by Reid and Wilkeson and those in the *Times* (London) and Philadelphia *Morning Post* are also listed in Sect. IV., the last two under *Anon.*

Boston *Evening Transcript*; Chicago *Times*; Cincinnati *Gazette* (by Agate, i.e., Whitelaw Reid); New York *Times* (by Samuel Wilkeson); New York *Tribune*; New York *World*; Philadelphia *Morning Post*; Richmond *Enquirer*; San Francisco *Alta California*; *Times* (London); Washington *Intelligencer*.

VIII. SECONDARY WORKS

For the sake of completeness this list is included, but works from it are rarely cited, and the text has been based upon the original works.

Balch, W. R., *Battle of Gettysburg*. Phila., 1885.

Bates, Samuel, *Battle of Gettysburg*. Phila., 1875.

Battine, Cecil, *Crisis of the Confederacy*. London, 1905.

Beecham, R. K., *Gettysburg, the Pivotal Battle of the Civil War*. Chicago, 1911.

Bingham, H. H., *Second and Third Days of the Battle of Gettysburg*. Harrisburg, 1894.

Bradford, Gamaliel, *Confederate Portraits*. Boston, 1917.

Idem, *Union Portraits*. Boston, 1916.

Catton, Bruce, *Glory Road*. Garden City, 1954.

Idem, *This Hallowed Ground*. Garden City, 1956.

Chesney, C. C., *Military View of Recent Campaigns*. London, 1863.

Cowell, A. T., *Tactics at Gettysburg*. Gettysburg, 1910.

Dalbiac, P. H., *American War of Secession*. London, 1911.

Davis, Burke, *Gray Fox*, N.Y., 1956.

Day, W. E., *Campaign of Gettysburg (By "Miles")*. Boston, 1912.

Ditterline, T., *Sketch of the Battle of Gettysburg*. N.Y., 1863.

Dodge, T. A., "The Gettysburg Campaign." *United Service Magazine*, July 1885.

Dowdey, Clifford, *Death of a Nation*. N.Y., 1958.

Downey, Fairfax, *Guns at Gettysburg*. N.Y., 1958.

Drake, S. A., *Battle of Gettysburg*. Boston, 1892.

Draper, J. W., *History of the American Civil War* (3 vols.). N.Y., 1867–70.

Eckenrode, H. J. and Conrad, Bryan, *James Longstreet*. Chapel Hill, 1936.

Evans, C. A., ed., *Confederate Military History* (13 vols.). Atlanta, 1899.

Fox, W. F., *Regimental Losses in the American Civil War*. Albany, 1889.

Freeman, D. S., *Lee's Lieutenants* (3 vols.). N.Y., 1942.

Idem, *Robert E. Lee* (4 vols.). N.Y., 1935.

Geer, Walter, *Campaigns of the Civil War*. N.Y., 1926.

Greeley, Horace, *American Conflict* (2 vols.). Hartford, 1864–67.

Knox, T. W., *Decisive Battles since Waterloo*. N.Y., London, 1889.

Livermore, T. L., *Numbers and Losses in the Civil War*. Boston, N.Y., 1901.

Lonn, Ella, *Foreigners in the Confederacy*. Chapel Hill, 1940.

Lossing, B. J., *Pictorial History of the Civil War* (3 vols.). Phila., 1866–68.

Minnigh, L. W., *Gettysburg: "What they did here."* [N.p.], 1910.

Nelson, A. H., *Battles of Chancellorsville and Gettysburg*. Minneapolis, 1899.

Paris, Comte de, *History of the Civil War in America* (4 vols.). Phila., 1876.

Pollard, E. A., *Second Year of the War*. N.Y., 1864.

Rhodes, J. F., *History of the Civil War*. N.Y., 1917.

Ropes, J. C. and Livermore, R. C., *Story of the Civil War* (4 vols.). N.Y., 1894–1913.

Sander, Constantin, *History of the Four Years' Civil War*. Frankfort-on-the-Main, 1865.

Sanger, D. B. and Hay, T. R., *James Longstreet*. Baton Rouge, 1952.

Sanger, D. B., "Was Longstreet a Scapegoat?" *Infantry Journal*, xliii, 39.

Stackpole, E. J., *They met at Gettysburg*. Harrisburg, 1956.

Steele, M. F., *American Campaigns* (2 vols.). Wash., 1919.

Stine, J. H., *History of the Army of the Potomac*. Phila., 1892.

Storrick, W. C., *Battle of Gettysburg*. Harrisburg, 1946.

Swinton, William, *Campaigns of the Army of the Potomac*, N.Y., 1866.

Tucker, Glenn, *High Tide at Gettysburg*. Indianapolis, 1958.

Vanderslice, J. M., *Gettysburg, Then and Now*. N.Y., 1897.

Williams, K. P., *Lincoln finds a General* (4 vols.). N.Y., 1949–56.

Wise, George, *Campaigns and Battles of the Army of Northern Virginia*. N.Y., 1916.

Wise, J. C., *Long Arm of Lee*. Lynchburg, Va., 1915.

Young, J. B., *Battle of Gettysburg*. N.Y., 1913.

IX. THE BATTLEFIELD AND THE MONUMENTS

On the battlefield as a historical document, see Appendix F. The numerous markers and the inscriptions on monuments also have served as sources of information, though they rarely supply data not elsewhere available. John B. Bachelder of the Gettysburg Battlefield Association probably was chiefly responsible for the markers. The inscriptions on the monuments were generally prepared by the representatives of the organization erecting the monument, with the collaboration of the Association. The markers and inscriptions, like other human documents, are subject to error, and must be used with due caution.

Notes and References

THE notes are arranged by Parts and Sections, and quotations are identified by the first two words, thus freeing the text of troublesome marks of reference.

PART 1
EARLY MORNING—MOSTLY CONFEDERATE

Section

1. Anon., 19th Mass. typescript; Ward; Sawyer.
2. OR, ii, 359; Longstreet's writings; Alexander, SHSP, V, 235 — "I was . . ."; OR, ii, 320 — "The general . . .".
3. Harrison, Longstreet's writings.
4. Dooley; Harrison; W. W. Wood; H. T. Owen; Richmond *Enquirer*, July 24, 1863; Sanger-Hay; D. E. Johnston.
5. OR, ii, 447.
6. Stiles, 227 — "make no mistake."; Lee's favorite post (NCRegs, v, map after p. 100) was a little north of the Point of Woods; he could not have been at the Lee Monument since the view from that point is much restricted by trees. Scheibert and Poague also put Lee near the Point of Woods.
7. Fremantle, 197 — "tall, broad-shouldered . . .".
8. Besides seeming to be ignorant of the severity of losses in Longstreet's two divisions, in Heth's division and in Scales's brigade, Lee did not know of the shortage of artillery ammunition (see OR, ii, 321). Fremantle, 193, 199, 205 — "all full . . .", etc.; Shotwell, OLOD, 80 — "How joyous . . ."; Dunn Browne, 184 — "The enemy . . ."; Hunton, 86f — "I threw . . ."; Stewart, 92 — "each soldier . . ."; Dawson, 93 — "You are . . ."; OR, ii, 152 — "almost total . . ."; Gordon, 137 — "the zenith . . .". For Wright's report, see Appendix E. AW, 421 — "when the . . ."; SHSP, iv, 156f — "This determination . . ."; SHSP, iv, 153f — "much depressed." Long, *Lee*, 287.

10. Sorrel, 23, 32, 57, 92 for the quotations and much of the information on Longstreet. Imboden, 428 — "my old . . .".

11. On the conference, see Long, Taylor, Alexander *Mem.*, Longstreet's writings, Sanger-Hay. AW, 429 — "The enemy . . ."; other sources quote the words somewhat differently. AW, 432n — "To have . . ."; AW, 429 — "General, I . . ."; Sanger-Hay, 180 — "dignified, yet . . .".

12. Harrison; D. E. Johnston; H. T. Owen. Mrs. Pickett is apparently based on Harrison. H. T. Owen — "sprinkling of . . .".

13. Harrison, 64ff; J. S. Wise, 69; Sorrel, 54, 155f; Dawson, 91; Fremantle, 197; L. C. Pickett's writings; Hunton. The quotations are from Sorrel.

14. On Kemper, DAB; J. S. Wise, 329 — "Judging by . . .". On Garnett, DAB; Alexander, B & L, iii, 365; H. T. Owen. On Armistead, DAB. A. R. Hancock, 69 — "Hancock, good-by . . .".

15. H. T. Owen, W. W. Wood, Shotwell, McCulloch. Bachelder's *Isometrical Drawing* marks a base for Pickett's division at the junction of the two runs. The exact line of the march and the point of the base are doubtful. That the base should have been at Bream's Mill, as sometimes stated, seems to me unlikely, since that point was too far in the rear. Apparently, however, the division did not march directly from its campsite to the battlefield.

16. Gart Johnson, 246; Doubleday, 187.

18. DAB; Sorrel, 127; Alexander's writings.

19. J. C.. Wise; Gibson, *Artillerist's Handbook*; Benton; Roberts.

20. Alexander's writings, esp. his reports; "Troop Positions (Interviews)." Alexander, B & L, iii, 361f — "as inoffensively . . .".

22. Sources as for #15.

23. Reports in OR bearing on these brigades; NCRegs., Dunaway, Love, McFarland, Lindsley, Rowland, T. B. K., Ashe, Hoke, J. B. Smith. Taylor, *Four Years*, 104 — "They were . . ."; OR, ii, 671 — "Depressed, dilapidated . . .". The seven "fresh" brigades I count as Pickett's three, Lane's, Thomas's, Posey's, and Mahone's.

24. DAB; Pettigrew; Freeman, *Lee's Lieutenants*, iii, 78n — "very pleasant . . .". On Fry, *Hist. of Ala. and Dict. of Ala. Biog.*

25. Brown, *Univ. Grays*, 10f — "always impulsive . . ."; Love, 34 — "Damn 'em! . . .". Underwood, 39 — "splendid uniforms." On 26th N.C., see OR; L. G. Young, both items; Underwood, 114; NCRegs, v, 599ff. On 1st Va., see Loehr; Dooley, *Introduction.*

26. Alexander's writings; "Troop Positions (Interviews)."

27. On Pendleton, Fremantle, 197, 218; Sorrel, 121; Susan Lee; Fishburne; Harrison 84f; Sanger-Hay, 415; Poague.

28. Alexander's writings.

29. Sources as for #15.

30. J. W. Brown, i, 370.

31. I have made a careful study of the times given for the opening of

the cannonade. They vary by five and a half hours, according to witnesses that would ordinarily be rated as of high historical competence. General R. H. Anderson in OR gives the time as 3.30; Captain Coates, also in OR, gives the time as "about ten a.m."

PART 2
LATER MORNING—MOSTLY UNION

Section

1. Meade, *Life*, 103 — "All well . . .".
2. DAB; Meade, *Life*; Smith, *19th Maine*; Reid. Gibbon, *Recs.*, 145 — "Because he . . .".
3. See also Appendix F.
4. J. D. Smith, 77 — "General Hancock . . ."; Walker, *Hancock*, 21 — "The smoke . . .". Ibid., 43, 112. OR, i, 73 — "Can't wait . . .". Lyman, 107.
5. Walker, *Second Corps*, and the regimental histories. Toombs, 294 — "The men . . ."; Page, 65 — "There was . . ."; Oliphant — "drilled, punished . . .". Willson, 169 — "Remember Harpers . . ."; on 1st Minn.: Searles, Lochren (their figures differ a little); Ford, 1of — "farms, factories . . ."; Aldrich, 147 — "the largest . . .". On Phila. Brig.: Banes; Anon., *In Mem. Webb*; G. J. R. Miller; Trial, 88, 95, 141, 276, 304; Pa. at G, i, 558; Plummer; OR, i, 826f, 856, 432.
6. OR, i, 318f. This is a boastful report; you would gather from it that Gates's two regiments repulsed the charge almost unaided. On the 151st, see OR, i, 326ff; Vanderslice, 115f. J. C. Williams — "nine monthlings . . ."; Sturtevant, 746 — "I was . . .".
7. See OR. Arnold is usually credited with six guns, but Reichardt states that one had been already disabled. Since he is writing from a close-up point of view, he is to be preferred to the more general statements that come from Hazard or from Hunt.
8. See OR. OR, i, 421, Harrow signs himself as commanding the Second Division.
9. DAB; Gibbon, *Recs.*; Woodruff; J. D. Smith, 77 — "he had . . ."; Lyman, 107 — "steel cold,". On Hays; DAB; Oliphant; Hays, *Life*. W. Scott, 6 — "a princely . . ."; Walker, *Second Corps*, 228f — "His extraordinary . . .".
10. J. D. Smith, 79; Battlefield Monuments; Warren-Bachelder map; OR, reports of the various units involved. (The battle-order of Harrow's brigade is established from OR as being different from that given on the monuments and by Warren-Bachelder.) On the slashing, see OR, i, 319; Doubleday, 197; Gibbon, *Recs.*, 134. The distance 239 feet is established in Trial. Paris uses the term *en potence*.
11. Swallow gives the fullest description of the fortifications, but is of

little validity for July 3, since he inspected the fortifications after they had been further strengthened on July 4. Shields, 453 — "about knee-high"; Bruce, 274 — "with one . . ."; Lochren, *Narrative*, 364f — "made a . . ."; Silas Adams, 260 — "Every Man . . .". See also *Maine in the War*, 481; OR, i, 321, 340; Cowan, Anon., *In Mem. Webb*; Mulholland.

12. Shields, 450, tells of Hays's worry for his right flank. On the cutting of trees in the rough ground, Cowan in Anon., *In Mem. Webb*.

13. On Hunt: DAB; Fitzgerald; his own articles.

14. Osborn, both his article and OR; OR, i, 891. McGilvery's report in OR is rather confused (See Appendix H).

15. DAB, OR. For the Monocacy Creek incident, see Ward. Testimony in Trial indicates that some of the men did not recognize Webb.

16. Sawyer, 117 — "a battle . . ."; Banes, 166 — "the rank . . ."; Haskell, 50 — "shattered, without . . ."; Reid, 96 — "grim and . . ."; Bardeen — "if the . . ."; Trial, 219 — "I was . . ."; Haskell, 3f — "With the . . .". See also Goss, 198; OR, i, 855.

17. McDermott, 29; Reid, 96; Plummer, 178f. NY at G, ii, 800; Rogers-Delavan, 57; Rogers, 35. Bruce, 287; Meade, *Life*, 105; Paris, 208. There was fighting around the Bliss barn on two days; on the fighting of July 3 see Walker, *Second Corps*, 288; OR, i, 467–471.

PART 3
NOON-DAY LULL

Section

1. OR, i, 308 — "The morning . . .". Hill, 261 — "Of shoulder . . .". Of Lee and Napoleon, see Freeman, *Lee*, i, 456. Pettigrew, 11 — "The invention . . .".

2. Trimble, SHSP, xxvi, 126 — "General Longstreet . . ."; see also Swallow for mention of the written orders. Scheibert, *Drei Monate* — "I plan . . .". Pickett in command, see Moore, H. T. Owen. OR, ii, 614 — "in readiness . . ."; OR, ii, 557 — "a favorable . . .".

3. Moore; Kimble; Houston-James; Dooley; OR, ii, 385, 999, 647, 666. Harrison, 91; Finley. OR, ii, 320 — "Pickett's and . . ."; OR, ii, 359 — "Heth's division . . .". See Scheibert, *Bürgerkrieg*, for some good notes on Confederate tactics. On Lee and Jomini, see Swift. On co-ordination of Pickett and Pettigrew, see Fry, Kimble, J. T. Jones. On Pickett's change of direction there are suggestions in Robbins, 105; Loehr, 36; Harrison, 183. These do not seem to me very helpful; Harrison declares that the change of direction was to avoid a ravine, but there is no such ravine.

4. SHSP, xli, 40.

5. W. W. Wood — "We saw . . .". Moore; AW, 431f. W. W. Wood — "commanding officers . . .".

6. Shields, 454 — "It needed . . .".

7. London *Times*; Scheibert, *Drei Monate*; Fremantle. W. W. Wood — "They were . . ."; Doubleday — "the flower . . ."; Mayo, 328 — "from being . . .". Shotwell, *Papers*, 4 — "the men . . .". Poague, 74; J. H. Walker; Dooley 102; Underwood, 26NC, 97.

8. Kimble, 460 — "June Kimble . . .".

9. Shotwell, *Papers*, 10; Houston-James; H. T. Owen; Loehr, SHSP, xxxiv, 33; Harrison, 90.

10. See Appendix G.

11. NCRegs, i, 543; R. S. Thompson, 108f; Page, 154f; N.Y. *Herald*, July 7, 1863, 3–5; W. W. Wood.

12. Benedict, 463; Dunn Browne, 187; Reid, 98; McDermott, 29; Crotty.

13. Aldrich, 211 — "It was . . ."; W. Scott, 8 — "At noon . . ."; Trial, McKeever — "while the . . ."; Aldrich, 211 — "All was . . .". Seville, 81; Trial, 80; Banes, 194; Bruce, 287f. Toombs, 290; Anon., *19th Mass.*, 234; Bruce, 288.

14. Sturtevant, 291.

15. On Cushing: Haight; Fuger's writings. On Brown: Sturtevant, 698, 229. On Haskell: Haskell, *Introduction* and elsewhere.

16. On the lunch of Gibbon, etc., see Haskell 77ff. Gibbon, *Recs.*, 146 — "an old . . ."; Haskell, 78 — "in good . . ."; Haskell, 80 — "young North . . .". On the lunch of Garnett, etc., see Harrison, 95f. Shotwell, *Papers*, 4; Napier, 192; Rhodes, 199, 208.

17. Trimble, *Diary*; Bachelder *Isometric Drawing*; Anon., "The Great Battlefield" — "Placing a . . .".

18. DAB, Trimble, *Diary*, 12. Swallow, 565 — "Many of . . ."; J. B. Smith, 355 — "I miss . . .".

20. AW, 430 — "Never was . . .". Longstreet's writings; Alexander's writings. For the texts of the notes (quoted in three different ways by Alexander) I have used the *Alexander Letters* which were presumably prepared carefully from the originals. Fremantle, 211. Alexander, *Mem.*, 421 — "overwhelming reasons . . ."; ibid., 422 — "What do . . ."; ibid., 422 — "both cheerful . . .".

21. OR, ii, 352 — "nearly one . . ."; Aldrich, 219 — "Between our . . .".

22–23. *Field Artillery Tactics*, and other manuals. OR, 754f; Scheibert, *Drei Monate*, 89; Benton 487, 468; Hunt, *Art. Administration*.

24. Swallow, 566 — "damage and . . .".

25. Hunt's writings.

26. Jacobs.

27. Brown, *Univ. Grays*, 38.

28. *Reb. Rec. Docs.*, 119.

29. Hyde, 200; N.Y. *Times*, July 6, 1863, 1–5 — "There was . . .". Morgan, 207; *Com. Conduct of the War*, 451; Meade, *Life*, 106;

Plummer, 180; Trial, 258; Rhodes, 208; Rogers-Delavan, 57. Rhodes, 208 — "on the . . .". NY at G, 665.

30. Harrison; Shotwell, *Papers*, 14; Shotwell, OLOD.

31. W. M. Owen, 248. OR, i, 51, 733 — "Received, 1.30 p.m." Brown, *Univ. Grays*, 38.

PART 4
BETWEEN THE SIGNAL-SHOTS

NY at G, 665 — "There she goes!" McDermott, 30; B & L, iii, 362 n.; W. M. Owen, 255; Sturtevant, 315; Devereux; R. S. Thompson, 101; J. G. B. Adams, 68.

PART 5
CANNONADE

Section

1. Buell, 93 — "It reminded . . .". Jacobs, 41; Harrison, 96; Morgan, 207; Trial, 258; Rhodes, 208; Rogers, 57. B & L, iii, 373 — "indescribably grand." Gibbon, *Recs.*, 147; Haskell, 82f; Moore.

2. R. S. Thompson, 101 — "Down! Down!" Shields, 453; NY at G, 801; Page; Haskell, 83; H. W. Jackson, 179. Anon. *19th Mass.*, 237 — "keeping their . . .". Howard, i, 436; Rogers, 57; Walker, *Hancock*, 139; Mulholland.

3. Hunt, B & L, iii, 372; Osborn; Pa. at G, ii, 912f; OR, i, 365.

4. Tyler, 109; N.Y. *Times*, July 6, 1863, 1–5; OR, i, 874, 878f; Livermore, 260. Meade, *Life*, 106f — "Gentlemen . . .".

5. Benedict, 466; Morgan, 208.

6. OR, i, 352, 603; Buell, 93 — "The enemy . . .". Anon., *Fifth Mass. Batt.*, 655.

7. Gibbon, *Recs.*, 149; Rhodes, 209; B & L, iii, 385ff.

8. Page, 149; L. A. Smith, 303, 394; Plummer, 180; Haskell, 89; Shields, 464; J. B. Young, 295f; Gibbon, *Recs.*, 178; Sturtevant, 600; B & L, iii, 374; Lochren, *Narrative*, 377; D. E. Johnston, 207. Washburn, 52 — "It was . . .". Shields, 451; Willson, 182; Toombs, 299.

9. Wilcox; J. H. Smith, 190; Dooley, 103; W. W. Wood. Shotwell, *Papers*, ii, 8 — "Pickett's division . . .". OR, ii, 650, 671; Fry. D. E. Johnston, 217 — "of a . . .". Brown, *Univ. Grays*, 38ff — "My mother . . .".

10. Silas Adams, 260 — "All we . . .". Haskell, 90.

11. OR, i, 885, 888; Anon., *Fifth Mass. Batt.*, 652; Osborn; Haskell, 84; J. S. P. Cook, 334 — "with folded . . ."; Washburn, 52 — "most of . . .". Shields, 450f; Anon., *In Mem. Webb*, 89. Bates, 155 — "That sandwich . . .". Howard, *At. Mo.*, 67; OR, I, 51, i, 1069 — "The fire . . .".

12. W. W. Wood; Bright, 234; R. H. Irvine, 391; R. T. Jones, 270 —
"Yes, but . . .".

13. Bright, 299, including quotations.

14. L. G. Young, OLOD, 555; OR, i, 544, 794, 801, 831, 706. Howard,
i, 436. Osborn — "it was . . .".

15. Bachelder, *Notes*; Rhodes. H. W. Jackson, 179f — "The men . . .".
Walker, *Hancock*, 141. J. B. G. Adams, 70 — "Volunteers are . . .";
Anon., *19th Mass.*, 236 — "Come, Jelison . . .". Benedict, 466;
Morgan, 208; NY at G, 1274ff; Anon., *In Mem. Webb.*

16. W. Scott, 9 — "This soon . . ."; Gates, 470 — "smoking and . . .".
Anon., *19th Mass.*, 236 — "The water . . .".

17. Dunn Browne, 202; Craighill; Parks; Hoke, 508ff; Benedict, 465;
Com. Conduct of the War, 410.

18. Gibbon, *Recs.*, 149; Haskell, 84ff (including the quotations).

19. OR, reports of McGilvery and his battery-commanders; Anon., *Fifth
Mass. Batt.*

20. Haskell, 109; OR, ii, 389; B & L, iii, 364f; Alexander, *Mem.*, 423.

21. Osborn (including quotations); *Com. Conduct of the War*, 333,
451; Hoke, 371n; Bachelder, *Third Day's Battle*; Howard, *At. Mo.*,
67.

22. Alexander is quoted from *Alexander Letters.*

23. OR, ii, 480; B & L, iii, 374.

24. Washburn, 52. On Cushing: Bachelder, *Notes*; Trial; Fuger.
Rhodes, 210; Morgan, 208.

25. Finley — "You'll get . . ."; J. H. Smith, 190 — "He was . . .".

26. Alexander, SHSP, iv, 238; B & L, iii, 364. The quotations are from
Alexander Letters.

27. F. R. Galloway; OR, ii, 612, and *passim*. OR, i, 373 — "an
hour . . ."; *Com. Conduct of the War*, 313 — "a little . . .". OR, ii,
435 — "caused immense . . ."; Ross, 663 — "had done . . ."; Pollard,
631 — "The Yankees . . .". Scheibert, *Drei Monate* — "Pulververschwendung"; Anon., *Fifth Mass. Batt.*, 652 — "Viewed as . . .".
Trial, Webb, 316; Stribling, 60.

PART 6
SECOND LULL

Section

1. Osborn — "a singularly . . .". Page, 150; Anon., "The Great Battlefield."

2. On Pickett's "letters," see Appendix B. AW, 430 — "General,
shall . . ."; ibid., — "My feelings . . ."; OR, ii, 360 — "I gave . . .";
AW, 431 — "I shall . . ."; L. C. Pickett, *Pickett and his Men*, 301 —
"If old . . .".

3. Haskell, 95; Shields, 452. Aldrich, 211f — "All the . . ."; W. Scott

— "Now, boys . . .". NY at G, 907. W. Scott — "Well, Scott . . .". Trial, 159, 243; Devereux; Washburn, 52; Bachelder, *Notes*. On Cushing's wound, Bachelder, *Notes*, and Trial, Fuger.

4. Bright, 230 — "Mount your . . .". Bright, 229, on the number of mounted men.

5. Dooley, 105 — "There are . . .". W. N. Wood; Dawson, 96; "Harry," 522; Finley. Dawson, 96 — "Run, you . . .". Dawson, who was British, wrote this passage in words that no American would have used (e.g., "hare" for "rabbit"); I have ventured to re-word it. H. T. Owen — "a brief . . ."; R. W. Martin — "Men, remember . . ."; Easley — "as he . . ."; R. W. Martin — "Did you . . ."; NCRegs, ii, 356 — "Now, colonel . . .".

6. Lindsley.

7. N.Y. *Times*, July 4, 3–2 — "The news . . .".

8. On Confederate strength the chief sources are the Battlefield Monuments; OR, ii, 387, 667, 671; Heth.

Estimates of Union strength are worked out piecemeal from OR, regimental and brigade histories, Battlefield Monuments, Bachelder's notes, and other sources. Haskell's over-all estimate (p. 72) of something under 6000 men for the Second and Third Divisions on the morning of July 3 seems to be considerably too high, although we must remember that three and a half regiments were on Cemetery Hill.

10. Toombs states that the 12th N.J. was the only regiment of the division to be armed with the smooth-bores. Anon., *Fifth Mass. Batt.*, 636, and Anon., *19th Mass.*, 250, give instances of Union soldiers hit by buckshot, thus showing that some of the Confederate troops in the charge were using smooth-bores. On the breech-loaders, see Page, 151. On bayonets, see McCarthy, *Minutiae*, Stewart, 200; Shotwell, OLOD, 91.

11. Alexander, *Mem.*, 424 — "Go and . . ."; ibid., for the other quotations.

12. As usual, estimates of time differ; Buell, 94, gives twenty or thirty minutes; Silas Adams, 260, ten minutes; Haskell, 111f, fifteen minutes. H. T. Owen — "Forward! . . .".

PART 7
ADVANCE

Section

1. W. Scott, 10; Rhodes, 211; R. S. Thompson, 110; Sturtevant, 299; Kimble, 460. On the problems of Pettigrew's advance: L. G. Young (both items). On intervals: OR, i, 437; Ashe, 144; Gibbon, *Recs.*, 179; L. G. Young. On Armistead: Dawson, 196; Poindexter; Lewis, 79; OR, ii, 1000.

2. Cowan's writings, including OR, i, 690; Banes.
3. OR, i, 439, 445; W. Scott, 10; Shotwell, *Papers*, 10; Scheibert, *Drei Monate, Bürgerkrieg*; Doubleday, 199; J. D. Smith, 79; Washburn, 52; Banes, 190; OR, i, 439 — "an appearance . . .". Pa. at G., i, 117; Dodge, 17; Trial, 219. McDermott, 31 — "Let your . . .". Gates, 471; R. S. Thompson; NY at G, 802. J. D. Smith — "Thank God! . . .". Wilson, 184 — "Beautiful, gloriously . . ."; Hays, *Life*, 439; Wilkeson; Rittenhouse, 10. Anon., *"The Great Battlefield"* — "A great . . .".
4. J. H. Walker, 222; Shotwell, *Papers*, 11; ibid., OLOD, 90; Bright; McCulloch; Loehr, *1st Va.*; J. H. Smith, 191; H. T. Owen; Houston-James; Hunton; Mayo; Rittenhouse, 10. OR, ii, 386 — "on the mountain." Rafferty, 30 — "The mark . . .". Anon., *Fifth Mass. Batt.*, 655, 665 — "We had . . .". Easley; Stewart, 101; Hunton, 100n; OR, ii, 387. On re-dressing, OR, ii, 360; Poindexter; J. H. Walker.
5. OR, ii, 644. On Brockenbrough: L. G. Young (both items); Bond; J. T. Jones; Houston; Lane, SHSP, xxiv; Walker, *Hancock*, 142; H. T. Owen; NCRegs, ii, 43f; F. A. Howell; McFarland; T. B. K., Richmond *Times*, Apr. 11, 1867; Dunaway; Anon., CV, Feb., 1898. Although the number of items here cited on this brigade is considerable, most of them are brief and unsatisfactory. OR, ii, 651 — "not a . . ."; OR, i, 893 — "I fired . . ."; NCRegs, ii, 43f — "shafts of . . .".
6. Longstreet's writings; Finley.
7. Pa. at G., i, 117.
8. F. A. Howell; Ross, 662; London *Times*. On troops along the sunken road: Buell, 95f; Hoke, 372; Rowan; Shields, 455f; Walker, *Second Corps*, 297. On 8th Ohio: Walker, *Second Corps*, 294n; Sawyer. On Armstrong; Talbot; NY at G, 79, 890. Simons; Dunaway, 92f. The question of whether the 8th Ohio met Brockenbrough's brigade must be decided by a *reductio ad absurdum*, i.e., there was no other body of troops for each of them to meet.
9. Ashe, 146f; W. W. Wood.
10. Bright. On stragglers from Pickett's division, see Bond (all items); Fleming, Easley. Fremantle, 212 — "a perfect . . .".
11. OR, ii, 647; Swallow, 568; Fry.
12. H. T. Owen; Rhodes, 211; Shields, 457; Silas Adams, 26of; W. Scott, 11; *Maine in the War*, 481; Ward, 199ff. Mayo — "Don't shoot . . .". Morgan, 209; OR, ii, 386, Trial, 304 — "But it . . .".
13. W. A. Montgomery; Clark, *Hampton Batt.*; OR, i, 1023. Shotwell, *Papers*, ii, 13 — "In a . . .". Mayo — "everything was . . .". On what was said: H. T. Owen; Irvine; W. N. Wood, 45; Shotwell, OLOD, 92; Stewart, 111.
14. Morgan, 211; Sturtevant; Benedict; OR, i, 349f, 352f.

15–16. Gibbon, *Recs.*, 150ff; OR, i, 386, 437ff, 445; Haskell; NY at G, 666; Loehr, SHSP; Finley; Mayo; Irvine; Shotwell, 91; Fry, 93. The movement of Kemper's brigade to the left is most clearly described in Union sources, but also can be made out from Confederate sources. Hall (OR) and Haskell both conceived it as an ordered maneuver, its purpose to effect a concentration in front of the Angle.

17. Irvine; Shotwell; OLOD, 91; Fry, 93; J. H. Moore.

18. Swallow, 568 — "Virginia and . . .". Bachelder, *Notes.* Porter and Stewart both tell the story of Monte, but somewhat differently; I have taken Porter's version; Stewart could have had the story only by hearsay.

19–20. OR, i, 318, 450; Mayo; Harrison, 41ff; D. E. Johnston, 211.

21. Seville, 81, 83; Page; OR, *passim.*

22. Dooley, 106; Easley. H. T. Owen — "mingled mass . . ."; OR, ii, 386 — "recoiled."

23. Fuger; Morgan, 212; Bachelder, *Notes.*

PART 8

HIGH-WATER MARK

Section

1. Trial is the most detailed source for the fight at the Angle, and OR and Haskell must constantly be used. Archer's men at the Angle: see Finley, Moore, J. B. Smith. Stockton's experiences, see his testimony in Trial. On the ebbing back after the first rush, see Finley; Trial, Stockton; OR, ii, 386.

2. Peters; Finley; CV, Feb., 1906, 196.

3. Trial, esp., Hamilton, Porter, Roberts, Webb, Banes, Haskell, 104 — "Halt!".

4. Lewis, 84; Trial, esp., McDermott, Lynch, Read; Finley; R. W. Martin, Bachelder, *Third Day's Battle*; Swallow, 569; Stewart, 102; Robbins, 107; McDermott, 316.

5. Trial, esp., McDermott, Fuger, Buckley, Webb, McKeever. McDermott; Anon., *In Mem. Webb*, 31. Trial, McKeever — "It was . . ."; Trial, McDermott — "We thought . . .".

6. Trial, esp., Wilson, McDermott, Garrett; Harding; Easley. Harding's account is not so credible as Easley's.

7. London *Times*; T. B. K.

8. Trial, esp., Devereux, Hill; Devereux.

9–10. H. T. Owen; Devereux; Anon., *In Mem. Webb*; Trial, Devereux, Hill.

11–12. Trial, Hill — "They were . . .". Anon., *In Mem. Webb*, 24 — "Take the . . .". Cowan's writings, NY at G, 82; Devereux; Anon., *19th Mass.*, 239; Morgan, 213; Walker, *Second Corps*, 298. The quotations are from Cowan, Anon., *In Mem. Webb*.

13. Walker, *Hancock*, 161; *Com. Conduct of the War*, 443; Gibbon, *Recs.*, 168 — "All yelling . . .".

14. H. T. Owen — "covered with . . .". Ashe, 146ff; Sawyer, 131; Small, 106; Scheibert, *Drei Monate*, 89f; McFarland, 557ff; Aldrich, 216; Montgomery, 440ff; John A. Graves; Underwood, 72; W. D. Reid; Willson, 345f; Seville, 82; Morgan, 211; NY at G, 907; B & L, iii, 391f; Searles, 82; L. P. Young, NCRegs, 126ff; Page, 152. Love, 44 — "For God's . . ."; Swallow, 568 — "fought with . . ."; NY at G, 802 — "within a . . ."; J. T. Jones, 134 — "Come over . . ."; Toombs, 300 — "smooth-cheeked lad."

15. Based mostly on Haskell, with quotations from that source. See also OR, and Trial, Map.

16. Bright; NCRegs, ii, 44; Alexander *Mem.*, and SHSP, iv, 202; W. M. Owen; OR, ii, 376, 382, 384, 389, 435; OR, i, 446; B & L, iii, 389.

17. Sturtevant; Benedict; Stine, 527f; OR, i, 348ff. Talbot, 92; NY at G., 907. Benedict, 469 — "the pivot . . ."; ibid., 478 — "Glory to . . .". OR, ii, 386 — "receiving a . . .". On Hancock's wound, see Walker, *Hancock*, 300; Sturtevant, 319, 703; Morgan, 215; Benedict, 477.

18. Trial, esp. Mannes, Lynch, Stockton; Sturtevant, 303; Plummer, 100, 180; Haskell; B & L, iii, 389; H. T. Owen; Livermore, 261f; Devereux. J. D. Smith, 82 — "in some . . .". Lochren, *Narrative*, 371. Devereux, 17 — "Whichever side . . .".

19. Fleming; Wilcox; Benedict, 473; OR, ii, 615. On Union reinforcements, OR, i, 801, 544, 513, etc.; Ropes-Livermore, iii, 482.

20. Washburn, 52; Love; Flowers, 260; Ashe, 150ff; Trimble, SHSP, and *Diary*. T. B. K. — "General Trimble . . ."; ibid., "My God . . ."; OR, ii, 666 — "within a . . .". Shotwell, OLOD, 94. Trimble, SHSP, 127 — "No, the . . .". OR, ii, 659f.

21. NY at G, 1324ff; OR, i, 753. J. H. Smith; Lochren, MOLLUS, 53; Douthat. The quotations are from Smith.

22. OR, ii, 322 — "effectually protected . . .". See also OR, ii, 724, 697. U. S. Grant, *Memoirs*, i, 556.

23. Small; J. D. S. Cook, 334f; OR, i, 472; Trial, Stockton; Swallow; Seville, 83; Ashe, 157; Page, 156; *Com. Conduct of the War*, 454; Haskell, 140; Devereux. Haskell, 112 — "Major ——, lead . . .", and other quotations. Lochren, MOLLUS, 54 — "A strange . . .". Haskell, 112 — "thrusts, yells . . .". Bachelder, *Descriptive Key*, 36; Banes, 191; Trial, esp., Webb, Whittich, Roberts, Read; Lochren, 54.

PART 9
REPULSE

Section

2. Bright; Poague.
3. *Com. Conduct of the War*, 454. Buell, 96 — "By God . . ."; Osborn — "no two . . ."; Anon., "The Great Battlefield" — "We have . . ."; J. D. S. Cook, 335f — "As the . . .".
4. Shotwell, OLOD, 94. Kimble — "For about . . .". Sturtevant, 450; Osborn; Harrison, 101; J. H. Moore; Benedict, 476; Wilkeson. Oliphant; Wm. Allen; Poague, 76.
5. Cowtan, 210; NY at G, 271f; Banes. Haskell, 120f — "See them . . ."; ibid., 117ff — "How is . . .".
6. Trial, Stockton, Russ; R. H. Irvine; Sturtevant; Benedict, ii, 478; Lochren, MOLLUS, 54; J. H. Walker, 221. Trial, Russell — "One of . . ."; Goss, 218 — "Doggoned if . . ."; Trial, Mannes — "We can . . ."; N.Y. *Times*, July 8, 1863, 1–3 — "Where are . . .".
7. Wilcox; Fleming; George Clark, 230; Sturtevant, 313f; Stine, 528; Benedict, ii, 476; Clark, *Hampton Batt.*, 143; NY at G, 1329; Shotwell, *Papers*, 15. Benedict, 473ff — "wandering across . . ."; Anon., *Fifth Mass. Batt.*, 653 — "a ridiculous . . .".
8. Trial, McKeever — "After the . . ."; Sturtevant, 506 — "I forgot . . .". Oliphant. Shields, 464 — "Boys, give . . .".
9. Poague, 75f, including the quotations.
10. Banes, 192, "as the . . .". Trial; Haskell, 115. Bingham, Letter — "Say to . . ."; Bingham was not sure whether the word used was "grievous" or "serious". Morgan, 215ff. Livermore, 264 — "We've enfiladed . . .". OR, i, 366 — "I did . . .".
11. Colston — "The whole . . .". Fremantle, 214. J. H. Moore — "Colonel, rally . . ."; ibid. — "General, I . . ."; Shotwell, OLOD, 95 — "Are you . . ."; Loehr, *1st Va.*, 38 — "General, let . . ."; Bright — "General Pickett . . ."; ibid. — "General Kemper . . ."; London *Times* — "General, I . . ."; H. T. Owen — "It's all . . ."; Colston — "Don't whip . . .". Fremantle also heard these words (see Appendix I). Fremantle, 214 — "All this . . ."; ibid. — "Very well . . .". The officer whom Longstreet thus addressed in irony was thought by Fremantle to be Pettigrew, though he is uncertain. It seems unlikely to me that Longstreet would have been thus brutal to a wounded man. I think it more likely to have been Wilcox, since the words addressed to Longstreet are about the same as those which Wilcox addressed to Lee.

Dowdey, 300, states that during the afternoon Longstreet took "a couple of swigs" of Fremantle's rum, and that "it is possible" that he was "more confused" than has been recognized. Granted that almost anything is "possible," one should point out that Longstreet could certainly not have had any of Fremantle's rum until about 3.30, since they were separated. McLaws, 88; H. T. Owen; McNeilly; Fremantle, 215. H. T. Owen — "Then commenced . . ."; ibid., for the following quotations.

12. Whitelaw Reid — "Ah! General . . ."; *Com. Conduct of the War*, 408, 394.

13. Sturtevant, 314.

14. Wilkeson. Willson, 187 — "so thickly . . .". Cowan, Anon., *In Mem. Webb*; Paris, 214; Swallow, 572; Trial, Webb.

15–16. On Union casualties the sources are given in the text, except that OR should be somewhat more emphasized. On Confederate casualties, see Appendix A. On casualties of individual regiments, see Hunton 99; Richmond *Enquirer*, July 15, 1863; Pollard, 283; H. T. Owen; Shotwell. On company losses, L. G. Young, OLOD; NSRegs, i, 590, 693, v, 599ff; Underwood, 114; Bond, NCPubs.; Richmond *Enquirer*, July 17, 1863; Flowers. Houston–James — "We gained . . .".

17. Bruce, 288; Banes, 191. Lochren, MOLLUS, 54 — "the bayonet . . ."; J. D. S. Cook, 335 — "A curious . . .". Fry; I. T. Miller; Trial, 222; Lochren, *Narrative*, 371. Trial, 288 — "There were . . .". Bachelder, *Descriptive Key*, 39; Trial, 173.

18. On estimates of prisoners, see Benedict, 470; Morgan; Gibbon, *Recs.*, 183; *Com. Conduct of the War*, 458.

19. OR, i, 353 and OR generally. Pickett, *Pickett and his Men*, 316. As to which officer was unwounded, see W. N. Wood, 48; London *Times*; Crocker, 130; Hunton, 99; Houston–James. OR, ii, 651 — "in Archer's . . ."; W. J. Martin, 45f — "defective organization"; Harrison, 104 — "a loss . . .".

20. OR, i, 377 — "There were . . .". OR, ii, 647; London *Times*; Loehr, CV. NY at G, 907 — "Harpers Ferry." OR, ii, 282; Trial, McDermott, 235; *Medals of Honor issued by the War Dept.* Shields, 464; Cowan, Letter, July 2, 1913.

21. Haight, xii; *Medals of Honor issued by the War Dept.*, Buell, 104.

22. B & L, iii, 421 — "General, this . . .".

PART 10

AFTERWARDS

Section

2, 3, 4. See Lee's reports and letters in OR, esp., I, 51, i, 752. Lee's Dispatches, 110 — "I am . . .". Pickett, *Pickett and His Men*, 316 — "my spirit-crushed . . ."; ibid., 317f — "with all . . .". On the shad-bake, see Freeman, *Lee's Lieutenants*, iii, 658ff. Freeman, *Lee*, iv, 112 — "I thought . . .". On Garnett, Harrison, 184f. The brief notes on later careers are from DAB and other standard works. *Com. Conduct of the War*, 444 — "did more . . .". Cowan, Anon., *In Mem. Webb*; OR, i, 428.

5–6. Hays's *Life*, 411 — "Harpers Ferry . . .". Trial, 187 — "very angry"; ibid., 276 — "If they . . .". Walker, *Second Corps*, 522 — the Second . . ."; ibid., 557 — "mustered out . . ."; Sturtevant, 438 — "afterwards conducting . . .".

PART 11
THE STORY OF THE STORY

Section

1. Dunaway, 93 — "If old . . ."; *Lee's Dispatches*, 110 — "It is . . ."; Gibbon, *Recs.*, 272 — "It is so . . .".
2. OR, iii, 1075 — "we have . . .". Richmond *Enquirer*, July 24, 1863 (reprinted in *Reb. Recs. Docs.* 108ff). For the attack upon North Carolina see also Pollard, 282; *Lee's Dispatches*, 108; Harrison, 99; Hunton, 97; William Swinton, *Twelve Decisive Battles of the War*, 344. For the North Carolina defense, see L. G. Young, OLOD; T. B. Kingsbury, OLOD, i, 194; Montgomery, 442; Bond's writings. The Virginia counterattack is well expressed by G. L. Christian. For Lee's expression of opinion, see B & L, iii, 421.
3. *Lee's Dispatches*, 108. For early attempts to "explain" the defeat see Early; Figg, 133; Harrison, 92f, 98; Pollard, 631. Pickett, *Pickett and his Men*, 307 — "sixty to . . .". The controversy is fully reviewed in Sanger–Hay. Augusta *Daily Constitutionalist* (quoted Sanger–Hay, 346) — "who have . . .". Alderson — "Longstreet, not . . .".
4. See Cockrell, Geer, 455–7; Poague; W. W. Wood.
5. On the Union controversies, see various articles in B & L, iii; Stine, 527f; Benedict, 482ff; *Reply of the Phila. Brig.*, Trial, 57 — "Did you . . ."; Trial, 37 — "Where did . . ."; Trial, 55 — "I thought . . .".
6. La Bree, 356ff; L. A. Smith.

Index

Rank is indicated as of July 3, 1863. Standard abbreviations are used.

343